Alphabets to order...

The Fellowship of Bohemian Scribes.

AN HOUR

For

* SIMULTANEOUS * WRITING *

Throughout the World.

Address

A. J. R.

Lock Box 248.   New York City, U. S. A.

ALPHABETS TO ORDER:

the literature of

nineteenth-century

typefounders' specimens

Alastair Johnston

OAK KNOLL PRESS

THE BRITISH LIBRARY

2 0 0 0

First Edition

Published by Oak Knoll Press
310 Delaware Street
New Castle, Delaware
USA

and by The British Library
96 Euston Road
London NW1 2DB
England

ISBN: 1-58456-009-6 (USA)

ISBN: 0-7123-4702-X (UK)

Title: Alphabets to Order
Author: Alastair Johnston
Editor: Mary Hallwachs
Publishing Director: J. Lewis von Hoelle

British Library Cataloging-in-Publication Data
A CIP record is available from The British Library

Library of Congress Cataloging-in-Publication Data:
Johnston, Alastair, 1950–
Alphabets to order: the literature of nineteenth-century typefounders' specimens/
Alastair M. Johnston.
        p.   cm.
    Includes bibliographical references (p.) and index
    ISBN: 1-58456-009-6
        1. Type and type-founding — United States — Specimens — History — 19th century.
2. Type and type-founding — Great Britain — Specimens — History — 19th century.
3. English Literature—19th century—History and criticism. I. Title.

Z250.A2 J63 2000
686.2'24'09—dc21   99-048068

Typeset by the author in the Miller types of Matthew Carter.
The 2-line initials are by Vincent Figgins.

The cover shows 'Fantasy of a Billsticker' by John Parry, London, 1835, by kind permission
of The Alfred Dunhill Museum, 48 Jermyn Street, London SW1, England

Printed in the United States of America on 60# archival, acid-free paper meeting the require-
ments of the American Standard for Permanence of Paper for Printed Library Materials.

Contents

Acknowledgments

THIS BOOK BEGAN IN 1979 as two lectures, one on the roots of concrete poetry, given at California College of Arts & Crafts, and another on the origins of display type, delivered at the University of California at Berkeley. My main research was carried out in the library of my friend & long-time partner in Poltroon Press, Frances Butler, whose generosity is matched only by her savage insight. Examination of rare specimen books was made at Columbia University's own Butler Library, which houses the American Type Founders Collection, formed by Henry L. Bullen; at the Newberry Library in Chicago; at the Huntington Library in San Marino, California; at the Houghton Library in Harvard University, home to the Bentinck-Smith Typographical Collection; at the Kemble Collection of the California Historical Society (thanks to Bruce Johnson and Patricia Keats), and at the San Francisco Public Library (whose rare books librarians, Johanna Goldschmid, Susie Taylor, and Andrea Grimes, have been diligent and generous). Examination of the British specimens in the St Bride Institute Library of the City of London was made possible through the kindness of the Librarian, James Mosley, who pointed out items of interest and shared his vast knowledge of the subject with me. Reproductions of rare specimens have been made through the kind permission of these friends and institutions.

Further refinement of the ideas expressed herein was made after delivering lectures at Columbia University as a guest of Terry Belanger's book arts program, at the Monotype Conference in Cambridge, England, and at the 'Eclecticism and Modernism' Conference in New York (thanks to Steve Heller who also requested an abridgment for *The New York Times* Book Review).

Valuable comments on the various drafts or chapters of the manuscripts were made by J. Alfred Carlock, Peter Dreyer, Bruce Johnson, Dawn Kolokithas, John Lane, and Steve Lavoie. Ruth McGurk found typos. The late Roger Levenson was generous with his own research materials; Janet Ing Freeman and Peter Isaac kindly sent me unpublished manuscripts that pertained to my research; David Pankow accepted an earlier version of Chapter 3 for publication in *Printing History*, the journal of the American Printing Historical Association; the staff of the Mark Twain Project at the University of California at Berkeley kindly tracked down references to Wales McCormick in Twain's notebooks and writings; Nicolas Barker's erudite comments prodded me along some profitable paths of exploration. I am especially grateful to him for his continued enthusiasm and insightful reading. Organization and rethinking was the result of long discussions with Darcy DiNucci, who helped me finalize the mass of accumulated material. Frances Butler took many of the photographs. To all of these individuals goes my sincere gratitude.

My thanks to the judges of the Premio Felice Feliciano in Verona for the honourable mention in 1991, and to three editors whose initial enthusiasm and ultimate rejection only made the work stronger: Mark Rakatansky at MIT Press, Bill McClung at The University of California Press, and Dr Peggy Smith at the Printing Historical Society. Finally thanks to John von Hoelle of Oak Knoll and David Way of The British Library for their confidence in my work.

AMJ

Illustrations

ILLUSTRATIONS

*All illustrations are shown approximately actual size,
however original margins have not always been indicated.
Grateful acknowledgment is made for permission to reproduce the illustrations
from the collections of the St Bride Printing Library, London (figs. 3–6, 8–14, 16–24),
Columbia University Library, New York (frontispiece, figs. 15, 27–31),
Frances Butler, Berkeley (figs. 2, 7, 11, 25, 26, 32–41).*

OPTIMIS PARENTIBUS

David & Christina Johnston

Introduction

Matter grows under our hands. – Let no man say, – 'Come – I'll write a *duodecimo*'
– Laurence Sterne, *The Life & opinions of Tristram Shandy*, 1762

THE LETTERFORMS of our roman alphabet are as subject to change as any other graphic imagery. Typefounders' catalogs display the fashions and innovations in type & technology, and almost incidentally have textual content. To the casual browser, these specimen books appear to consist of mindless maundering and teasing elliptical fragments. Many scholars have commented on the evolution of type forms depicted in type specimen books, but none has examined them for their literary content. In his introduction to *The Type specimen of the Vatican Press, 1628* facsimile (Amsterdam, 1967), Hendrik Vervliet says, 'The text is of no importance in itself; it serves only to display the types'.

Concerned with the pure form of the letters, scholars avoid interpreting the laborious concoction, compilation & hand-composition of what often appears to be nonsense. Considered as literature, however, typefounders' specimen books reveal a great deal.

My approach is more speculative than the studies of nineteeth-century type by Nicolete Gray and others, for I felt a disparity between the seriousness of the scholars and the 'Hot Box Gone Mad' approach of typefounders who composed their specimens in the stick. The specimens have much in common with the volumes in the legendary 'Library of Babel' in the short story of Borges: 'For every sensible line of straightforward statement, there are leagues of senseless cacophonies, verbal jumbles and incoherences'.

Read with a poetic as well as a typographic sensibility, the spontaneous texts of nineteenth-century typefounders' specimen books anticipate later trends in concrete poetry, cut-up writing, and even performance art, but to quote Marie Antoinette's milliner (recalling King Solomon), 'There is nothing new but what has been forgotten'. Now-worn paths in typography and poetry were first made in book form by typefounders who, like graffiti artists, had nothing in particular to say but an overwhelming need to say it.

The founders' purpose was to display the virtues of their types to potential customers. But the typefounders were literary men and could not simply let the types speak for themselves. They play with language in their specimen books, and often their subconscious voices murmur through what otherwise appear to be randomly chosen texts. They describe their types, show us how to use them (the faces themselves often suggest the words), discuss the history of printing, and reveal their reading habits, from the meanest classified ad to the most enduring works of literature. Current events, from the jingoism of politics to the sanguinary partisanship of war, from frivolous fads to the latest technologies, are fodder for the composing stick.

The nineteenth century was 'a period, all told, in which the businessman defeated and annihilated the philosopher and poet,' according to the Boarding-House Philosopher.[1] Conspicuous consumption even extended to printed matter. The explosion of manufacturing bestowed a cornucopia of products on the burgeoning bourgeoisie. Marx titled a chapter in *Capital*, 'The fetishism of the commodity and its secret.' Throughout the century, as progress and commerce grew hand in hand, the expansion of Empire also seemed limitless and brought the thrill of the exotic home to British hearths. The solemnities of the Queen's Jubilee of 1887, no less than the enchantments of the Crystal Palace in 1851, carried over into the department store, according to Thomas Richards.

There was a typographical explosion at the beginning of the nineteenth century, and, for this reason, I begin my study there. Sweeping changes occurred in printing as a result of the industrial revolution. With the diversification of manufactured goods, advertising and packaging raised their infant cries for attention. The press, geared to a full-scale consumer war, played a pivotal role in the purveying of goods and services to the populace. The devising, cutting and casting of new typefaces accelerated at a staggering rate. The book types that previously had sufficed for poster work

1. Don Amaranth de Fraile in *Belarmino & Apolonio* by Ramon Perez de Ayala (Madrid, 1921; English edition, University of California Press, 1971).

were replaced by bolder versions for less-sophisticated readers. There were, in addition, new eye-catching inventions: the slab serif, sans serif, and shaded and decorated types. Their introduction led, in turn, to changes in reading, not only in scale and pace, but in the readers' understanding of emphasis through type weight & colour.

With the arrival of display types, the specimen books became the playground of the compositors.

It's clear that the compositors of these specimen pages were discarding language as blithely as painters came to discard the object in the early twentieth century. The typefounders' self-reflexiveness in the pages of their books shows us how to deal with language, and how new types, as they came into play, altered the way we look at words, hear, and think about them.

But the 'word as image' notion is fraught with over-investigation to determine how much one approximates the other, as a visual manifestation, or by covert 'signifiers' (*caveat lector*).

Types do speak to us through their shapes. Through our cultural upbringing, we bear a largely unconscious visual reading to the permutations of the roman alphabet. There are a million nuances to be discerned in the naked type between calligraphy and geometrically constructed letters, or between ductal and glyptic forms. From the time of their creation, typographical letterforms continue to acquire associations: through their use, through their colour. This racial identity, or subtext, is distinct for each typographical variation. Some letterforms generate a more powerful response. The early, uncomplicated display types – bold, slab, and sans serif – continue to pile up connotations.

The eclectic typography of typefounders' specimens is divorced from the traditional book, being less rigid and more personalized.

A similarly chaotic approach to type was that of German poet Hugo Ball in his poem 'Die Karawane' (Berlin, 1917). Its success as a visual statement prompted Ball to pronounce the oft-quoted homily: 'The word and image are one'. Ball rejected past languages with their implied social structure. He wanted to escape the symbolism of language by making typefaces speak for themselves. When something is ideologically grounded, people are less apt to notice it. By making his poem unnaturally visible, Ball pointed out the ideological basis of all letterforms.

But it is undoubtedly a mistake to assume that a thread runs from the catalogues of types produced in the nineteenth century through to the modern movements associated with concrete poetry. There may be similar parallel paths in language and literature that could have had unconscious effects on each other, but it is far easier to trace connections in reverse as I found myself doing in the course of my research. This approach caused me to look for certain types of language fragments and patterns in the specimens, and consequently I may have overlooked others.

I came to typography though poetry and was well aware of the modern experiments with language and letterforms before I fully comprehended the impact of printing type on the way the manuscript is altered between the voiced work and the printed book. While I am now convinced that there was no vital connection between anonymous compositors setting up texts for specimen books and later similar discoveries by language-oriented poets lost in admiration of their typographical errors, or minimalists equally astounded by their own ability to create patterns with the fixed spacing of a typewriter, the parallels I have found are all the more forceful because the discoveries were made independently. Dadaism and Surrealism, however, were movements that grew out of broader cultural contexts than simply poetry, and I feel that in this case, the specimen books reflect a ground-swell of nonsense that can be traced back for decades into popular culture.

Dadaist Richard Huelsenbeck's idea of a topographic use of type to suggest sound, tone, emphasis, inflection, etc, derives partly from Stéphane Mallarmé. But the visual syntax of Mallarmé in his careful modulation of blank space as silence in *Un Coup de dés jamais n'abolira le hasard* (1897; first separate edition, Paris, 1914) was antithetical to the Dadaists' use of chaos in typography to reflect the world turned upside down by war. While the Dadaists eschewed the careful control and modulation of Mallarmé's *mise-en-page* and went beyond the 'freeing of words' of Marinetti, strictly speaking, Dada typography continues the tradition of *Parangonage*, or aligning types of different face and size on the same line, a technique that appeared in French press advertising particularly between 1860 and 1880,[2] and 'crazy type' compositions in American ephemera.[3]

2. The connection is noted by François Caradec in 'Dada sans/avec parangon' in *Dada et la typographie* (Paris, 1970).
3. See, e.g., 'First Annual Outing Typothetae of Buffalo, Saturday, July 31st, 1897. Official Programme' reproduced at the time in Lockwood's *Printer & Bookmaker*, and on the centenary in *The Ampersand*, vol. 16, #2 (San Francisco, 1997, p.13).

Abstract sound poetry was widely emulated until it peaked typographically in two French movements: Lettrisme & 'Pataphysique. Separated from meaning, the abstract poem collapses reality. In *Courrier Dada*, Raoul Hausmann wrote, 'The great step by which total irrationality was introduced into literature took place with the introduction of the phonetic poem'. Explaining the application of typography, he continued:

> I had used letters of varying sizes and thicknesses which thus took on the character of musical notation. Thus the optophonetic poem was born. The optophonetic and the phonetic poem are the first step towards totally non-representational, abstract poetry.

'Optophonetic' implies that the pictographic qualities of letterforms support the sound. Whether actual or imaginary, to assign specific qualities to letterforms is treading on thin ice. If the audience for this sort of thing is not trained, the connotations are artificial and superficial. While everyone shares the associations of the printed culture of their era, Ball's use of Gothic faces implies a different optical/visual connection than that made by Victorians like Pugin and Ruskin. As Henri Foçillon says, in *La Vie des formes en art*, 'In the life of the mind there is a region in which forms which are defined with the utmost exactitude nevertheless speak to us in very different languages'. The earlier Gothic revival of spidery type forms was assumed to recall the spiritual transcendence of the twelfth century, but how could the Victorian bourgeois guess at the relation of mediæval man to God? (As Wilde noted, 'The only spirit which is entirely removed from us is the mediæval.') To me Ball's *Die Karawane*, with its cacophony of dark Jugend voices, suggests the profusion of tongues one would encounter crossing North Africa by caravan.

Other accidental resemblances occur far earlier. John Wilkins, for example, in *Essay towards a real character, and philosophical language* (London, 1668) proposed a language for scientists that would incorporate universal symbolism from mathematics and chemistry, while his contemporary, Bishop Sprat, the historian of the Royal Society (founded by Charles II in 1660), wanted to 'survey ancient and modern sources of imagery in order to determine which are depleted and which are still viable for modern usage'.[4] According to

4. Quoted by Barbara M. Stafford, *Voyage into substance: Art, science, nature, and the illustrated travel account, 1760–1840* (Cambridge, MA, 1984), pp. 35–6. See also her chapter 4.

Stafford, 'The radical restriction of figured language was central to the ideology of the Royal Society ... Sprat upheld the view that literary images must be concrete and based on direct sense experience. ... Sprat makes clear that visual and linguistic tasks are identical.' Two hundred and fifty years later, Ball said 'The word and image are one.'

Dadaism as Nonsense poetry was strongly rooted in English literature that bloomed (notably among men of the cloth) in the eighteenth century with the writings of Reverend Laurence Sterne, for example his 'Chapter of chances' in *Tristram Shandy*, vol. IV, chapter 9, the promised chapter on 'the right and wrong end of a woman', or chapter XIV, following 'Pish!', and Horace Walpole's self-published *Hieroglyphic tales* (Strawberry Hill, 1785), written to amuse his girlfriends. The languages used by the Laputans and the Houyhnhnms in Reverend Jonathan Swift's *Gulliver's travels* (London, 1726) are also part of this tradition. In the nineteenth century, a pinnacle was reached by the Reverend Charles Dodgson (Lewis Carroll) in *Alice's adventures in wonderland*, two decades after the irreverent Edward Lear had published *A Book of nonsense* under the alias Derry Down Derry in 1846.

A STARTLING ARRAY of new typographic forms was created at the turn of the nineteenth century. However, the scarcity of specimen books and the profusion of variant states among those extant make it difficult to date the introduction of new types. The specimen books were issued without dates to avoid annual obsolescence. Where there was a printed date, it was often excised by the founder, or a cancellation title page provided. Paper watermarks are of some help, but a printer might hold stock of dated watermarked paper for several years before printing on it. A founder might leave his specimen texts standing, or would print enough leaves to bind up several editions of his book, adding pages as his stock of types increased, and oversewing them onto new copies of the specimen book.

Evidence of the founders' methodology is seen in the recurring typographical errors that remain through several editions of a specimen book. Robert Thorne, a pioneer in the cutting of fat face types (which are about 25% bolder than bold face types) and a for-

mer pupil of Cottrell, misspelled 'Teingmouth' in his 1803 specimen. William Thorowgood retained this error in the specimen
issued after he took over the Fann Street Foundry. Thomas Cottrell,
himself, was subjected to variations on his name by his contemporaries, and no one knows for certain how he spelled it. Other examples of careless proofreading expose themselves through several
states of a specimen issued over a number of years.

The public became aware (for the first time in history) of the
names of famous fine printers. Society was abuzz with the latest
talk of the Continental press, particularly the work of G.B. Bodoni
at Parma. Even the monarch, King George IV, caught 'the Bodoni
Hum', as T.F. Dibdin noted. Dibdin was parodied in *Bibliosophia* by
his fellow clergyman, James Beresford. Elsewhere (in *Miseries of
human life*, volume 2 [London, 1810]), Beresford wrote of 'The
mental famine created among poor students by the modern luxury
of the press – hot-pressed paper – Bulmer's types – vignettes in
every page, etc...'.

Technology, as well as typography, was in transition. At the turn
of the nineteenth century, printing slowly transformed from a
handcraft into a fully mechanized industry. Machine-made paper
was manufactured by the Fourdrinier brothers in England by 1804.
In 1799 Lord Stanhope perfected the iron handpress; by 1814
Koenig's steam cylinder press was printing *The Times*. In the late
1820s, publishers' cloth bindings began to appear, and for the first
time books were marketed as completed products, rather than collated gatherings of sheets. In addition to increased leisure time and
widespread literacy (thanks to the Education Act), lamps burning
sperm whale oil allowed evening hours to be devoted to reading
novels and periodicals, along with the *Bible*.

THE ANGLOCENTRIC FOCUS of my work has a two-fold explanation: firstly, most nineteenth-century innovations in letterforms
were made by British and American foundries[5]; secondly, although
I am conversant with Romance languages, I did not have access to
a sufficiently wide sample of German, Dutch, French, Italian, or
Spanish specimens to include them in my survey. However, I did
notice that European founders, in their specimens, tended to follow
the lead of their western counterparts.

5. An exception is the Latin or
Runic style introduced by
Deberny in 1854.

I also came across some best-selling authors now forgotten by us: the prolific Charles Knight, a friend of Dickens, who singlehandedly wrote whole encyclopedias; C.G. Leland, a scholar who wrote wildly popular dialect verse; and Samuel Griswold Goodrich, author of almost 200 children's books, who was as renowned as Twain in his lifetime. Leland and Goodrich both grappled with the problem of their successful American editions being pirated in Europe. Goodrich, who claimed to have seven million books in print at one point, hired the young Nathaniel Hawthorne to ghostwrite one of his most popular works, a world history. Later, Hawthorne characterized him as a 'maggot who feeds on rich cheese.' The piousness of Goodrich's Peter Parley books undoubtedly led to their being forgotten by later generations, but there was such a feeding frenzy around the Peter Parley name that remainders of miscellaneous books would be reissued with 'Peter Parley' in the title, while Thomas Tegg of Cheapside and other unscrupulous publishers would generate their own Peter Parley items, in addition to piracies, aware of the lack of copyright protection. Goodrich received some money from Tegg in 1832, but went on to give him several manuscripts for which he was later unable to collect any income.[6]

In addition to literature and its branches, publicity printing, in the form of posters and packaging, underwent a transformation in the nineteenth century and consequently radical changes in reading were wrought by the introduction of display types. In showing printers how to deploy their types, the founders demonstrated a new approach to language.

I chart the popularity of Cicero's 'Oration against Catiline' as a specimen text, the use of the Lord's Prayer, and the discussion of the printer's craft and its history in the specimen books. Two remarkable prototypical concrete poetry works (Caslon's *Epitome specimen,* which I discuss in chapter 7, & Marder-Luse's *Specimen of candy stamps,* the subject of chapter 9) span the mid-century and link the self-conscious poetry of the Georgian era to the logopandocie of the high Victorian compositors. The later chapters recreate the American printer's milieu in the last quarter of the century from the specimen texts. Together, the chapters survey the many aspects of the literature of nineenth-century typefounders' specimens.

6. See further, Daniel Roselle, *Samuel Griswold Goodrich, creator of Peter Parley. A study of his life and work* (New York, 1968).

Readers are encouraged to wend their own paths through specimen books, and find personal threads of interest to trace, as each type presents its face for approval. Just about anything you seek will be found in the specimen texts: literary allusions, puns, patriotism, homilies, statistics. You will be surprised, as I was, to find how long ago some ideas were expressed, like the bishop foreshadowing Ball, or Cocteau's echo of Cicero. The very idea of printing, in fact, was hinted at by Cicero (who felt his own greatest achievement was putting down Catiline's rebellion), as I found in this passage from John Johnson's *Typographia* (1825, I:75):

> Cicero, in his *De Naturā Deorum*, has a passage from which Toland supposes the moderns took the hint of printing. The author orders the types to be made of metal, and calls them *formæ literarum*, the very words used by the first printers to express them. In Virgil's time, brands, with letters, were used for marking cattle, &c. with the owner's name.
>
> In the second book, he gives a hint of separate cast letters, when he speaks of 'some ingenious man's throwing the twenty-four letters of the alphabet, (made either of gold or other metal) by chance together, and thus producing *The Annals of Ennius*'.

Like the sculpture slumbering in the block of marble, the wisdom and humour lie dormant in the typecase. Cicero's idea was restated by Cocteau, who said, 'The greatest work of literature is no more than an alphabet in disorder', and nowhere is this more apparent than in the literary creations of nineteenth-century typefounders.

But if one author has allowed the close reading of these texts as literature it is, of course, James Joyce, and his covey of exegetes. Anything and everything is possible in Joyce and the interpretation of his works. He set an anchor for future scholars to constantly return to *his* story and an attempt to understand his world view, his referents. In *The Stoic comedians: Flaubert, Joyce and Beckett* by Hugh Kenner (1962:36) we find a parallel between Joyce's pigeonholes and the controlled chaos of the nineteenth-century typefounders' specimen texts:

> There presides over this phantasmagoria precisely the faith that presides over the eighteenth century's rationalism, the faith that we can register all relevant phenomena in some book where we can find them again: in a dictionary, where human speech is dissociated into words which can be listed in alphabetical order, or in an encyclopedia, where human knowledge

is broken up into discontinuous fragments to be registered on a similar principle.

Finally, as I have worked on this book for well over a decade, I perhaps at times seem to overstate my case or detour in pursuit of the hairy unknowable; may I once again then invoke Laurence Sterne, one of the first authors to fully comprehend the capabilities of typography as a vehicle for expression. He said:

It is the nature of an hypothesis, when once a man has conceived it, that it assimilates every thing to itself, as proper nourishment; and, from the first moment of your begetting it, it generally grows the stronger by every thing you see, hear, read, or understand. This is of great use.

AMJ

Le plus grand chef-d'oeuvre littéraire

n'est qu'un alphabet en desordre.

–Jean Cocteau

Double Pica Roman.

Quousque tandem abutere, Catilina, patientia nostra? quamdiu nos etiam furor iste tuus eludet? quem ad finem sese effrenata jactabit audacia? nihilne te nocturnum præsidium palatii, nihil urbis vigiliæ, nihil timor populi, nihil consensus bonorum omnium, nihil hic munitissimus habendi senatus locus, nihil horum ora vultusque moverunt? patere tua consilia non sentis? constrictam jam omnium horum conscientia teneri conjurationem tuam non vides? quid proxima, quid superiore nocte egeris, ubi fue-

ABCDEFGHIJKLMNOPQ
RSTUVWXYZÆŒ

ABCDEFGHIJKLMNOP
QRSTUVWXYZÆ

ABCDEFGHIJKLMNOPQRSTUVX
£1234567890

1

How long, O Catiline,
wilt thou abuse our forbearance?

... Let us return to a thoughtful consideration of the situation which faced Cicero
(a shady character) and his associates at the moment of the Catiline conspiracy.
– Graham Greene, *A Sort of life*

QUOUSQUE TANDEM ABUTERE, Catilina, patientia nostra?
quamdiu nos etiam furor iste tuus eludet? ad quem finem
effrenata audacia jactabit sese?' (*How long, O Catiline, will you
abuse our forbearance? How long, too, will your fury elude us? To
what length will your unbridled audacity go?*) William Caslon
introduced these opening lines of M.T. Cicero's 'Oration against
Catiline' into his type specimen sheet of 1734, and with the success
of his types, other founders found their tongues, albeit in Latin.[1]
More than any other formula, type specimens in the nineteenth
century employed this text, affirming Juvenal's observation that
'Catiline is everywhere.'[2] Many students would have learned the
speech by heart in school; as it is also usually the first piece in editions of Cicero's *Orations*, many other students would not have
gone past it. As J.W. Mackail[3] says of Cicero,

> Before his time, Latin prose was, from a wide point of view, but one among
> many local ancient dialects. As it left his hands, it had become a universal
> language, one which had definitely superseded all others, Greek included,
> as the type of civilised expression.

Caslon's use of Cicero had no less an effect. Just as his type had a
lasting impact on British typography, Caslon's choice of text
achieved totemic status for typefounders' specimens (*Figure 1*).

One theory has it that Caslon chose the Latin text for its initial Q,
as he was anxious to flaunt the graceful tail of this usually neglected

1. Why would a quote about a traitor retain such a mystique unless the air of conspiracy was familiar to typefounders? 'The history of English type-founding before Caslon is a weak & fitful accompaniment to the continental: it cannot be told separately', according to Harry Carter and Christopher Ricks in their foreword to E. Rowe Mores's *Dissertation upon English typographical founders & founderies (1778)* (London, 1961), p. lxvi.

For the history of English language type specimens before the era of this study, see W.T. Berry and A.F. Johnson, *A Catalogue of specimens of printing types by English and*

Scottish printers and founders, 1665–1830 (Oxford, 1935), Talbot Baines Reed, *A History of the old English letter foundries (1887)* (revised by A.F. Johnson: London, 1952), and Horace Hart, *Notes on a century of typography at Oxford, 1693–1794* (Oxford, 1900). On William Caslon, see Johnson Ball, *William Caslon master of letters* (Kineton, Warwickshire, 1973).

2. *Satire* XIV, lines 41–3.

3. J.W. Mackail, *Latin literature* (New York, 1923). According to Montaigne, Cicero's habit of wrinkling up his nose indicates a scornful disposition.

4. Garamond himself joined Cicero and St Augustine as a designation of a body size. See Nicolas Barker, 'The Aldine roman in Paris, 1530–34,' in *The Library*, fifth series, XXIX, 1:19 (Oxford, 1974).

5. Talbot Baines Reed, *A History of the old English letter foundries* (1887, revised by A.F. Johnson: London, 1952), p.263, note 3.

I have quoted Reed verbatim here, though he has dropped commas and capitals from the original, and says 'adopted' where Wilson has 'chosen'.

letter. (In following his lead, other founders made the tails of their 'Q's even more attenuated, until Bodoni virtually broke it off.)

Cicero's name would also be familiar to printers as a type size. Since the sixteenth century, Continental printers had referred to (what we call 12 point) pica as 'cicero,' after a popular typeface cut by Claude Garamond for Estienne's printing of Cicero in 1538–9.[4]

Alexander Wilson, the professor of astronomy who cut types for the Foulis brothers' press at the University of Glasgow, divulged the reason for using Latin: the relative infrequency of ascenders and descenders produced smooth ribbon-like lines of uniform colour. T.B. Reed[5] quotes the 1833 specimen of the Glasgow Foundry:

> 'In conformity', says the preface, 'with ancient immemorial usage we have in Part I displayed our Founts in the Roman Garb – the venerable *Quousque tandem* – but lest it should be supposed we had adopted the flowing drapery of Rome for the purpose of shading or concealing defects, we have in Part II shown off our founts in a dress entirely English.' This had already been done to some extent in the specimen of 1772.

In a departure from tradition, Thorowgood & Co. (1821) give prospective customers some English text in Double Pica No. 2:

> How far, O Catiline, wilt thou abuse our patience?
> How long shall thy frantic rage baffle the efforts of
> Justice? To what height meanest thou to carry thy
> daring insolence? Art thou nothing daunted at the
> ABCDEFGHIJKLMNOPQRSTUVWXY   £1234567890
> *ABCDEFGHIJKLMNOPQRSTU*   *MAN*   *MAN*

The first successful founders in the United States were former employees of Alexander Wilson, and doubtless emulated him for more than sentimental reasons. James Ronaldson's preface to his specimen of 1822 (Philadelphia) reads:

> To the Printers of the United States. Gentlemen,
>   The following specimen deviates from the custom of English Founders: the practice has been, to employ a particular latin sentence; perhaps the object was to enable printers to compare the size of one letter with another, and latin having few ascending and descending letters, shows type to the most advantage. Only a line of the latin is given in this for the purpose of comparing the size; and the specimen is in the language you will principally employ the type in, trusting its reputation to its own intrinsic merits.

Ronaldson's logic was not seen, however, and type specimens continued to be set in the by-now familiar Ciceronian complaint. If the choice of a different Ciceronian oration seemed like an innovation, few noticed. By 1834, in fact, even Ronaldson's successors, Johnson and Smith, had abandoned efforts at English composition and returned to '*Quousque tandem...*'.

The London founders, who led the way in the new styles (and also in sales) set the format. In his 1815 specimen book, Vincent Figgins departed from the tradition, as reported by T.C. Hansard in his *Typographia* (1825:317):

> The emulation to excel in cutting a new type of any particular feature, and the various fashions which, unfortunately for the printers, have been started and patronized, have left the specimen of a British letter-founder a heterogenous compound made up of fat-faces and lean-faces, wide-set and close-set, proportioned and disproportioned, all at once crying 'Quousque tandem abutere patientia nostra?' One founder, Mr. Figgins, has, however, broken the spell by showing specimens in our own *vulgar* tongue: still the 'Quousque' must be partly retained in order to show, by a comparison, the getting in, or driving out powers of his founts.[6]

Hansard campaigned against the Ciceronian formula: he goes on to denigrate the 'innovations' in type design made with the introduction of contrasted shading, and continues:

> Perhaps this *equivoque* (*How long* etc.) will appear the best reason that can be given for supposing that no new specimen of type can be exhibited but by this scrap of Latin, which contains about the very worst selection of characters that could have been chosen to exemplify the perfection of a fount. The proportion of vowels and liquids to other letters is much greater in the Latin language than in the English, and it must therefore be a fallacious mode of making us duly acquainted with the relative elegance and order of the various forms of types adapted chiefly for our own language.

Hansard then summons a quotation from the garrulous bibliomaniac Thomas F. Dibdin (1817, II:381-2) to deliver the *coup de grâce*:

> The Latin language, either written or printed, presents to the eye a great uniformity or evenness of effect. The *m* and *n* like the solid surloin upon our table, have a substantial appearance: no garnishing with useless herbs, or casing in coat of mail, as it were, to disguise its real character. Now, in our own tongue, by the side of this *m* and *n*, or a *t* at no great distance from it, comes a crooked, long-tailed *g*, or a *th*, or some gawkishly ascending or descending letter of meagre form, which are the very flankings, herbs, or dress-

6. The 'getting in, or driving out powers' must refer to the economy of fit of the respective types. *Typographia* (one of many works with the title) is an entertaining collection of Hansard's opinions about matters typographical, bibliographical and historical.

ings, of the aforesaid typographical dish, *m* or *n*. In short, the number of ascending or descending letters in our own language, the *p*'s, *l*'s, *th*'s, and sundry others of perpetual recurrence, render the effect of printing much less uniform and beautiful than in the Latin language. Caslon, therefore, and Messrs. Fry and Co., after him, should have presented their 'specimens of Printing Types' in the *English* language: and then, as no disappointment could have ensued, so no imputation of deception would have attached.

It must be noted that Figgins, in the samples that Hansard lauds, carefully chose words with neither ascending nor descending letters, retaining the *typographical surloin* of his 'main man' Dibdin.

Scraps and fragments of 'Quousque tandem', in its original and corrupted forms, appeared in founders' specimens throughout the nineteenth century. In 1837, for a change, the Boston Type and Stereotype Company (which keeps the English spelling of 'vigour', but can't decide whether to retain hyphenation or not) quotes Sallust's opinion, from *The Conspiracy of Catiline*, IV, 2, in Double Pica Antique:[7]

7. I checked a dozen contemporaneous translations of Sallust, and, not finding the quote, conclude it was made by a literate compositor.

> Lucius Catiline was descended of an illustrious family; he was a man of great vigour, both of body and mind, but of a disposition extremely profligate and de praved. From his youth he took

The nineteenth-century founders slowly began to discard Cicero as a specimen text, trying out the Lord's Prayer and other neutral standbys. By the end of the century, however, such reverence for tradition was completely forgotten.

2

Pan-religious Paternosters

By this art you may contemplate the variations of the 23 letters.
– Robert Burton, *The Anatomy of melancholy*, 1621

JOSEPH, THE FOUNDER OF THE FRY DYNASTY, and a Quaker, was described by Updike as a 'typographic Vicar of Bray' for the stylistic flip-flops of his foundry's output.[1] First he went into part-nership with Isaac Moore, who cut a Baskerville copy that in some ways surpassed the original (the italic is more florid, the roman more sparkling in its contrast and tightly articulated ductus). After Moore's departure around 1776, Fry reverted to copying the Caslon style that, despite the inroads made by Baskerville's innovations, endured in popularity. Printers resisted the delicate Baskerville style which was more fragile than the serviceable, sturdy Caslon model. Fry proudly proclaimed in his specimen that the Caslon imitations could be mixed with the originals and no one would notice. The Caslon foundry was not amused and the two rival foundries traded barbs in the prefaces to their specimens. (Fry's 1766 and 1785 specimens follow Caslon, too, in setting forth the 'Quousque's.)

Fry's type, like Caslon's, was popular in the American colonies. After the War of Independence, as Americans began to produce an adequate supply of type domestically, imports were still considered superior. Isaiah Thomas of Worcester, Massachusetts, had a Bible set at the Fry foundry and shipped to him in standing pages: an expensive and perilous proposition.

In 1782 Joseph Fry admitted his sons Edmund and Henry to the family firm, and in that year bought a collection of exotic types at the sale of the James Foundry, which had been stocked with Dutch types in 1710 and had absorbed most of the remnants of the older

1. *Printing types*, 1937, II, 118–20.

2. *Ibid*, p. 120. T.B. Reed lists the following types purchased by Fry: 6 Blacks, 4 Hebrew, 3 Rabbinical, 3 Greek and 1 Alexandrian, 1 Arabic, 1 Irish, 2 Ethiopic, 2 Samaritan, 2 Scriptorial, Union Pearl, Court Hand, & 35 flowers. (*A History of the old English letter foundries*, p. 302.)

Fry's Samaritan #7 is very like that cut by Dummers for Caslon, however, Reed says it is the type cut for the London *Polyglot* of 1657 (p. 63, fig. 33). For a facsimile of the James Sale Specimen, see Mores, *A Dissertation*, p. 14.

English foundries by the time of its dissolution.[2] These types formed the core of Fry's collection, which was displayed to full advantage in his son Edmund's book *Pantographia* (London, 1799). Edmund followed in his father's footsteps and trained as a doctor, but never practiced due to deafness. When Joseph retired from typefounding he started the famous chocolate business in Bristol. The foundry became so prominent that the street it stood on was renamed Type Street.

Aided by his father's superb holdings of non-Roman types, and inspired by a love of learning, Edmund Fry began a study of the physical appearance of other languages. Having studied punch-cutting and typefounding, he devoted himself to producing series of characters for which he had no practical use. But in terms of comparative grammatology – the 'science of writing' (which Derrida himself said is impossible to define) – the multiple examples of variant alphabets from each culture reward study.

Pantographia was the result of sixteen years of philological research. Although uncritical in its inclusion of spurious alongside real languages, the grammatolatry, or worship of letterforms, of its author is manifest on every page. Among the many variants within one language or group of alphabets can be found twenty varieties of Chaldean! For alphabets that Fry didn't possess, or couldn't create by adding sorts to an existing fount, he had wood facsimiles cut. *Pantographia* is important in its depiction of philology and typography at a moment when book types were about to be augmented by display types: those characters whose primary function was no longer legibility and the conveyance of information, but the appeal to the eye which would render them useful to advertising. The full title of this remarkable work is *Pantographia; containing accurate copies of all the known alphabets in the world; together with an accurate English explanation of the peculiar force or power of each letter: to which are added, specimens of all well-authenticated oral languages; forming a comprehensive digest of phonology.* The work is dedicated to Sir Joseph Banks, President of the Royal Society.

Pantographia typifies the longing for all knowledge that led to the founding of the Royal Society in England in the late seventeenth century. The society met regularly to watch scientific experiments, helped the government with problems from ventilating prisons to measuring the alcohol content of spirits, and funded voyages of exploration. With the expansion of the British Empire into Asia, curiosity about non-English peoples led to an interest in their languages. While communication was only the first step toward exploitation, some members of the British scholarly elite had a genuine interest in the not-yet-subjugated peoples of the world. Books like Captain James Cook's series of *Voyages* were eagerly studied for the information about the customs and beliefs of peoples encountered by British explorers. *Pantographia* follows in the tradition established by the Jesuits' Congregation of the Propaganda Fide in Rome at the end of the sixteenth century for the display of what were then called 'exotic' languages.

For the purposes of comparison, Fry's sample texts are set in the Lord's Prayer. Fry may have received his inspiration from the James Foundry's specimen. (If he received some of their metal as standing type, it may have been already composed for him.) Fry's piety is writ large in his reiterations of the *Paternoster*, but there was a precedent for such a litany. The use of the Lord's Prayer as a specimen text was a tradition at the Oxford University Press (where Bishop Fell had established the fabled collection of type).[3] In 1668 Bishop Wilkins compiled 72 versions of the Lord's Prayer, giving future scholars of a religious bent a head start.[4] Caslon used the Lord's Prayer as the text for many of the exotic types in his 1763 specimen.

In *Pantographia*, Fry attempts to record all known languages in a remarkable array of alphabets. Some question that this staggering work can be considered a type specimen, as a minority of the types are real – many of the more exotic alphabets are represented by woodcuts – and among them are several sizes and variant settings of a single type, for example of Jackson's arabic, which is used for Malayan #1 & #5, Persian #2, Tartaric #1, and Turkish #1.[5] But on the title page, Fry identifies himself as a letter-founder, so we can assume he means this work to be a specimen.

The work is comprehensive (as the exhaustive title suggests): it includes 39 Greeks and 12 Latins, 21 English (12 are variant versions of the 'Our Father' from different Bibles; the last is an engrossingly unreadable Secretary script[6] [*Figure 2*]), 20 Chaldeans, 11 Hebrews, 9 Syriacs and 9 Saxons, 8 Egyptians, 7 each of Tartaric, Samaritan, Phenician, Persian, Armenian, and Irish, 6 Malayans,

3. The earliest known specimen sheet – that of Erhard Ratdolt (Venice, 1476) – is set in the 'Ave Maria'. On the Fell types see Harry Carter and Stanley Morison's *John Fell: the University Press and the 'Fell' types* (Oxford, 1967).
    In Eastern religions, repetition is virtue, so the invention of printing in China, for mass-producing block-print images of the Buddha, can be seen as furtherance of devotion.
4. Oxford's specimens of 1693 and 1695 have 45 forms of the Lord's Prayer and 19 different languages. In 1700 the *Oratio dominica* exhibited the same text in over 100 languages. (Reed, p. 146.)
    Wilkins intended to logically organize all human knowledge into a single hierarchy and then invent a written character capable of communicating this information visually. Wilkins's experiments & documentation of smoke signals, sign language, and geometric cryptograms formed the basis of early cryptography during the English Civil War.
5. Pointed out by John Lane in a letter to the author, 13 August 1991. Joseph Jackson was apprenticed to Caslon.
6. Cottrell's Engrossing, which was shown in Luckombe's *The History and art of printing* (London, 1771). Stower's *The Printer's grammar* (1808) included a large sampling of Fry's collection with his comments, as well as types from other founders.

78

ENGLISH 21.

And whereas by Indenture
of afsignment bearing date
on or about the sixth day of
June in the Year of our Lord
one thoufand seven hundred
and eighty seven made bet
ween the said Edmund Fry
of London of the one and

ECCLEMACH.

A friend	*Nigefech*	A bow	*Pagounach*
The beard	*Iscotre*	To dance	*Mefpa*
The teeth	*Aour*	Seal	*Opobabos*
No	*Maal*	Yes	*Ike*
Father	*Aoi*	Mother	*Atzia*
Star	*Aimoulas*	Night	*Toumanes*
One	*Pek*	Six	*Pekoulana*
Two	*Oulach*	Seven	*Houlakoala*
Three	*Oullef*	Eight	*Koulefala*
Four	*Amnahou*	Nine	*Kamakoual*
Five	*Pemaka*	Ten	*Tomoïla*

and 6 Arabics.[7] The African languages – showing how far traders had penetrated the continent – are represented by a Hottentot, the 'click' language of the Bushmen in South West Africa (which doesn't jibe with the version described in the *Encyclopedia Britannica*), some numbers in Gambian, a Portuguese-sounding Angolan, Amharic, and Abyssinian, and some offhand remarks, typical of the time: 'The principal languages of Africa are, the Egyptian, Fetuitic, or of the Kingdom of Fetu, the Mauritanian or Moroccan, and the jargon of those savage nations inhabiting the deserts.' The Ethiopic or Amharic, which Fry cut himself, he ascribes to a Cushite shepherd, which would elevate that anonymous pastoral character to a rank with Sequoyah, the only other mortal to have devised an alphabet (Cherokee) from scratch.

Fry attempts to record all known languages, including Savanna,[8] Savoo, Nova Zemblan,[9] and Ecclemach (*Figure 2*), 'the language of a colony of North California, which differs widely from those of all their neighbours, and possesses more resemblance to our European tongues, than to those of North America'. From Cook's *Voyage*, vol. 3, we learn the language of the Friendly Isles, while another picturesque South Seas scenario is conjured by the Atooi lesson from Captain Cook's *Last voyage*, from which we learn to say 'Tehaia waheine? Eroemy ooroo. Homy ehoora.' ('Where's a woman? Fetch breadfruit. Give me a dance.')

Of the texts set in Roman, apart from the 34 examples of such simple sailor vocabulary, 131 are transliterations set in Roman (with accents), including Psalmanazar's Formosan, a fictitious language (debunked by the author himself in his posthumously published *Memoirs* of 1764) which Fry cites from the *Oratio dominica* (Amsterdam, 1715), without comment.

The fact that Fry's linguistic pipe dream was, not surprisingly, somewhat beyond his capabilities as a typefounder doesn't take away from the marvels of his *magnus opium*. Fry's work is better thought-out than the quotidian specimens of other founders. Among the splendours are three alphabets attributed to Charlemagne, an Alexandrian Greek erroneously ascribed to Wynkyn de Worde,[10] Fry's Italic (with its splendidly contorted tail to the 'g'), Armenian #5, which is composed of cavorting men and beasts,[11] and the twenty Chaldeans, as used by Adam (#2, #3), Noah, (#5), and

7. Two of the Hebrews were cut at Type Street for the Frys; four sets of Hebrew, purchased at the James sale, were not shown in *Pantographia*. Fry had cut six Hebrews, along with eight Greeks, and eight Blacks. Two Arabics came from William Martin, two from Caslon, one from Jackson, and a Nagari from Charles Wilkins, according to John Lane (letter to the author, 13 August 1991).

8. From the natives of Georgia, it resembles a West African dialect, or perhaps it is related to Gullah Creole.

9. See especially John F. Shade, *Historia Zemblica* (New Wye, 1959).

10. Wynkyn de Worde, an immigrant from the Rhineland, took over Caxton's business in Westminster and was first to use italic type in England, but there is scant evidence that he operated a foundry.

11. Anthropomorphic initials in Armenian survived from manuscript into letterpress. See, e.g., the fine wood-engraved initials accompanying *bolor* types of Christoffel van Dijck shown in György Haiman's *Nicholas Kis. A Hungarian punch-cutter and printer 1650–1702* (San Francisco, 1983), pp. 407–8.

12. It is the mysteriously named 'Writing of the crossing of the river', of Cornelius Agrippa. See E.A.Wallis Budge, *Amulets and superstitions* (London, 1930), p. 404. *Cf.* also the Gnostic alphabet on page 211, and the Hebrew alphabet shown by Budge at page 229.
13. Cut by Moxon, according to Reed. See also Rowe Mores, p. 33, and Moxon (1962:365–70).
14. That the publication of the Domesday Book was subject to delay may be gathered from a droll note from the contemporary antiquary E. Rowe Mores, who had mentioned Cottrell's fount of Norman for the intended Domes-day-book which will, at the present rate, 'hardly be finished by domes-day'.

Abraham (#7, #8). Chaldean #9 is a 'display' type, purportedly 'the same on which the tables of the law that were given to Moses, were written'. Chaldean #10 is apparently a Kabbalistic alphabet.[12] Fry quotes Sigismondo Fanti from Poinsinet de Sivry's *Recherches nouvelles sur la science des médailles* (Maastricht, 1778), 'that this alphabet is of very great antiquity, having been used by the Hebrews in the wilderness, in the time of Moses'. But, like Moses, we have reason to be wary of the Egyptians: they bear no resemblance to the Demotics shown in Diringer's *The Alphabet*. Fry's Cadeaux are French decorative capitals which date to the fifth century. The Irish #6,[13] Samaritan, Saxon #2, one Arabic, and some of the Hebrews and Greeks are 'cast at the Letter Foundry in Type Street', and the Russian #1 was also cut at Type Street (making it the first Cyrillic cut in England), but the Thibetan is copied from the second volume of the *Alphabeta varia/typis sacræ congregationis de propaganda fide* (the specimen of the Roman press which promulgated Catholic doctrine in foreign languages), and many others are taken from English and Dutch editions of *Oratio dominica,* and from Fournier's *Manuel typographique* (1764–6).

In addition to Moore's handsome roman and italic (which permeate the book in the 131 transliterations of alien Lord's Prayers into phonetic English), Cotterel's [*sic*] Domesday is reprinted from Luckombe's *History and art of printing* (1771:174), with many typographical errors, and in Fry's Appendix we find Jackson's Domesday, which was used instead of Cottrell's, with this legend:

> In page 50 of this book, I have given a specimen of the Norman character, cut by Cottrell, which was intended for this celebrated national work. The present is an impression from the same types that the folio edition of Domesday was printed with, and is composed from that part relating to the county of Dorset, p. 84–6. This letter was cut by my late friend Joseph Jackson, in a manner more successful than his fellow-labourer: he also engraved a variety of types for the Rolls of Parliament, a work which will ever reflect honor on the good taste of the present reign.
>
> I am indebted to my friend and antiquary, J. Nichols, for enabling me to gratify the curious with this specimen.[14]

The Appendix includes Achastlien,[15] Acheen –'one of the languages spoken in the island of Sumatra, taken from the comparative vocabulary' (of Marsden), including the Acheen for *white, black, die, cocoa nut, husband, wife, night, good, fire, water,* and *rice*; two versions of Batta, also from Sumatra (and also from Marsden); Barman, from the kingdom of Ava in Ceylon (copied from the Jesuits' two-volume *Alphabeta varia*); Bengallee (copied from the *Oratio dominica*); Courlandic (which sounds like hick Livonian); two Lampoons (from Marsden) as spoken in Sumatra, including the words for *rice, hog, I, god, white, black, die, water, cocoa nut, fish, moon*; Monks, which is an ornamental blackletter contributed by John Nichols from the *Gentleman's Magazine;* Sclavonian, or Ancient Russian, which was inadvertently omitted from the Russian section; and Rejang #1 *&* #2, from the island of Sumatra with a wonderful bug-like incipit mark, again drawn from William Marsden's *History of Sumatra* (London, 1783).

Among the real types, though not the real languages, we find Bishop Wilkins's 'curious and ingenious' Philosophic, cut by Joseph Moxon in 1668.

The repetitious use of the Lord's Prayer provides a phonological means of comparison that is slightly more compelling than a certain fragment of Latin. One hardly tires of reading the many minor variations of Anglicised versions of 'Our Father' in these handsome transitional types. Seeing the Lord's Prayer in Vandal must have been quite reassuring to Fry's readers. (Celtic is presented in a stirring poem from Ossian, who enjoys the company of Psalmanazar.)

Pantographia is an important reference and starting point for the study of language as well as letterforms, although Fry often confuses language with typographical diversity, and within languages, many of the texts are dialect variations. This is clear from the first of the Scots 'languages':

> Our fader, vhilk ar in hevin: hallovit be thy name: thy kingdon cum: thy vil be doin in erth, as it is in hevin. Gif uss yijs day our daily bred, and forgif us our sinnis, as we forgif them than sin agains us. Et led us not into tentation: bot delyver us from evil. Amen.

15. The words for one to ten in this language of a 'colony of Northern California', apparently 'a very difficult tongue', taken from the vocabulary of Pérouse; however, according to Kroeber's *Handbook of North American Indians*, vol. 8, this is the same tongue as Ecclemach, both being early names for the Essalen tribe inhabiting the Carmel Valley.

Several of the phonetically transcribed languages of the *Pantographia* – such as Lusatian, Lettice, or Ethiopic #2 – are tongue-twisters that echo the raving Panurge when he is first encountered by Gargantua, and adumbrate Kurt Schwitters's *i-Sonate mit Urlauten,* or 'Ur Sonata':

LUSATIAN.
Wosch nasch, kensch sy nanebebu, wss weschone bushy me twove: pos hish knam krailestwo twojo: so stany woli tuoja, takhak manebu, tak heu nasemu: klib nasch schidni day nam shensa, a woday nam wyni nashe, ack my wodawamij wini kam naschim: neweshi nass dospitowana: a le winoshi nas wot slego psheto twojo jo to kralestvo atra moz, ata zest

Pantographia is a challenge to read aloud, and undoubtedly enjoyed popularity on this account as much as for any linguistic, philological, or typographic importance. As a literary form, the book is a tour-de-force, providing endless speculative springboards to the intercommunication of putative races.

3

Guard the mysteries!
Constantly reveal them!

It hath been shewed already how ineffectual it is for any other but Artists to take the oversight of Printing, and how easily the inspection of strangers may be eluded by any that have a minde to make a sinister use of that Art; and likewise how little better it is to call Printers to the assistance of others, since they are like to be but cold in their scrutiny, when their discoveries shall redound nothing to their own profit or reputation, but to the advantage of those that call them, whose hands will be thereby the more strengthened against them.
– *A Brief discourse concerning printing and printers*
(London: printed for a society of printers, 1663)

OF COURSE, a topic of great interest to printers is printing itself, and texts about 'the black art'[1] began appearing in specimen books around the beginning of the nineteenth century, mostly in the form of accolades to the art and speculation on its history.

The origins of the art were long cloaked in secrecy. As Oxonides said, 'The Art of Printing, which has given light to most other things, hides its own head in darkness.'[2] Gerard Meerman paraphrased this (in *Origines typographicæ*, The Hague, 1765), according to Bowyer, in his *Account of the origin of printing with remarks* (London, 1774): 'It may seem somewhat strange that the original of Printing has hitherto eluded all the researches of the learned; and that this art, which has given light to all others, should itself remain in obscurity.'

The first printers concealed their work from industrial espionage. As the epigraph above shows, printers had their own reasons for keeping trade secrets, so it is appropriate that this particular paranoiac shade attend the development of what was the harbinger of the age of mechanization.

1. 'Black Art' is a corruption of necromancy or black magic but has been appropriated by printers to refer to our own inky conjurings. See James Alexander, *The Literary conjuror: an enigmatical, though, in almost every instance, a literally true story, illustrated by a copious glossary, and other matters highly entertaining* (Cork, 1808).
2. Letter to the *Weekly Miscellany*, April 26, 1735.

Early printers kept their secrets even in the face of persecution by the Church, which mistrusted this new & powerful source of information. The irresistible connection between Gutenberg's capitalist business partner, Johannes Fust, and Doctor Faustus had fermented into the notion that the first printer sold his soul to the Devil in exchange for the secret of printing. Henry Lemoine tells the story[3] in his *Typographical antiquities* (1797:7):

3. Quoting Zapf's *Annales typographicæ augustanæ ab ejus origine 1466 usque ad annum 1530. Accedit F.A. Veith diatribe de origine et incrementis artis typographicæ* (Augsburg, 1778).

> Some writers relate that Faustus having printed off a considerable number of copies of the Bible, to imitate those which were commonly sold in MS. Fust undertook the sale of them at Paris, where the art of Printing was then unknown. As he sold his printed copies for 60 crowns, while the scribes demanded 500, this created universal astonishment; but when he produced copies as fast as they were wanted, and lowered the price to 30 crowns, all Paris was agitated. The uniformity of the copies increased the wonder; informations were given to the police against him as a magician; his lodgings were searched; and a great number of copies being found, they were seized: the red ink with which they were embellished, was said to be his blood; it was seriously adjudged that he was in league with the devil; and if he had not fled, most probably he would have shared the fate of those whom ignorant and superstitious judges condemned, in those days, for witchcraft; from thence arose the origin of the story of the Devil and Dr. Faustus.

John McCreery versifies the story in his poem, 'The press' (Liverpool, 1803):

> When the new treasure FAUST to Gallia bore,
> Her sons with jealous eyes the work explore;
> The capital convulsive terror shook,
> Scared at the numbers of the sacred book;
> Nor could the holy theme their fears dispel
> Of some foul dealings with the guests of hell.
> Forth to the awful judgment hall they sped,
> And, bound in chains, the culprit artist led.
> A pious chief, in crozier'd armour drest,
> His keen abhorrence of the wretch exprest:
> 'Thou, who hast dealt with blackest imps below,
> 'Leagued against man with man's eternal foe,
> 'Repent,– and be to us the means explain'd,
> 'Say by what art these volumes thou hast gain'd.'
> FAUST with undaunted heart the prelate view'd,
> His eye bespoke a spirit unsubdued:
> 'With no infernal power did I consult,
> 'Of human labour this the great result.'

McCreery explains in a footnote:

> In this adventure, we seem to have the origin of the opinion, that printers
> have the occasion for the assistance of a supernatural personage in the
> progress of their labours, with whom all the rest of the world is most anx-
> ious to avoid any very intimate acquaintance. Had we not other complaints
> against his Satanic Majesty, than that of assisting John Faust to bring to
> perfection the Art of Printing, we certainly should have no right to stigma-
> tize him as being of so malignant a disposition as he is commonly repre-
> sented. The PRINTER'S DEVIL is a character almost identified with the
> origin of the art, and we may consider ourselves peculiarly fortunate in hav-
> ing a guardian exclusively assigned to us, from whom, notwithstanding his
> general bad conduct to other people, we have so little to apprehend, and
> who is commonly our faithful assistant, both in our labours and in our plea-
> sures. From hence also the legend of the *Devil and Doctor Faustus*.

Fust was exonerated, but (according to Hansard) Samuel Palmer, in
his *General history of printing*,[4] 'mentions the incident relative to
the origin of printing'. As it turns out, the real 'Doctor Faustus' was
a con artist despised by Melanchthon, the Lutheran reformer and
educator, and referred to in 1532 as a 'great sodomite and necro-
mancer'[5] by the City of Nuremberg, who refused him safe conduct.
Though a veritable proto-televangelist, this Faust does have a connection to literature through his secret information-retrieval system
with which he claimed he could produce the lost comedies of
Plautus and Terence and that 'he could out-do Ezra's restoration of
the lost Scriptures by reproducing all the works of Plato & Aristotle,
should they ever be forgotten, and what is more, improve on them.'[6]
Faustus was a contemporary of the inventor of printing, and his
legend serves to remind us of the bedevilled mentality of the times.

Around 1790, William Blake wrote, in one of his 'Memorable fan-
cies' in *The Marriage of Heaven and Hell*, 'I was in Hell and saw the
method in which knowledge is transmitted from generation to generation.' Figgins (1815) describes how the clergy initially ascribed
the invention of printing to the Devil. Books were said to be 'written with the blood of the victims who devoted themselves to Hell,
for the profit or fame of instructing others'. Figgins's source for this
material is Henry Lemoine's *Typographical antiquities* (London,
1797).[7] Of course, the clergy had other, less godly, reasons for oppos-
ing the spread of printing. The paragraph from which Figgins lifted
his quote is worth giving more fully:

4. Palmer's book (called 'very inaccurate' by Bigmore and Wyman & 'exceedingly super-ficial' by Dibdin), was largely compiled and completed by George Psalmanazar after Palmer's death in 1732:
'Mr. Palmer dying before he had completed his work, it was resumed by the famous George Psalmanaazar, who wrote all that relates to the English Printers, making Book III. in about 100 pages, without say-ing any thing of the Scotch or Irish; as also the last page of the preface, giving an account of Mr. Palmer's intention of treating of the practical part of printing'. ('Memoirs of Joseph Ames by the late Richard Gough, esq.' from Dibdin's edi-tion of Ames's *Typographical antiquities* [1810:I:33].) Dibdin spells Psalmanazar's name in different ways.
5. E.M. Butler, *The Myth of the magus* (Cambridge, England, 1948), p. 121.
6. *Ibid.* Unfortunately Faustus was never given the opportuni-ty to demonstrate his ability to recreate lost books. A later rendering of the supernatural in the early printing office can be found in Mark Twain's final novel, *No. 44, the mysterious stranger* (Berkeley, 1969).
7. Lemoine was an eccentric London bookseller & transla-tor. Though derived from other writers, his book made use of more continental sources than his contemporaries in Britain.

Before the invention of this divine art, mankind were absorbed in the grossest ignorance, and oppressed under the most abject despotism of tyranny. The clergy, who before this æra held the key of all the learning in Europe, were themselves ignorant, though proud, presumptuous, arrogant, and artful; their devices were soon detected through the invention of typography. Many of them, as it may naturally be imagined, were very averse to the progress of this invention; as well as the brief-men, or writers, who lived by their manuscripts for the laity. They went so far as to attribute this blessed invention to the devil; and some of them warned their hearers from using such diabolical books as were written with the blood of the victims who devoted themselves to Hell, for the profit or fame of instructing others.

We can sense sympathy for the Devil emerging in the printers' ongoing battle with the Church. The Oxford Printing Press has an 'origins of printing' article in their specimen (London, 1852)[8] that includes the disclosure: 'Faust had the policy to conceal his art, and to this it has been supposed we are indebted for the tradition of "The Devil and Dr. Faustus", handed down to the present times.'

Another relic of the Faust legend is the application of the term Printer's Devil to the printer's apprentice. Such satanic sentiments hung around 'the black art' well into the Age of Reason.

By the end of the eighteenth century, though, information about the true origins of printing slowly trickled out, amid a wash of speculation. James Watson, one of the first to write in English[9] on the origins in his *History of the art of printing* does so 'as one carrying a Lantern in a dark Night, that I may communicate to others the Light by which I myself walk.' (1713:7) Indeed, we can trace in type specimens the dawning of general knowledge about the art, as well as the printers' pride in it.

In 1774 William Bowyer the Younger, who printed at the sign of Cicero's Head in London, published *The Origin of printing, in two essays: I. The Substance of Dr. Middleton's dissertation on the origin of printing in England; II. Mr. Meerman's account of the first invention of the art (with appendices on books in Hebrew, Greek, and the early polyglotts).* As the title suggests, all the writers of this era were madly glossing each other's works, so tentative assertions gained in authority by repetition.

Viewed without the scientific aids of later bibliographers, the remoteness of the 'true' origins of printing sanctioned such accounts as Mr Meerman's, who remembered – over 320 years after the

8. The Oxford Printing Press (not to be confused with Thomas Hailing's Oxford Printing Works of Cheltenham) was a branch of M^{essrs} Partridge & Oakley of Paternoster Row, located in the Oxford Mews off the Edgware Road.

In T. Adams' *Typographia* (Philadelphia, 1845:16), which was compiled mainly from English sources, we find a paraphrase of the same legend. 9. After Richard Atkyns's *Original and growth of printing* (1664), and Joseph Moxon's *Mechanick exercises on the whole art of printing* (1683–4). Watson's preface was written by John Spotswood, Advocate, and the historical portion of his text is a condensed translation of De la Caille's *Histoire de l'imprimerie* (Paris, 1689). A.F. Johnson, footnote to T.B. Reed, p. 257.

introduction of moveable type – the original wooden characters he had played with as a child. This partially substantiated his crediting a Dutchman, Laurens Janszoon Coster, with the introduction of moveable types. But Gutenberg partisans stood firm. The controversy up to 1884 is covered in Bigmore and Wyman (following the very confusing account given in 1842 in Timperley's *Encyclopedia*), where we learn that Christoph Besold (in *De bombardis: ac item de typographia, dissertatio historica*, Tübingen, 1620) doubted that the Germans could have learned the art of printing from the Chinese, and so must have invented it independently, and that Bernard Mallinckrodt (in *De ortu ac progressu artis typographicæ*, Cologne, 1640) took a poll and found an overwhelming majority in favour of Mainz over Haarlem as the birthplace of Occidental typography. (John Johnson [1824:I:39] summarizes Mallinckrodt's tally: 'For Mentz: 109; Against Haerlem: 13; Neuters: 11.') For these scholars at least, the matter was settled.

Although key documents on the history of the origin and development of printing had been collected by Christian von Wolf in *Monumenta typographica* (Hamburg, 1740), there was still an air of mystery surrounding it, and a reluctance on the part of printers to state anything factual, due, perhaps, as much to ignorance as to a desire to protect secrets.

By the nineteenth century, brief paragraphs of printing lore began to appear in specimen books. In these passages, often quoted from contemporary writers, typefounders comment on the growth of the art, extol its virtues, & speculate on the roles of the first principals in the industry. The couplet by Lew Welch (from his poem 'Theology'), with which I titled this chapter, captures the cautious yet boastful position the typefounders took in relation to their art.

Vincent Figgins issued a type specimen in 1815 that showed three pages of Pica types set up in such a paragraph, drawn from *The History of the house of Austria* by the Reverend Archdeacon Coxe: 'The consequence of this happy and simple discovery was a rapid series of improvements in every art and science, and a general diffusion of knowledge among all orders of society'.[10]

Figgins also quoted Hansard's glowing accolades of his work, as well as articles on Earl Stanhope and the introduction of composition forme rollers. (These pages are retained in Figgins' 1832 book.)

10. William Coxe (1747–1828), Archdeacon of Wiltshire, *A History of the house of Austria from… 1218 to 1792* (2 vols, London, 1807; second edition, corrected, 6 vols, 1820), was later quoted by T.C. Hansard in *Typographia*, and Timperley in his *Encyclopedia of literary & typographical anecdote*. The corrected second edition was printed by Hansard & includes this footnote at page 421 of volume 1: 'A controversy has arisen concerning the first discoverer of the art of printing, between the three towns of Haerlem, Mentz, and Strasburgh, each from a natural partiality attributing it to their own countryman. The dispute, however, has turned rather on words than facts; and seems to have arisen from the different definitions of the word printing. If we estimate the discovery from the invention of the principle, the honour is unquestionably due to Laurence Costar, a native of Haerlem, who first found out the method of impressing characters on paper by means of carved blocks of wood. If moveable types be considered as a criterion, the merit of the discovery is due to John Guttenberg of Mentz; and Schepfer, in conjunction with Faust, were the first who founded types of metal. The modern improvement of stereotype printing may be considered as a recurrence to the first and simple principles of the art.'

In Great Primer Script, Figgins resurrected the gripes about the church, in a paragraph quoted from an unpublished memoir of Charles, Earl Stanhope, that had been quoted in Hansard's *Typographia* (1825:62):

> Printing, from its commencement, has always had some opponents, actuated from selfish interests; who, in many cases, possessed such influence over their fellow-men as to corrupt their judgments and decisions, whenever the question of its advantages or disadvantages to mankind came to be agitated. The monks, in particular, were its inveterate opposers, the great majority of them acting upon the spirit of an avowal made by the Vicar of Croydon, in a sermon preached by him at St. Paul's Cross, when he declared 'We must root out printing, or printing will root out us'. Happily, this superior art withstood their hostility, and it became the main engine by which their artifices, invented to keep the people in superstition and ignorance, were detected and punished.

Gutenberg is credited for being the first printer, but is usually considered a xylographer (or printer from woodblocks), while Peter Schoeffer steals the glory for casting the original metal types. An antique (slab serif) shown by Richard Austin and Son's Imperial Letter-Foundry, Worship Street, Finsbury Square, (in the St Bride copy of the specimen book from 1819 with the date excised and a price list dated 1827 inserted) credits this thesis in Long Primer (*Figure 3*):

> The art of printing was invented by the GUT-TEMBERGS at MENTZ, about the year 1450, who used types cut in wood, but all authorities concur in admitting PETER SCHOEFFER their son in law to be the inventor of cast metal types; and we may suppose the whole art of letter founding as he produced an alphabet of matrixes and cast metal types: printing and type founding was first practiced in England by W. CAXTON an Englishman in 1471 & fi fl ff ffi ffl , : ; . - - ! ? ') °

In 1835 Figgins quotes this paragraph in English Ronde:

> Peter Schoeffer of Gernsheim, perceiving his master Faust's design, and being himself ardently desirous to improve the Art, found out the methods of cutting the characters in a Matrix, that the letters might easily by singly cast, instead of being cut. He privately cut Matrices for the whole Alphabet; and when he showed his Master the letters cast from those Matrices, Faust

ANTIQUE.

NONPAREIL,

ABCDEFGHIJKLMNOPQRSTUVWXYZ

LONG PRIMER,

The art of printing was invented by the GUT-TEMBERGS at MENTZ about the year 1450, who used types cut in wood, but all authorities concur in admitting PETER SCHOEFFER their son in law to be the inventor of cast metal types; and we may suppose the whole art of letter founding as he produced an alphabet of matrixes and cast metal types: printing and type founding was first practiced in England by W. CAXTON an Englishman in 1471 & fi fl ff ffi ffl ,:;.--!?')°

ABCDEFGHIJKLMNOPQRSTUVWXYZ

ABCDEFGHIJKLMNOPQRSTUVWXYZ
£1234567890

ENGLISH,

The art of printing was invented by the GUTTEMBERGS at Mentz, about the year 1450, who used types cut in wood, but all authorities concur in admitting that PETER SCHOEFFER their son-in-law was the inventor of cast. fi fl ff ffi ffl

ABCDEFGHIJKLMNOPQRSTUV WXYZ& ,:;.-!? £1234567890

TWO LINE ENGLISH,

ABCDEFGHI
JKLMNOPR!
STUVWXY.-'
1234567890

AUSTIN and SON'S Imperial Letter-Foundry,
Worship Street, Finsbury Square.

11. On Peter Schöffer's possible role as a typefounder, see Harry Carter, *A View of early typography* (Oxford, 1969), pp. 103, 9.
   This 'extract from the family papers of J.F. Faustus of Aschaffenburgh (circa 1620)' was quoted in Bowyer & Nichols' *Origin of printing*, where Nichols comments: 'The signification of Schoeffer, in Latin, is Opilio; in English, Shepherd – Gutenberg signifies, in English, Goodhill. – John Faust or Fust, is by many supposed to have derived his name from Faustus, happy; and Doctor Faustus seems to carry an air of grandeur in the appelation; but very erroneously so; for John Faust, or Fust, is no more than John Hand, whence our word Fist.' *Cf.* Palmer (1732:17) and Timperley (1842: 107–8). For a clearer modern interpretation of Faust von Aschaffenburg's 'distorted version of the lawsuit and of Gutenberg's role in the invention,' see Janet Ing, *Johann Gutenberg and his Bible* (New York, 1988), pp. 42–4.

was so pleased with the contrivance, that he promised Peter to give him his only daughter Christina in marriage, a promise which he soon after performed.[11]

In 1849, Neill & Co. of Edinburgh employed the same quotation, indicating the source as 'testimony preserved in the family by Jo. Fred Faustus of Ascheffenburg':

Though a variety of opinions exist as to the individual by whom the art of printing was first discovered; yet all authorities concur in admitting PETER SCHOEFFER to be the person who invented *cast metal types*, having learned the art of *cutting* the letters from the Guttenbergs: he is also supposed to have been the first who engraved on copper-plates.

As late as 1893, the Benton-Waldo Foundry of Milwaukee still suggested (in 30 point Royal Script):

> *There is a statement current that*
> *Schoeffer was the first founder, but*
> *The manufacture of Printing Type*
> *has been brought to a greater degree of*

(The text ends there.) In 'The Press', McCreery credits 'Faust', rather than Schoeffer, with casting the first metal types:

> To give to distant times a name more dear,
> To spread the blessing thro' a wider sphere,
> SCHOEFFER and FAUST with kindling ardor fired,
> Lent the strong aid that thirst of fame inspired;
> The stubborn block, with rude unchanging form,
> One end could answer, but one task perform,
> Till FAUST, with all his powers of genius ripe,
> Struck the fine die, and cast the moving type,
> That ever, as the curious artist will'd,
> In some new station some new office fill'd.

McCreery, however, admitted his methodology proceeded according to 'the names that rose to court the rhymes'.
   'Faust' was also given the laurel by that non-practicing master of the art, William Thorowgood, in his *New specimen of printing types* (London, 1834), in a piece displaying his 'Double Pica Script on inclined body (without segments of Letters or Combinations)' that contains a reference to the Helmasperger Instrument, a brief in legal jargon summarizing a lawsuit brought against Gutenberg by

Double Pica Script on inclined body.

The invention of Printing took place in the early part of the 15th century, and it long remained an undetermined point, concerning the place where and the person by whom it was then discovered. The best authorities place the event between the years 1440 and 1450.

It was a long controverted question by many learned antiquarians, whether Guttemberg or Faust was the inventor of the art, till happily the original instrument was found, by which it appears, the former only associated the others with him for the sake of their purses, he not being able to proceed without on account of the great expence attending the cutting of blocks of wood, which after they were once printed from became entirely useless for any other work. This instrument which is dated November 6, 1455, is decisive in favor of Guttemberg; the honor of inventing single types, made of metal, is ascribed to Faust wherein he received much and valuable assistance from his servant and son-in-law, who invented the punches, mattrixes,

Thorowgood, London.

12. The second paragraph comes almost verbatim from Luckombe's *The History and art of printing* (London, 1771), with the important difference of 'former' being substituted for 'latter', thereby shifting the invention from Faust to Gutenberg. Luckombe's information was adapted from several sources: 'The Historical part is collected from the ingenious Mr. MOXON, and other able Writers on this noble Art, to the publication of the late industrious antiquary Mr. AMES, in his Typographical Antiquities of Printing, together with the collected judgments of the learned Dr. MIDDLETON, Mr. ATKYNS, Mr. WATSON, Mr. PALMER, &c. &c. wherein the pleas of the invention are impartially given.'

A snippet of this text was used by William Hagar & Co (New York, 1826).

13. The types are usefully identified as to foundry of origin. Book types from Miller, Wilson, and Caslon & Livermore are set forth, blackletter from Thorowgood and Figgins, Wilson's fine 'Glasgow Homer' Greek, and some of the exotics of Dr Fry. Greek as seen in the specimen books is often set out in the start of Homer's *Iliad*. Hebrew was traditionally set in the opening of Genesis.

On James Moyes, see Iain Bain, 'James Moyes's Temple Printing Office of 1825', *Journal of the Printing Historical Society* 4 (London, 1968), and Berry & Poole's *Annals of printing* (London, 1966) where

his partners (*Figure 4*):[12]

> The invention of Printing took place in the early part of the 15th century, and it long remained an undetermined point, concerning the place where and the person by whom it was then discovered. The best authorities place the event between the years 1440 and 1450.
>
> It was a long controverted question by many learned antiquarians, whether Guttemberg or Faust was the inventor of the art, till happily the original instrument was found, by which it appears, the former only associated the others with him for the sake of their purses, he not being able to proceed without on account of the great expence attending the cutting of blocks of wood, which after they were once printed from became entirely useless for any other work. This instrument which is dated November 6, 1455, is decisive in favor of Guttemberg; the honor of inventing single types, made of metal, is ascribed to Faust wherein he received much and valuable assistance from his servant and son-in-law, who invented the punches, mattrixes,

Elsewhere in the same book, quoting John Johnson (1824, 1:76), Thorowgood ponders the bountiful advantages bestowed on mankind by the introduction of printing, in English No. 2:

> Of all the discoveries which have been made, we conceive the reflecting mind will admit that none have tended more to the improvement and comfort of society than that of printing; in truth it would almost be impossible to enumerate the advantages derived by all professions from the streams of this invaluable fountain, this main spring of all our transactions in life. It was justly said by a celebrated writer, that were the starry heavens deficient of one constellation, the vacuum could not be better supplied, than by the introduction of a printing press.

The preface to James Moyes's *Specimens of the types commonly used in the Temple printing office* (London, 1826), is a 'Summary of the origin of printing.'[13]

Another fragmentary narrative is found in Alexander Wilson's Sons specimen of 1812. They applaud the art preservative in an excerpt from Philip Luckombe's *The History and art of printing* (London, 1771, following Watson) set in the Wilsons' Script (another one of many examples of aposiopesis we encounter in specimen texts, with a typographical error in the last partial word) (*Figure 5*):

> *The usefulness of the Art of Prin-*
> *ting is so universally acknowledged, it*
> *needs no proof; every one knows, wi-*

SCRIPT.

The usefulness of the Art of Printing is so universally acknowledged, it needs no proof; every one knows, without the invention of this Art, the productions of great men would have been confined in the possession of a few, and of no utility to posterity. In short, what would the Moderns know of the sciences did not Printing furnish them with the discoveries of the Ancients? All the elogiums we can bestow on the invention, and the honours we pay it, are far deficient of its merit; and, we believe, few will deny it when they consider the vast expences which our forefathers were at to procure manuscripts, of which we have given a few instan-

A B C D E F G H I K L M

they note that the wrapper of his scarce specimen portrays the new premises – built after an 1824 fire in Moyes's Hatton Garden office – the first printing office constructed as such.

thout the invention of this Art, the productions of great men would have been confined in the possession of a few, and of no utility to posterity. In short, what would the Moderns know of the sciences did not Printing furnish them with the discoveries of the Ancients? All the elogiums we can bestow on the invention, and the honours we pay it, are far deficient of its merit; and, we believe, few will deny it when they consider the vast expences which our forefathers were at to procure manuscripts, of which we have given a few iustan-

In 1830, Howe, a minor founder and stereotyper in Philadelphia, sets out each style & size in the paragraph from Johnson beginning, 'Of all the discoveries which have been made,' quoted above. The book also includes Cicero's unforgettable lambasting of Catiline.

Thomas Curson Hansard, a popular British authority on printing during the nineteenth century, is quoted in William Miller's specimen book of 1834, along with a paragraph on the value of printing as a 'permanent means of communication.' John Knox is quoted in Vincent Figgins's 1828 specimen (from the essay by Stanhope that was quoted by Hansard):

> 'The art of Printing', says Dr. Knox, 'in whatever light it is viewed, has deserved respect and attention. From the ingenuity of the contrivance it has ever excited mechanical curiosity; from its intimate connection with learning, it has justly claimed historical notice, and from its extensive influence on morality, politics, and religion, it has now become a subject of very important speculation'.

The full quotation, given by Johnson (1824, I:3) and Timperley (1842:111), continues with an analogy between printing and gunpowder, and mentions the multitude who wish neither invention had been brought to light, 'for the increased number of books distract rather than improve the mind'.

Earl Stanhope's iron handpress, which revolutionized printing, & composition forme rollers, another great technological advance, were celebrated for the first half of the nineteenth century in laudatory paragraphs. The dedication of Caleb Stower's *The Printer's grammar* (London, 1808) to the Earl, the praise of Hansard in *Typographia* (London, 1825), & of William Savage in *A Dictionary of the art of printing* (London, 1841), attest to the importance of Stanhope's contributions to the improvement of the art.

A page from John Johnson's *Typographia* (1824, II:7) on Aldus & Italic was chosen by several founders to demonstrate their italics.

When the founders wished to demonstrate verse in open settings, invariably the choice would be something along the lines of

> What light is yon, that shines so bright,
> And rivals all the stars of Night?

or

> Behold the Press! from which pure fountain springs
> The talent that upholds the Throne of Kings!

from Johnson's *Typographia* (I:78; I:608), found, for example, in the *Specimen of book-work type, submitted by William Lake, 50, Old Bailey* (London, 1837) in types from Caslon. This specimen also includes the quotation, 'Printing took its rise about the middle of the fifteenth century, and in the course of a few years reached that height of improvement which is scarcely surpassed even in the present times', from Coxe's *History of the house of Austria* (1820, I: 421). Coxe's short excursion into the effects of printing on civilization – expansion of knowledge, general spirit of improvement in every art and science, &c. – was typical of the times. Studiedly noncommittal pastiches of then-current knowledge, which at that time in England was little more than the 'subject of very important speculation', were favoured by printers reluctant to side with Gutenberg or Coster, but eager to extoll the benefits of the invention of the art.

John Remfry, in *Specimens of printing types, ornaments, &c.* (London, 1840), ponders the turn of events:

> The discovery of the Art of Printing may be regarded as the commencement of a new era in the history of mankind. The shackles, by which the minds of the multitude had been bound for ages, were then thrown off; and men of all classes began to read and think for themselves. In the present highly-improved state of the art, the press is an engine of immense power; and it is highly probable that in a few years the entire population will be able to read, and a person who takes no pleasure in reading will be a rare phenomenon.

14. Illustrated in Nicolete Gray, *Nineteenth century ornamented typefaces*, 1976:41.
15. 'Hereby, tongues are known, knowledge groweth, judgment increaseth, books are dispersed, the Scripture is read, stories be opened, times compared, truth discerned, falsehood detected and with finger pointed, and all (as I said) through the benefit of printing'. Foxe's *Book of martyrs*, 1641 ed., I:927.

(Despite his plea for literacy, Remfry's 5-line Tuscan Egyptian [*sic*] reads 'MURCURY'.)

The importance of typography to the dissemination of literature is trumpeted in Thorowgood and Co.'s *Specimen of printing types*, issued in London around 1840, which states categorically in Brevier Grotesque Shaded:[14]

LETTER FOUNDING AND PRINTING ARE THE TWIN PROFESSIONS WHICH CONTRIBUTE MOST TO THE LUXURIES OF LITERATURE.

Since Foxe's *Actes and monuments of these latter and perillous days* (1563),[15] many authors had extolled the benefits of printing, but, in general, during the early Victorian period, the founders are plagued with banality. The verbal style of *parvum in multo* still found favour with many founders, particularly when welling from the flamboyant quill of T.C. Hansard. Because the texts are, after all, only there to give colour to a page of type and show the impression of a full page, they often tend to high-sounding gobbledegook, running abruptly off the bottom of the page, never to be continued. The Montreal Type Foundry offers the following paragraph on 'the black art' in Great Primer Secretary in its 1849 specimen book:

> By means of the Printing Press, man may speak to all kindreds, and tribes, and peoples, and tongues, and make his voice be heard, with simultaneous power, beyond the Atlantic waves, and upon the shores of the Caspian Sea, and amid the population of Europe. Nay, he may speak to accumulating generations after death with all the freshness and force of eloquence. Printing gives to man a sort of ubiquity, and eternity of being; it enables him to outwit death, and enshrine himself amid a kind of earthly immortality. His words that breathe, and thoughts that burn, are enshrined and embalmed; and with him thousands hold profitable or hurtful communion till time is no more. If, then, we are loudly called upon to be careful what we speak and what we do we are doubly warned to beware what we throw into the press, and invest with a power to endure, and strength to pass every sea, and to visit every people. It is to this we are indebted for the promulgation of the arts and sciences, and for every other social and intellectual blessing. In short, it may be asked, what is there, that tends to improve the moral and physical condition of man, that is not fostered by the all powerful energies of the Press!

And in Double Pica Church Text and Great Primer Black Shaded:

> The history of the Art of Printing is enveloped in mystery; this Art, which commemorates all other inventions, which hands down to posterity every important event, which immortalizes the actions of the great, and which, above all, extends and diffuses the word of God to all mankind; this very Art has left its own origin in obscurity, and has given employment to the studies and researches of

... Of what we may never know.

Another anacoluthon slowly unfolds in the scarce *A Specimen of types & ornaments, used in the printing-office of Joseph Aston, Exchange, Manchester* (ca. 1808). More of the story is revealed in each diminishing size, as in the fireside word game where each participant has to recite the list handed on by the previous speaker without error or omission and then add another item to pass on. The superfluity of commas, indeed, suggests a faltering delivery, as if the compositor were attempting to recall the previous section before tacking on the next. By the time we reach Nonpareil we have learned this much:

> The invention of Printing, was an event of the greatest possible consequence to mankind. The sun of knowledge, then burst the thick clouds of ignorance and superstition, and diffused its cheering light upon the world. Typography became the star, which pointed out the way to science; a way, which, till then, had been only trod by the few, whose riches had commanded, or whose devotion to seclusion, had procured them access to the MSS. which contained all the remains of the learning of the preceding ages.

Even as the Faustian legends charmed and intrigued nineteenth-century readers, scholars were bringing a greater variety of analytical tools to bear on the debate over the rival claims of Haarlem and Mainz. Moreover, the Great Exhibition of 1851 focussed attention on the origins of printing in England. A new awareness of more recent printing history was created by the revival of Caslon Old Face by the Chiswick Press in 1840.[16] Recognizing that there was a potential market for period typography, the Caslon Foundry reissued these types in 1857, four years after R. Besley & Co, who operated the Fann Street Foundry, had reissued a revived transitional face (Richard Austin's cutting, in fact, which they termed 'Old Face' solely because of its age, not realizing its importance in the transition to modern types), complete with long 's' and, in the largest size (Great Primer) ranging figures.[17] The subject matter of the Besley

16. Janet Ing Freeman, 'Founders' type and private founts at the Chiswick Press in the 1850s', in *Journal of the Printing Historical Society* 19–20 (London, 1985–87), p. 70.

As early as 1856 John K. Rogers' Boston Type Foundry was offering Caslon types, though in their *Supplementary Specimen Sheets*, issued that year, they confused the long 's' and lowercase 'f'.

17. The sizes from Pica down to Brevier have old style or non-ranging figures; the English has a 'transitional' set that retains the old style alignment yet keeps the balanced weight of the lining numerals.

setting (taken from Stower 1808:17) relates to the by-now familiar argument over priority (*Figure 6*):

> FROM the whole of this investigation, it appears perfectly fair to attribute the origin of the invention to Haerlem, the improvement to Mentz. The natural and pleasing account of the discovery made by Koster has greatly the advantage over the confused and contradictory evidence in behalf of Guttemberg or others. The servant of Koster may easily be imagined capable of conveying the art in a surreptitious manner from Holland to Germany; but we must be much more credulous to conceive of the magistrate as defrauding another country of the invention and setting up a

In 1888, James Conner's Sons of New York composed this in Pica Backslope Athenian:

> The Noble Art and Mystery of Printing was first Invented and Practiced by John Faust, in the City of Mentz, in High Germany, about the Year of our Lord 1451.

In the United States, founders were running articles on Stanhope's inventions fifty years after his death. In their 1867 specimen, for example, Farmer, Little and Co. of Boston (established by Elihu White in 1810 after he emigrated from London) discuss the Earl's advances in stereotyping and proposals for logotype setting:[18]

> Composition, as probably the reader knows, is the method of arranging types in the proper form for use. This, ever since the invention of moveable types, made by Laurentius Coster, in 1430, has been done by hand. A movement toward economy in this respect was, indeed, made some sixty years ago, by Charles, the third Earl Stanhope, inventor of the Stanhope Press, and of the process of stereotyping which is still in use. His plan was to make the type-shank thicker than usual, and cast two or more letters upon its face instead of one. This, his Lordship rightly considered, would save labor, if available combinations could be determined; since, using such types, it would frequently happen that the compositor would need to make but one movement for two or three or even four letters. The desired economy, however, was not secured.

Elsewhere in their book, Farmer, Little provide useful snippets on make-ready, distribution ('If you drop one type, pick up two'), and 'Respectability among printers'.

In Scotland, James Marr & Co. of Edinburgh, successors to Alexander Wilson, utilize a piece, 'Learning in the reign of James I,' about the origin of letters among the Greeks (It first appears in a

18. Stanhope was backing the idea of Henry Johnson and John Walter who printed *The Times* in 1782 from logotypes at the Logographic Press. (H. Hart, *Charles Earl Stanhope and Oxford University Press*, p. 407 and note by James Mosley.)

There are obvious practical reasons for the non-acceptance of the new logotypes: the founders would have had to cast larger founts, requiring more punches and matrices, while printers would have needed special job cases with a new layout for the expanded fount.

R. BESLEY AND Co.'s OLD-FACE ROMANS.

GREAT PRIMER.—OLD FACE.

FROM the whole of this inveſtigation, it appears perfectly fair to attribute the origin of the invention to Haerlem, the improvement to Mentz. The natural and pleasing

1 2 3 4 5 6 7 8 9 0

ENGLISH.—OLD FACE.

FROM the whole of this investigation, it appears perfectly fair to attribute the origin of the invention to Haerlem, the improvement to Mentz. The very natural and pleaſing account of the diſcovery made by Koſter has greatly the advantage over the confuſed and contradictory evidence in behalf of Guttemberg or others. The ſervant of Koſter may eaſily be imagined to

1 2 3 4 5 6 7 8 9 0

PICA—OLD FACE.

FROM the whole of the investigation, it appears fair to attribute the origin of the invention to Haerlem, the improvement to Mentz. The natural and pleasing account of the discovery made by Koster has greatly the advantage over the confused and contradictory evidence in behalf of Guttemberg or others. The servant of Koster may be easily imagined capable of conveying the art in a surreptitious man-

1 2 3 4 5 6 7 8 9 0

SMALL PICA.—OLD FACE.

FROM the whole of this inveſtigation, it appears fair to attribute the origin of the invention to Haerlem, the improvement to Mentz. The very pleaſing and natural account of the diſcovery made by Koſter has greatly the advantage over the confuſed and contradictory evidence in behalf of Guttemburg and others. The ſervant of Koſter may eaſily be imagined capable of conveying the art in furreptitious manner from Holland to Germany; but we muſt be much more

1 2 3 4 5 6 7 8 9 0

LONG PRIMER.—OLD FACE.

FROM the whole of this inveſtigation, it appears fair to attribute the origin of the invention to Haerlem, the improvement to Mentz. The natural and pleaſing account of the diſcovery made by Koſter has greatly the advantage over the confuſed and contradictory evidence in behalf of Guttemberg or others. The ſervant of Koſter may eaſily be imagined capable of conveying in a furreptitious manner the art from Holland to Germany; but we muſt be much more credu-

1 2 3 4 5 6 7 8 9 0

BREVIER.—OLD FACE.

FROM the whole of this inveſtigation, it appears fair to attribute the origin of the invention to Haerlem, the improvement to Mentz. The natural and pleasing account of the diſcovery made by Koſter has greatly the advantage over the confused and contradictory evidence in behalf of Guttemberg or others. The ſervant of Koſter may easily be imagined capable of conveying the art in a furreptitious manner from Holland to Germany; but we muſt be much more credulous to conceive of the magiſtrate as defrauding another country of the invention, and ſetting up a

1 2 3 4 5 6 7 8 9 0

R. BESLEY AND CO., LONDON.

broadside of John Milne & Co, successor to Duncan Sinclair, Edinburgh, circa 1861, and several editions of James Marr's books, circa 1867, and recurs in the specimens of the Great Western Type Foundry of Barnhart Brothers and Spindler, Chicago.). From 1842 onwards, Marr employs this quote:

> It has often been a subject of wonder with those learned and ingenious persons who have written concerning the arts of the ancient world, that the Greeks and Romans, although they possessed a prodigious number of books, and approached very near to printing in the stamping of words and letters, and similar devices, should not have fallen upon the art; the first rude attempts at typography being sufficiently obvious, though much time and contrivance have been required to bring the process to the perfection in which it now prevails.

By the century's end, Catiline had become a remnant of a near-lost custom; it was only in the 'borrowing' between foundries that the traditions of the specimen books were maintained. Popular non-factual pieces on 'the origins of printing' recur in the books. One of the standbys is the piece beginning 'Of all the discoveries...' from Johnson's *Typographia*, first found in Hagar, New York, 1827, then in Howe of Philadelphia in 1830. It reappears in Thorowgood, 1834 (quoted above on page 34), in Baltimore in 1854, and in the specimen of the United States Type Foundry, New York, 1888, among others. A less self-congratulatory tone was adopted by James Conner, circa 1865, when he wrote:

> As the Art of Printing has without question, been of very great use in advancing learning and knowledge, the abuse of it, as of all other good things, has likewise produced many inconveniences.

Cincinnati appropriated this quote for their specimen in 1878.

By 1869, the specimens from the Bruce Foundry in New York consisted of dates and jumbled bibliographical information of interest to printers. My own research was made easier by an earlier scholar, Our Boy Tom, at the rival foundry of Collins & M'Leester. *The Proof-Sheet*, a promotional paper of the Philadelphia foundry, included a regular feature called 'Our Boy Tom's Pickings', which covered much miscellany. On page 8 of volume III, number 13, for July 1869, they ran this article:

[OUR friend Bruce having kindly sent us a copy of his handsome new Specimen Book, Our Boy Tom (who has a taste for abstruse studies) has made the following discoveries, and picked the subjoined items from the volume.]

On examination of the 166 pages in this book, I find that –
'George Bruce's Son & Co.'....occurs.... 195 times.
'Bruce's'.................. " ....172 times
'Bruce'.................. " .... 21 "
'George Bruce'............. " .... 18 "
'D. & G. Bruce'........... " .... 5 "
'G. Bruce'................ " .... 2 "
'David Bruce'............. " .... 2 "
'George Bruce & Co.'........ " .... 1 time.
'Bruce's Son & Co.'......... " .... 1 "
Making the total 'Bruce'...... 417

I have no doubt that it is Bruce's Book. The venerable 'Quousque tandem abutere' occurs only one hundred and twenty-six times, and the following items once each: –

. . . AN unknown printer of merit, never connected with Faust or Gutenberg, practised his art at Mentz as early as 1454.

. . . TWO kinds of ink and two impressions were used in printing the earlier books of Coster; a thin fluid watery ink for the wood-cuts, and a thick oily ink for the metal types. The accidental overlapping of the colors in printing proves both the double impression and the use of two kinds of ink.

. . . ELECTROTYPE plates for printing were made at the same time, without mutual knowledge or concert, by Professor Jacobi, of St. Petersburgh, and J.C. Jordan, of England, in 1839.

. . . STEREOTYPE plates were first made in 1725, by William Ged, a goldsmith, of Edinburgh.

. . . STEREOTYPING by the papier-maché process was invented by Genaux, of Paris, in 1829.

. . . STEREOTYPING was practically introduced into the United States by D. & G. Bruce, in 1813.

. . . LEADS for the widening of lines of type were first used by Peter Schoeffer, in an edition of Cicero printed at Mentz in 1465.

. . . CHARLOTTE GUILLARD was the first notable female printer. She was in business for fifty years in Paris – from 1506 to 1566 [*sic*],– and was celebrated for the correctness of her books.

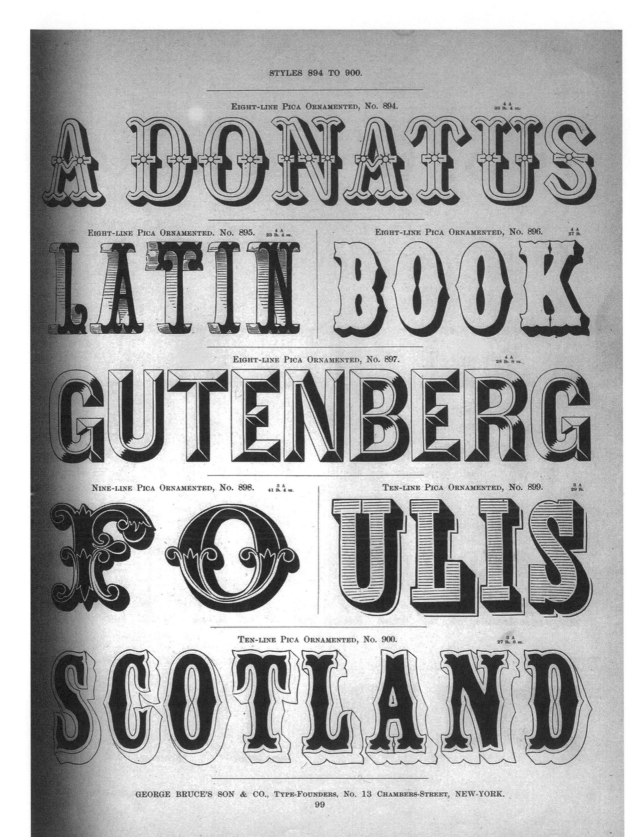

STYLES 894 TO 900.

EIGHT-LINE PICA ORNAMENTED, No. 894.

A DONATUS

EIGHT-LINE PICA ORNAMENTED. No. 895.   EIGHT-LINE PICA ORNAMENTED, No. 896.

LATIN BOOK

EIGHT-LINE PICA ORNAMENTED, No. 897.

GUTENBERG

NINE-LINE PICA ORNAMENTED, No. 898.   TEN-LINE PICA ORNAMENTED, No. 899.

FOULIS

TEN-LINE PICA ORNAMENTED, No. 900.

SCOTLAND

GEORGE BRUCE'S SON & CO., TYPE-FOUNDERS, No. 13 CHAMBERS-STREET, NEW-YORK.
99

. . . GREEK types of correct proportion were first made and used by some unknown German printers at a monastery near Naples, in 1546.

. . . HOE'S Rotary Press was first used on the Philadelphia *Public Ledger,* in 1847.

. . . WOMEN were employed, and commended, as compositors in Italy as early as 1481.

The arbitrary approach of the 1869 book was rectified with Bruce's specimen of 1878. Theodore L. De Vinne's *The Invention of printing,* which appeared in 1876, was incorporated, in different sizes and faces, as text into Bruce's specimen of that year. DeVinne's text (re-set to demonstrate various sizes and leading) occupies 168 leaves (often printed two-up). The glorious array of display types is set out in a mixture of printers' names and dates, places where printing was first practiced, quotes from Moxon and other works, and a hodge-podge bibliography of more than 370 works of books about books (*Figure 7*).[19]

In return for supplying the pertinent copy, De Vinne had access to the foundry for the typographical realization of his complex work. The text was not only the first important work on printing history published in the United States but also the most coherent text for a specimen book.

We see through the specimen books how printers began to arrive at a fuller awareness of their craft, its history and legends. By the end of the century, bibliographers were in full command of the facts. Coster partisans, however, wouldn't relinquish their claim.[20]

19. In addition, there are 352 pages of type and ornament. These specimen pages are printed on one side only. Five supplements were issued after the expanded specimen appeared in 1882 (the fifth is dated May 1887). At page 124, sixteen additional pages have been inserted with an original numeration: superior figures to the power of twelve (124^1–124^{12}), then $124^1/2$, $124^5/8$, $124^3/4$, and finally $124^7/8$.

The Poltroon Press library includes two differing editions of this Bruce specimen: one does not contain the De Vinne work, but instead has 16 pages of electrotyped illustrations of a cruder style pertaining to religious themes (perhaps this edition was destined for export to South America and the Catholic market). Between the variant states, there is a possible total of 576 pages, making it one of the most impressive type specimen books ever issued. The types are numbered and many bear copyright dates and the seal of the U.S. Patent Office.

20. The renowned Haarlem firm of J. Enschedé en Zonen claim the invention for their home town in their 19th-century specimen books. Johan Enschedé, himself, found the long-sought-for fragments of *Donatus* that linked the invention to Coster, but none bore dates. In 1972 Lotte Hellinga averred, 'No tangible link has been established between the Coster legend and the surviving early Dutch editions.' ('Further fragments of Dutch prototypography', in *Quarendo* II, 3, 183.) See also Hellinga's, *Laurens Janszoon Coster was zijn naam* (Haarlem, 1988). On the three types of printed matter ascribed to Coster, see Lotte Hellinga in *Bibliotheek leven*, vol. 52, p. 387, November 1967. That Coster's work may have involved stamping rather than moveable type is discussed by Dr Hellinga in a review of a Sotheby sale catalogue in the London *Times* (April 24, 1982). See also Christopher de Hamel's letter to the editor of 7 May 1982.

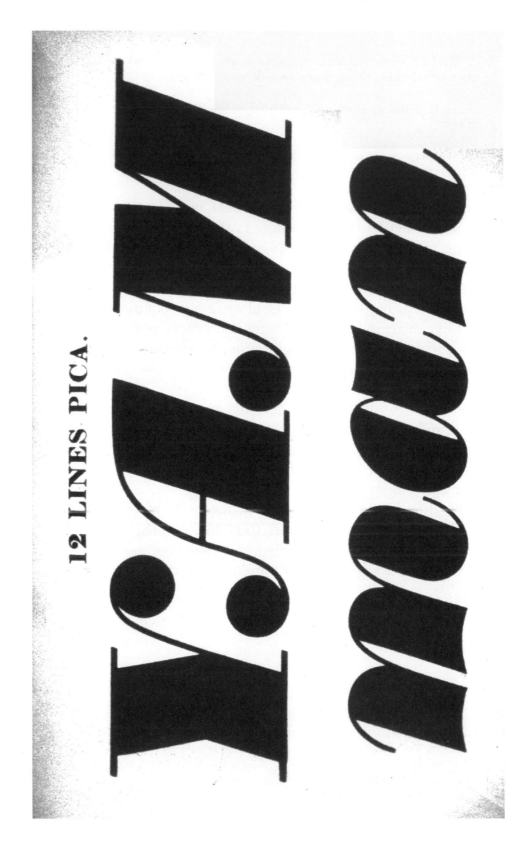

4

Typographical surloin

Next day the posters appeared in due course, and the public were informed, in all the colours of the rainbow, and in letters afflicted with every possible variation of spinal deformity, how that Mr Johnson would have the honour of making his last appearance that evening, and how that an early application for places was requested, in consequence of the extraordinary overflow attendant on his performances, – it being a remarkable fact in theatrical history, but one long since established beyond dispute, that it is a hopeless endeavour to attract people to a theatre unless they can be first brought to believe that they will never get into it.
– Charles Dickens, *Nicholas Nickleby*, Chapter 30

DURING THE TRANSITIONAL PERIOD from old style to modern, display types were no more than tentatively enlarged versions of book founts. The first large types were Cottrell's Letters of Proscription, circa 1760. T.C. Hansard (1825:359) from his more distant perspective, was able to look with amusement on the shock these novelties inspired:

> Mr. Cotterell [*sic*] from the time he was left to himself by Mr. Jackson, continued to increase his founts as low as *brevier*. But he also cut some founts of dimensions which till then were unknown; and which Mr. Mores calls 'proscription, or posting letter, of great bulk and dimension, as high as to the measure of 12 *lines of pica*!' What would these founders think of *posters* of the present day, when a single letter, Q, is made to fill a whole broadsheet for a lottery-puff?

Mr Mores' other comments on Cottrell's work are typically droll (1961:77): the brevier alluded to above is 'low enough to spoil the eyes'. Despite his curmudgeonliness (Dibdin called him 'crabbed and eccentric'), Edward Rowe Mores was a true original, and his devotion to researching the British typefounders laid the groundwork for Hansard, Reed, and later historians.[1]

1. 'His pedantry and occasional ill nature must be forgiven for his learning, humour, and preservation of facts, which, but for his attachment to a dry subject, would unquestionably have been lost.' William Savage, *Practical hints on decorative printing* (London, 1822), p. 67n.

James Callingham, in his *Manual of signwriting* (1871), credits
Caslon with the introduction of bulked-up roman letters in the
1785 *Specimen of large letters*. At three inches high, these were the
largest letters then made; in form they are proto-Clarendon, but
that style, with a bracketed slab serif, was not discovered to be typographically useful till later in the nineteenth century.

The early nineteenth-century advertisers' call for new types was
answered with new inventions: the boldface and fat face (about 25
percent bolder still) were followed by the slab serif and sans serif
(the serifs that the sans serif lacks are slab serifs) in increasing
sizes, then by shaded and decorated types. One reason for the boom
in display types was the tax on press advertisements, which meant
that more handbills & placards were printed.

In the Printing Historical Society's facsimile reprint of Figgins's
1815 specimen (1967:23), editor Berthold Wolpe provides a key to
the origin & presentation of many of these new modern & display
types: 'The large types were of course intended to be used mainly
on posters, but we find them also being used on the covers of books
of engravings. The displaying of names of towns in the specimens
invites their use on coaching placards.' These placards would be set
in the window of an inn where the mail coach would stop. Thus we
find 'Bury,' 'Dover,' and the clever near-anagram (*Figure 9*):

Remote
Atmore

The types soon lost the warm, modulated proportions of the transitional style, but they gained in humour. As the founders rapidly
abandoned the calligraphic origins of letterforms, they turned to
their mechanical construction. The application of thick serifs and
emboldened weight produced ridiculous effects when applied to the
lowercase letters such as 'a,' 'e,' and 's.' These ugly ducklings arrest
the gaze and often leave the viewer gaping in wonder. As Savage
said, in his *Practical hints on decorative printing* (1822:20–21):

> The founders have now introduced another change in the proportions of
> letters, and have gone to a barbarous extreme, from their first improve-
> ment. The rage is now which of them can produce a type in the shape of a
> letter, with the thickest lines, and with the least white in the interior parts.

5 LINES PICA, ITALIC ANTIQUE.

BLAKE, GARNETT, & CO.

2. See cover. '*The Metropolitan Paving Act* of 1817 was the first legal attempt to frustrate the indiscriminate pasting of advertisement bills on any suitable surface without permission.' Berry & Poole, *Annals of printing* (London, 1966), p. 208.

3. The work of John Soulby, Sr, for example, adheres to classical vase-shaped layouts with the heavy, larger types grouped near the top of the page. See John Lewis, *Printed ephemera*, Michael Twyman, *John Soulby, printer, Ulverston*, and Twyman's *Printing 1770–1970*.

4. Since I wrote this I came across corroboration of my thesis in Michael Twyman's 'Bold-looking type in the nineteenth century,' *Journal of the Printing Historical Society* 22, 1993.

5. Forerunner of the ironic one-word paintings of Ed Ruscha in the 1960s, which were mostly rendered in slab serif and fat face.

The new rage for eye-catching placards forever altered the typographical landscape, as seen in paintings of the time by the American Thomas Le Clear and the Englishman John Parry.[2] The urban scene was captured in a poem anthologized by Charles Timperley in his collection, *Songs of the press*:

THE STRAND — IN TRANSITU

THE *Strand*, deserted by its better half,
    As if the Plague had crept along its side,
In spite of graver thoughts, compels the laugh,
    Placards so oddly take the lettered stride:

For 'Birmingham', in type of glaring red;
    'Rowland's Macassar' with a scalp of hair;
'Air Pillows' for the weary, giddy, head,
    And heads of 'Saracens' for every fare.

The 'Tally Ho!' will start at half past one,
    The 'Intelligence' will travel void of fees;
'St. Dunstan's Steeple Chase',–'the Bolt and Tun',
    'Plans' for consolidating 'Siamese'.

'Hunt's is the cheapest and the best'.– Defiance
    To 'Warren's' opposite in letters large;
'New Saxony broad cloths', in which reliance
    Might, if once tried, be fixed with moderate charge.

In early appearances the new display types are awkwardly deployed, demonstrating the printers' difficulty with their effective presentation.[3] However, with the founders showing the way in their specimen books, the way we read and relate to letterforms soon took on a new dimension.[4] The increased scale of reading wrought by the new display types began to have an impact on the public as advertisers sought bigger and bolder types, or bill posters chose one word to emphasize in their handbills.

In the specimen books, some of the display faces fill an entire octavo page with three of their letters. In the confines of the specimen page, these large types become forceful geometric statements. One word, '**Gas**,' (*Figure 10*) in Sixteen-line Pica (replete with the contorted counter to the lowercase 'a') is a typical offering from Caslon & Catherwood.[5] Instead of a textured gray block, the page becomes a white area punctuated by a concentrated blot of black.

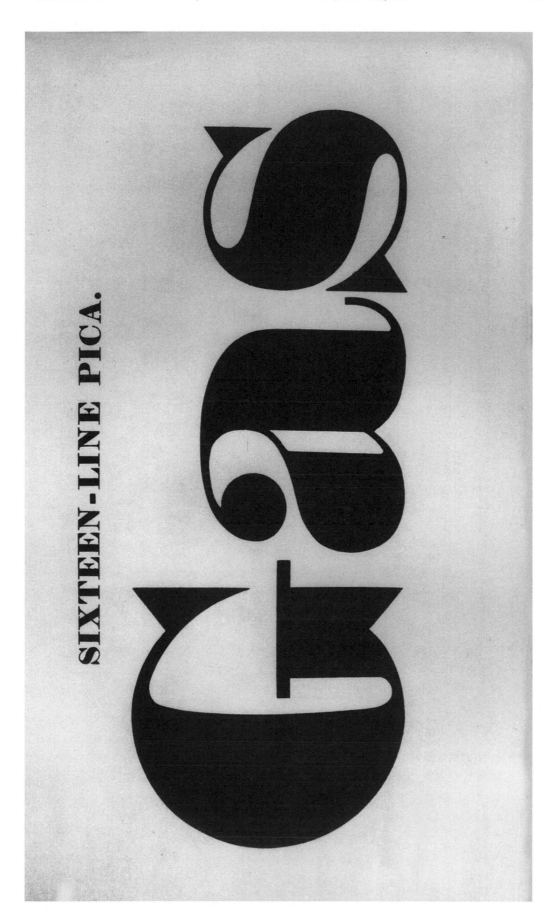

The reader confronting these pages for the first time is struck by the white space; with such large characters, the counters of the letter-forms assume positive form; so the normally invisible interiors of letters appear like abstract figures trapped in heavy black contours, and the magnified twists and turns highlight unusual interactions among them. The typefounders seemingly often combined the most awkward letters to heighten the absurdity of figure/ground relations created by the constrained scale of the quarto or octavo page. 'Man' can hardly display the variety of characteristics in a typeface. This mesmerization through scale and contrast is a new way of holding our gaze.

To demonstrate the potential uses of their types, the founders concocted texts announcing auctions, property to let, wanted posters, civic activity and legal notices. The abundant 'typos' suggest they were composed casually, and there is a strong current of the compositor's subconscious speaking through the pages. The *pi* of textual matter and the non sequiturs of mini-sermons followed by postillion cries or headlines give the books a Dadaist sensibility. Some suggest a highly personal serial poem, or are multi-voiced like good collaborative graffiti: disjointed and paratactic in the cut-up style.

The first to decry the new types was William Savage in his *Practical hints on decorative printing* (1822:74) where he answers his own rhetorical question:

> Whence, then, the inelegant & heterogenous nature of modern typography?
> ...Between the productions of the different Founders there is scarcely any affinity; and, when used together in the same page, the want of uniformity offends the eye. This evil has been much encreased by the recent introduction of the fat letter, which in Bill printing is a great improvement; but when used in books along with the lean, produces a great incongruity. The fatness has been carried to an unnecessary excess, and some founts have been cut, totally unfit for Book printing, which have nevertheless been used for that purpose. The fat letter has now been introduced into all the Foundries, so that a printer may have all his types from the same house, and yet mar his work, by blending the fat and the lean.

Savage lays the blame firmly at the door of the Fann Street foundry off Goswell Street: 'Robert Thorne has been principally instrumental in the revolution that has taken place in Posting Bills, by the introduction of fat types.' Hansard (1825:360) also condemned the new type, while he admired Thorne. In his comments on

Fry's 1823 specimen (1825:356), he says, 'the fat-face fashion...
ought to be eradicated from every type-foundry, and left for hewers
in wood alone'.

Hansard's attribution was later echoed by T. B. Reed, who relished
the deformity in his discussion of Thorne's work (1952: 293):

> Not sharing at the regret expressed by his brethren in the art at the new
> departure, he still further advanced upon it by the production of some ex-
> ceedingly thick and fat (and we may add unsightly) jobbing letters, which,
> though subsequently followed and even exceeded by others, were at the time
> unique for boldness and deformity.

But as Savage pointed out, the founders were only supplying a
demand, and didn't intend their types to be used in bookwork
(1822:21): 'If bad taste is to be attributed to any one, it properly
attaches to the printer for applying them to purposes for which they
were never designed.' In Thorne's 1803 specimen, he savours the
effect of his new modern types[6] with a resounding, full-page 'Smack.'

By 1823, even the founders themselves were balking at the new
bulkiness. Figgins warned in his specimen book that year (in Two
line Great Primer, Antique),[7]

> The increased fatness
> in JOB-LETTER is an
> improvement, but is it
> not in many instances
> carried to an extreme?

The Antique or slab-seriffed types were the first for which the
founders felt compelled to apologize. Although the added weight
was problematic in all the new emboldened types, some interesting,
quirky forms were created, but when the founders began to treat the
lowercase letters with elephantiasis, the efforts to deal with the convoluted counters of the 'a' and 'e' were disastrous. Bottlenecks occurred when the punchcutter strove to retain the proportions of the
humanist script on which roman lowercase letterforms were originally based. The only solution was to make the lowercase less bold
than the uppercase, so that the two inevitably looked mismatched.
In 1824, Fry, speaking of his Pearl Antique, mentioned 'the greatest
care and attention having been paid so as to render it as regular and
uniform as the nature of such characters will allow'.[7]

6. Illustrated by Twyman in the above article as figure 12.

7. Reprinted in the subsequent editions. See the facsimile, with an introduction and notes by David Chambers, *Specimen of modern printing types by Edmund Fry 1828* (London, 1986). *Cf.* McLean, 'An Examination of Egyptians', *Alphabet & Image* 1, and his review of Miller & Richard's Egyptian in *Typographica* 3.

In the following year, Hansard thundered against the new types of Fry, but is kinder to Figgins (1825:359–60):

> As his specimen bears equal rank with any for the number and beauty of its founts; so he has strayed less in to the folly of fat-faced, preposterous disproportions, than either Thorne, Fry, or Caslon. I consider his five-line pica german-text, a typographic curiosity.

Blake, Garnett (circa 1827) say of their Pearl Antique: 'The Antique Character, if well executed by the Founder and properly displayed by the Printer, is both useful and ornamental.' In their effort to accomodate customers, they announce (in Brevier Antique): 'The types cut at this foundry, are to the London standard for height and may be had Scotch height if required.'[8]

Thorowgood questioned his own judgment in issuing a large condensed fat face in 1834 which reads:

**PRINTING
TYPES?**

Who, however, can resist a page of massive lead types reading

**HOMER
munition**

as does Figgins' 6-line pica (or 72 point)?

The peculiar enjambment of these fattened modern letters also has a bold message. Each word or pair of words in caps and lowercase has a page to itself; the turning pages read like random leaves pulled from a top hat at the Cabaret Voltaire or the cacophony of thawing words on the deck of Pantagruel's barque (*Gargantua & Pantagruel*, IV, 56). Thorowgood's monosyllables read like such fragments or ice cubes. In 1821, he sounds off with:

RIS　　MES
mat　　hone

'RIS' is laughter, and 'hone'– apart from sharpening the founder's various skills – refers to the parodist, reformer and publisher William Hone (who reappears in Wells & Webb, 1840, and as a polychrome beauty in 25-line Ionian in Page's 1867 book). In his 1825 catalogue, Thorowgood commences another sequence with

8. See note on page 143 of Moxon's *Mechanick exercises* (Oxford, 1962), by Harry Carter & Herbert Davis.

Ma   GUN
Mat   Shot

Similarly, we find a sequence of surloin in the *Specimen of improved printing types* issued by Bower and Bacon (Sheffield, 1830):[9]

9. St Bride's has the only known copy.

Mn Mm Mun Mm MEN ment

And in increasing sizes up to 12 lines Pica (*Figure 8*):

YAM
man

which displays ball terminals on caps and the concave terminals of lower case in the italic. 'MAMA' is often invoked to display italic capitals, with and without swash terminals.

Messrs B & B anagram 'DEALER | LEADER'; a reversed fat face called White states, 'SOCIABLE | BOLDER', and, a bold modern:

Random
Medium

The attentive reader will have noticed that not all the cards are on the table, for the founders are sticking close to the 'm's and 'n's of 'typographical surloin' savoured by Dibdin. This seems to have been the easiest configuration for the founders, for they all follow suit, and only the bold let their quirkiest projectors hang out. Cicero is often reduced to one morsel, and a choice piece of surloin it is: 'Munitissimus'. In larger sizes of type it might be sliced to 'Muni' or merely 'Mun'. In 1835 Figgins refers to himself as 'Multinomial V. Figgins.' For a slightly expanded snippet of Cicero the returning vacationer is queried: 'Quousque tan'. Thorowgood's book of 1835 conjures

MANY
mannitum

and adds the cautionary

MENTIR

in 14-lines Grotesque, while the homesick compositor of Thorow-good's 1834 book offers a dreamy combination of Cicero *cum* coaching card (*Figure 11*):

ANGELIC.
Quousque
de Manchester

Among other choice cuts, Figgins' 1815 'HUME | Mentor' became Bower *&* Bacon's 1830 'Hume | *Mute*'.

Fragmentary language blossomed with the passion for archaeology in the early decades of the nineteenth century as *Daily Mail* readers set off to the Near East in search of the tablets containing the *Epic of Gilgamesh*. Alex Robb of Philadelphia issued his *Specimen of printing types and ornament* in 1846, with one or two words on each page, including these evocative pairs:

RITE	MIND	HOME	SIN	MERN	MET	WEM
short	strain	maine		mintus	bront	MAINE

and, in 8-lines Pica Ornamented:

MAYN
waine?

The three pages citing Maine and the play on it are signed S. Ecklin *&* Co. Philadelphia. Robb bound pages from his former partner Ecklin's book into his own specimen.[10]

'MAINE' persisted, not surprisingly, in American specimens of the first half of the century. Boston Type Foundry's 8-line Pica Ornamented (1820) reads

HUME
maine.

The New England Type Foundry (Boston, ca. 1834) proffers

BOSTON   *MAINE*
mansion   and couples it with   *ransom*

in 7-lines Pica Italic, as a retort to the English founders. Their particular flavour of surloin includes this fragmentary memory of the Colonial War from 1827:

10. According to Annenberg (1975: 219), Ecklin was a stereotyper who worked for either L. Johnson or Howe and Co.

FIVE LINES PICA ITALIC, No. 4.

ANGELIC.

Quousque de

Manchester

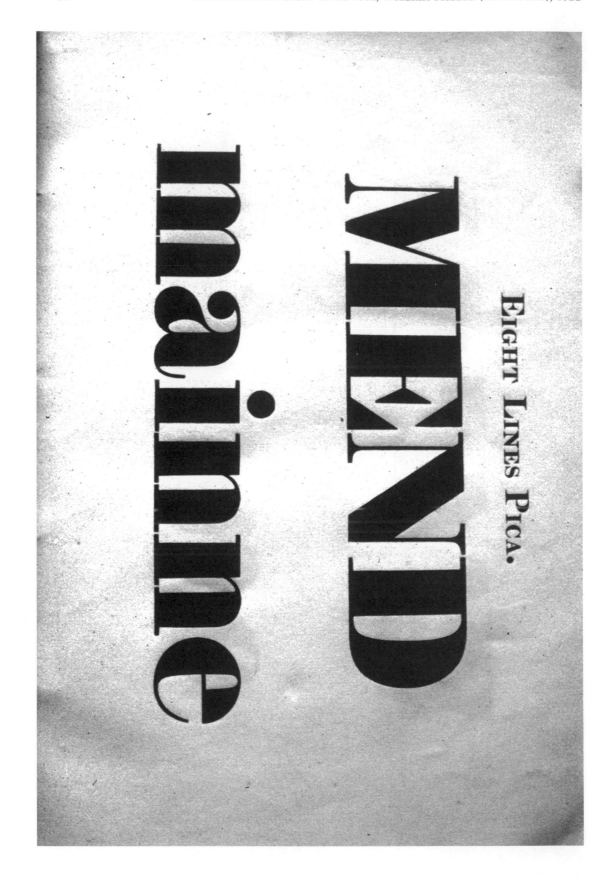

QUA!	HORN	MAN	AIM.	MEN	AM
model	horse	arms	come	mail	shot

William Hagar & Co. (New York, 1826) posit

NAYM	*MAR!*	HOME	DIE	DEIST!
maner	*miner*	maine	mite	MANY

A witty comment on the carelessness of founders in proofreading their own books was made in 1822 by William Miller in the Eight lines pica showing of his new modern face (possibly the work of Richard Austin) seen here (*Figure 12*):

MEND
mainne

But as Charles Smith pointed out in his fictionized autobiography, *A Working man's way in the world* (London, 1857), 'If anybody had a right to spell a word as he chose, it was a printer short of types'.

Founders used the same texts to make comparison easier for would-be purchasers. Since Figgins had established this prime order of typographical surloin ('MEND | Maine' appeared in 1821), Miller's reference may be an editorial comment on his rival's offering, or a parody. Figgins's choice of 'Maine' can hardly have been made to suggest a coaching card, unless it was intended to appeal simultaneously to French and American customers. But we may include it under the rubric of 'typographical surloin'.

To display their Egyptian types, Bower & Bacon (Sheffield, 1830) chose the surloin accoutrement

Bun

Shortness of space in setting larger sizes led inevitably to a series of cursory ejaculations that prefigure some American poetry of the 1960s.[11] An apex of minimalist poetry is found in *First premium wood types, cut by machinery; warranted superior to any ever before exhibited, & sold at reduced prices, by George F. Nesbitt, Tontine building, New York, 1838.*[12] One word poems like 'NODE' (*Figure 15*) and 'ITCH' sparkle in bold wood types. One page says '*read,*' but Nesbitt betrays his feelings about having anything to say in two pages reading

11. Aram Saroyan was the most celebrated exponent of this style. He was rebuffed by the Olivetti typewriter company when he asked for support, claiming their typewriter face was an integral part of his work. When he received an NEA grant for his one word poems such as 'lobstee' & 'lighght', there was outrage in Congress. However his four-legged 'm' (achieved with rub-on lettering) attains a new level of typographical surloin.

12. Several of Nesbitt's types appear to be copied from Wood & Sharwoods' monumental specimen of the same year, issued in London. (Similar, rather than identical faces occurred when a founder copied a style from a specimen showing only a few characters.) Nesbitt's 12 Line Pica Corinthian is cribbed from Blake & Stephenson, ca. 1833 (Gray p. 46); his 8 Line Pica Antique, Rose Oramental [*sic*] is adapted from Bower & Bacon's Egyptian Ornamental of 1826 (Gray fig. 63); his 8 Line Pica Antique, Tulip Ornamental, from an Egyptian Ornamented of Blake, Garnett, 1827 (Gray chart #32). Nesbitt's 11 Line Pica Antique Extra Ornamented appears to predate Wood and Sharwoods' (Gray chart #104, to which it is related). See also Dan X. Solo, 'The Influence of galvanism on type design', in *The Kemble Occasional* 19 (San Francisco, June 1978).

nul | mot

American founders and wood type manufacturers deploy their large types with witty brevity and reckless abandon. Darius Wells & Co. (New York, 1828) offer

SORE

which, as compositors know, is EROS in reverse.

The fertile world of nature is celebrated in 10-line Pica Roman:

MERD
plants

In this book, Wells[13] & Co. also suggests the poetic

LIFE
Trifle

13. Wells, inventor of the lateral router, exported wood type to Europe until British manufacturers were established in the 1840s. He had a flourishing trade all over the world.

14. As Rob Roy Kelly points out (1969:72).

15. Wells' 24 Line Antique Ornamented predates Bruce (1837) for this style; both were copied from Deberny & Peignot's Italiennes Ombrées series. For styles originating in wood see the backsloping Gothic Condensed and Zig-Zag illustrated in the next chapter (*Figure 15*).

Wells had the wood type market to himself until Nesbitt, a printer, offered, in his vast catalogue of 1838, 225 styles and sizes of wood type: the work of Edwin Allen, a mechanical genius, but not an artist.[14] In 1834, George Leavenworth added the pantograph to the router for the production of wood types (his business was absorbed by Wells in 1839). Another valuable innovation was the introduction of electrotyping by Thomas Starr in the 1840s. The wood type manufacturers created novel designs, some of which were adapted to metal by European founders – the reverse of the situation in the preceding decades.[15]

Ultimately, joining droll concision and typographical appropriateness, Darius Wells & Co. lament the tendency to increased pachydermitis, enjoining the other founders to revise their 'Quousques' &

quit

5

Saving face

Mr Fax said he should have thought, on the contrary, that *ex fumo dare lucem*
would have been, of all things, the most repugnant to his principles; and
Mr Mystic replied that it had not struck him so before, but that Mr Fax's
view of the subject was 'exquisitely dusky and fuliginous'.
– Thomas Love Peacock, *Nightmare Abbey*

TEXTS THAT ADVERTISED the qualities of the types they were
set in were a natural choice for typefounders' specimens. Such
passages ranged from exaggerated claims for the faces to shame-
faced apologies.

In addition to the Antiques, or slab serifs, and the 'dropsical' fat
faces (as Updike termed them), Script[1] was another class of letterform for which founders felt perennially obliged to offer excuses.
They would explain what a misbegotten idea it was, then humbly
suggest that their version was an improvement over previous efforts
– although one American founder admitted that the imports were
superior![2] Similarly when typewriter faces were introduced as
foundry type at the end of the century, they too were generally ex-
cused rather than recommended. The stub-pen styles introduced in
the 1880s – the sorriest of all script types – are so illegible that one
can hardly make out what the founders are saying at all.

Figgins stated the problem of well-fitting connecting strokes in
his 1821 book (using the long 's' throughout):

> *The plan upon which the English Letter-Founders have hitherto cast
> Scripts, is not capable of preserving that freedom of correctneß of connection
> so eßentially neceßary to the attempt at imitating Writing, with any toler-
> able Succeß.*
> *London, August 22, 1819*

1. I mean to distinguish Latin
scripts from italic, though
Stanley Morison in 'Towards
an ideal italic', *The Fleuron*, v,
p. 93, uses the term 'script' to
describe another series of cur-
sives (deriving from the same
source: the Italian chancery)
which he distinguishes from
italic. In his *Caractères de
l'écriture dans la typographie*
(Paris, 1927), Morison sets
apart scripts from the chancery
italics of Arrighi and Blado, &
the civilité founts of Granjon,
& denominates the types of
Pierre Moreau of Paris (1643)
as the first script types.

In his monograph on *Ichabod Dawks & his news-letter*
(Cambridge, 1931), Morison

traces Dawks's script back to one of Moses Pitt (London, 1672), thence back to Moreau (p. 21). The first English display type, Union Pearl of 1708, bears a family resemblance to the Dawks script type. The success of Dawks's *News-letter* was attributed to the 'rich invention' of his type which Morison terms a slightly more decorative, Anglicized version of the late-Italian chancery hand. It appeared around 1696. See further Morison, 'On script types', in *The Fleuron*, IV (London, 1925); Cottrell's Engrossing (my *figure 2*) is illustrated in Reed; Graham Pollard (in *Birrell & Garnett catalogue of typefounders' specimens, etc, offered for sale*, London, 1928, p. 81) mentions Caslon's Script type as one of the first to popularize the form in England, but Morison decries this particular letterform. Morison's essays are collected in *Selected essays* (Cambridge, UK, 1981). See also John Lane's article on Arthur Nicholls in *The Library*, 12/1991.

2. Bruce (1820), in a dig at Ronaldson, says British types were superior, as those of the 'foundry which principally supplied the United States, previous to 1817, were mostly so unfortunate as to have been since condemned by the proprietors of that respectable establishment.'

In 1835, Blake & Stephenson announced:

Sir, / The great inconvenience experienced by Printers in composing and correcting Scripts cast on an inclined body, has induced us to offer to the trade, two sizes, cast on a Square Body, and a New Principle.

In 1842, Thorowgood quoted William Savage to introduce his Great Primer Script on common square body:

Mr. Savage in his valuable work entitled a Dictionary of Printing, thus writes: "There is no character connected with our language on which so much labour has been expended within the last twenty-five years as on this. The old Scripts were so notoriously stiff and formal, that they could hardly be said to bear any other resemblance to writing than in the mere shapes of the letters; these were cast on a square shank, with all the ascenders and descenders hanging over their body, which is styled kerned. These kerned letters having no support, were liable on preßure to break off, and the fount became so disfigured thereby, that the use of Script was abandoned by almost common consent. In 1815 Meßrs. Firmin Didot and Sons introduced a new Script, cut with great freedom, and cast on a rhomboidal shank, with triangular blocks having a corresponding angle on one side, and the other two sides forming a right angle with which to justify the beginnings & endings of lines. In order to enable the printer to form complete words without any apparent junction, a great number of pairs of letters, parts of common

Four out of five of Thorowgood's scripts, however, were still cast on the common square body in 1863. The aggravating scripts which are the dickens to decipher and the devil to print without breakage, thwart the compositor, causing wrong fonts, so were generally reserved for specialty jobs. In the 1880s, founders introduced non-kerning scripts. Marder, Luse, in announcing their Spinner Script (in *The Inland Printer*, January 1884) said: 'By the absence of kerned letters, the hair lines are so well protected that they will stand as strong a pressure as any portion of the letter.'

Another requisite but little-used part of a printing office's equipment in the nineteenth century was a fount or two of blackletter. Originally the national British character, blackletter was supplanted by roman or 'white' letter (so-called because the massed effect is lighter on the page) due to the inability of early British printers to develop an adequate native typefounding industry, so that French and later Dutch types predominated in Britain.

By the beginning of the nineteenth century, blackletter was found only in places such as newspaper mastheads and legal notices, where it was used to impart suggestions of 'truth' and 'authority'. The allusion to the Bible still persists, for church printers were the last to relinquish the older letterform. Blackletter added a tone of admonition in a proclamation:

𝕹otice!

The swell effect of the new bold roman types imposed on black-letter gave it pachydermitis too. The fat blackletter was also offered in a more tolerable tooled state, with incised white lines,[3] but the number of typographical errors in the specimen books indicates that printers themselves found it illegible.

A Blake-Garnett specimen, circa 1827, has a two-line English Black lamenting:

> The Beauty of the Old English Character is entirely destroyed when cut of an extreme fatness: and this fatness cannot be of any advantage except in the larger sizes used in Posting Bills.

For the most part these jolly tragic types are found maundering in 'legalese' that, as marginal English, could be copy-fitted in the stick, like the 'Notice is hereby given …' in Fry & Sons' second edition of their 1786 specimen book. As more of the sentence is revealed in the dwindling sizes of the type, it becomes apparent that the notice is interminable. One is reminded of Dickens's famous case of Jarndyce and Jarndyce, as well as the doorkeeper in Kafka's short story 'Before the Law', a parable about the endless circularity of a well-oiled state bureaucracy. Another version, seen first in Caslon's 1734 specimen and again in 1746 (the definitive wording was arrived at by Caslon in 1763[4]), and copied by everyone else for a century, is quoted here with an abrupt ending from Figgins's 1815 book:[5]

> And it be hereby enacted, That the Mayors, Bailiffs, and other head Officers of Every Town and place corporate, and City within this Realm, being Justice or Justices of Peace, shall have the same authority by virtue of this Act within the limits & precincts of their Jurisdiction, as well out of Session as at their Sessions, if they hold any, as is herein limited, prescribed and ap-

3. The inline was introduced by John Bell in 1787, followed by Fry & Steele (in Stower's *Printer's grammar*), in 1808. See Allen Hutt, 'The Gothic title-piece and the English newspaper', in *Alphabet & Image*, 3, London, 1946.
4. See Updike, ii:104 and fig. 264. 'This was the first specimen-*book* issued in England,' says Updike, who notes the reprint in Luckombe. But it was Bishop Fell (Oxford, 1685) who issued the first specimen book in England.
5. Binny & Ronaldson used it in 1812 (see Silver, *Typefounding in America, 1787–1825*, pl. 3); see also Thorowgood's 1824 blackletter, illustrated in Updike, ii, pl. 335, & A. Bessemer's 1830 Great Primer Black, illustrated in *Journal of the Printing Historical Society* 5 (London, 1969).

Blacks.

FOUR LINES OPEN.

And be it f urther her eby enacted that the M ayors, Bai

EDMUND FRY.

B. & T.

In this 1815 specimen book, Figgins often abandoned hyphenation to give lines in larger faces a cleaner appearance, as many breaks were necessitated by the format. Other founders followed suit, sometimes using arbitrary hyphenation or irregular word breaks to accommodate the larger types in the (usually) octavo books. Arbitrary and non-hyphenated word-division were employed by the founders to obviate ugly linebreaks. By mid-century more founders were using the larger quarto format for their specimen books, but the traditional octavo size, and the odd linebreaks it necessitated,[6] held sway for a long time.

Fry's Four Lines Open Black in his 1824 book uses the Caslon text, subjected to the most radical whims of word division (*Fig. 13*).

Loud and soft typography

THE PHYSICAL SIZE of the type can also assert itself as a creative tool in the right hands. Bigger or bolder type seems to shout out to us, because it is more prominent. The diminuendo apparent in many specimen books dies away to pages of tiny grey type that strain one's vision. An earlier use of this implied emphasis and volume in speech is found in *The Miscellaneous essays and occasional writings of Francis Hopkinson, esq.* (Philadelphia, 1792) between pages 247–9, where he bellows his opinion in large sizes of text type. Earlier, of course, we find Laurence Sterne using dwindling sizes of type to indicate speeding-up speech, in his homage to Rabelais: the story of the Abbess of Andoüillets and the stubborn mule. Sterne broke all the rules of conventional typography in *The Life and opinions of Tristram Shandy, gentleman* (York & London, 1759–67) and created many new ones.[7] Thorowgood doffs his cap to the clerical crack-up in his Four Line Pica Italic Tuscan, shown in his specimen book of 1824:

MEMENTEIS

STERNE

MINISTER

... however he is later transmuted into NEST MINSTER!

6. Although early scribes broke words irregularly and without hyphens, the tradition of 'proper' word division was well established by the 1800s. Looking for non-typographic forerunners of this style, I noticed that arbitrary word division, without hyphenation, to facilitate layout in embroidery, may be seen in samplers going back as far as the Renaissance.

7. See my articles 'Poet as typographer', in *Ampersand*, XI:2 (San Francisco, 1991) and 'Typography and the science of nonsense', in *Ampersand*, XI:4 (San Francisco, 1992). The first author to use type size for emphasis was John Dee, the Elizabethan alchemist; see Frans A. Janssen, 'Author and printer in the history of typographical design', in *Quaerendo* 21 (Leiden, 1991).

The last word on the use of typography to indicate volume and inflection was that of Robert Massin in his design of Eugene Ionesco's *La cantatrice chauve* (Paris, 1964).

Thorowgood polishes his surreal humour in the 1843 *Selections from the specimen of the Fann Street foundry* (with the cover title *Designs for ornamental printing*), with the following in three sizes of Etruscan:

MANCHESTER FANCY DRESS ASSEMBLY
GROTESQUE EXHIBITIONS
❋
PHRENO-MESMERISM COMBINED WITH CLAIRVOYANCE,
DISSOLUTION OF THE LONG PARLIAMENT,
MECHANICAL ENGLAND, ORNAMENTAL FRANCE
❋
ATMOSPHERIC RAILWAY DIRECT FROM LONDON TO EDINBURGH.
CONCERT EXTRAORDINAIRE, 1,234,567,890 PERFORMERS!

One 'Atmospheric Railway,' promoted by I.K. Brunel in 1844, was built in South Devon and another in France.[8] But comical juxtapositions such as these are rare in the early specimens of the century.

In the *Specimens of printing types* by L.I. Pouchée (London, 1819), the upstart French founder uses the forum to excoriate the competition[9] in a belligerent apology for the typefaces he shows therein:

Address to the Printers

Printing has been known in England near Four Hundred Years, and has, from its vital importance to Society in the development of Learning, and the exercise and encouragement of Arts, Manufactures, and Commerce, long since created a very essential and extensive Trade in the manufacture and sale of Types (both for Home Consumption, and Exportation); and although only FOUR Type Foundries (exclusive of mine) are worked in London at this time, the jealousy of those who have had so long possession of the Trade would in its tenacious operation (as manifested in their treatment of me), seem to bespeak that they consider themselves EXCLUSIVELY entitled to all its advantages, 'AD INFINITUM'.

The exercise of such a feeling by Men possessing Large Capitals, UNACCUSTOMED TO COMPETITION, AND WHOSE MUTUALITY IN BUSINESS HAS BEEN RENDERED OPPRESSIVE BY A BOUNDEN ADHERENCE TO REGULATIONS, WHICH ARE AT VARIANCE WITH THE PRIMARY INTERESTS OF THEIR EMPLOYERS; WHILE THEY ARE NO LESS UNJUST IN THEIR EFFECTS UPON THE INDIVIDUALS WHO ARE WORKING AS JOURNEYMEN IN MOST BRANCHES OF THE TRADE; is capable of presenting many obstructions, which in the early progress of a Con-

8. P. Sadner, *Manuel classique de conversations Françaises et Anglaises*: 'Qu'est-ce que c'est ces chaumières à la suisse, avec la colonne à côté?' 'Elles furent construites pour servir d'atelier à un chemin de fer atmosphérique expérimental, qu'on a essayé sur cet ligne, mais qui n'a pas reussi.' I am grateful to Nicolas Barker for pointing this out to me. The Atmospheric Railway failed because rats ate the leather valve-flaps attached to the vacuum tubes.
9. Pouchée may seem to slight Richard Austin here, but while Austin was a long-established engraver of types, flowers, vignettes, and stock blocks, he mostly worked for other founders. His Imperial Letterfoundry issued its first specimen in the same year as Pouchée. The four founders referred to must be Caslon & Livermore, Thorowgood's Fann Street Foundry, Edmund Fry & Son, and Vincent Figgins. William Caslon IV's foundry sold to Blake, Garnett of Sheffield in 1819. See Reed, p. 355.

Thomas Barton, listed by John Johnson as a founder working at Stanhope Street, Clare Market, is ignored also, but no specimen from his foundry has survived.

TEN-LINES PICA.

MORE.

margin

Great Wild Street.

L. I. POUCHÉE,

cern of this nature, have the most harassing, and serious effects; the pressure of which, I offer as an apology for any defects that may appear in my first specimens; though I have great pride in knowing they will not suffer much in a comparison with those of other Founders.

Having thus let off steam, the still-frustrated Pouchée, a few pages into the book, demands a larger format (*Figure 14*):

MORE
Margin

He grumpily refers to, 'Two lines small Pica, erroneously termed DOUBLE PICA.' In his war against the established foundries, Pouchée introduced Didot's typecasting machine into England. The rivals bought him out in 1830 and destroyed the machine.[9]

In the same year as Pouchée's rant, Blake, Garnett juggled letters in an onomatopœic manner that is as memorable as Joyce's 'Mrkgnao!' It is tempting to think it is their rebuttal to the unwelcome alien:

mmmeeennn cccuuurrr

George Nesbitt of New York came up with 'RANT / FUONDER,' doubtless aimed at his competitor, Darius Wells. It is hard to believe that the huge typo 'FUONDER' was accidental, though it is in a face that causes you to rapidly avert your gaze.[10]

Seeing the possible decay of his book over time, not to mention the violence exercised upon specimens by printers who tear out pages or clip out lines, letters or cuts, Nesbitt has us contemplate

HOLES

in an 18-line condensed sans. Two decades later, Thomas MacKellar wrote a poem for the front of his specimens, beginning

Printer spare that book!
Cut not a single leaf!
You know not half the pains we took,
Or you'd regard our grief.

Among technical problems that plagued the founders were the

9. A.F. Johnson, 'The homes of the London typefounders', in *Selected essays on books & printing* (Amsterdam, 1970); on the destruction of the machine, see James Mosley, *Ornamented types* (London, 1993), p. 5.

10. Edwin Allen's Roman Grotesques (*Figure 15*, from Nesbitt's book) are a backsloping and forward-sloping italic joined at the middle. Gray's 2-line English Zig-Zag (her fig. 90) was cut by Figgins seven years later. Gray was unable to consult Wells or Nesbitt for her study.

The Gothic Condensed Backslope style was unique to wood type.

The only other wood type maker at the time was Debow, who sold Leavenworth's faces from 1835. In his 1837 book, Debow illustrated a 'GOHTIC CONDENSED' [*sic*].

15 Line Pica Roman Grotesque.

hardness of the metal and the thinness of the hairline serifs. Richard Austin's 'Address to printers' of 1819 (quoted by Berry & Johnson at page 76) lamented the unworkable quality of the new modern types with serifs as thin as razors:

> Besides this, in the drawing of the letters, the true shape and beauty are lost; and instead of consisting of circles, and arcs of circles, so agreeable to the eye, some of them have more the appearance of Egyptian characters than good Roman letter. For my own part, though I admire the improvements that have taken place in printing-presses, ink, &c. yet it is but labour thrown away on indifferent types; and I am bold to say, with all the pretended improvements in the face of types, the majority of them look worse when put to the test of work than those cut thirty years ago, and this at a time when arts have arrived at such perfection in this country.
>
> ... In point of economy, it is of much importance to the Printer to have the utmost durability united with the most elegant shape; thus enabling him the better to meet the reduced price now paid for printing.

Figgins stresses the hardness of his types in 1823:

> The various Founts
> contained in this book
> are cast with Metal,
> which ENSURES their
> DURABILITY
> *
> The Types manufactured at
> the Foundry of V. Figgins, are
> always cast with the most
> DURABLE METAL,
> and are warranted, in wear,
> to equal those of any foundry
> in the United Kingdom. 1823.

11. Copper was widely applied by the 1850s to preserve serifs and prolong the life of type via electroplating. The introduction of stereotyping in newspapers led to the decline of this practice. See 'Copper-facing: an incident in the history of typefounding' by Rollo G. Silver, *The Library*, Fifth series, XXIX:1 (Oxford, 1974), pp. 103–110.

Barnhart Bros & Spindler started a craze among American Founders when they introduced their 'copper-mixed type' in June 1876.[11]

Lithography, too, by this time was making deep inroads in the business of the letterpress printer. Harrild & Sons' *Specimen of new type, etc. Being a choice selection from the foundries of Messrs. Besley & Co., Caslon & Co., V. & J. Figgins, & Stephenson, Blake & Co., etc.,* distinguish the trades thus:

Pica Albert Text
The Letter Press Printer must be content with the commercial induce-
ment offered, in the power he has of producing large numbers with rapid

Great Primer Albert Text
The principal advantage of the Lithographer, is the facility he has for producing quickly a small number of Copies

As the specimens expanded, they tended to take one text and
repeat it for all of the book or newspaper founts. It must have been
a penance akin to writing lines in school for the young compositors
who set these paragraphs, such as one in MacKellar's book that
appeared 67 times, beginning 'Experience proves that the apprentice foreshadows the workman, just as surely as the bend of the
twig foretells the inclination of the tree.'

By the second half of the century, when the plethora of available
display types and the sheer volume of the specimens allowed for a
lot of slackness in the composition, it was clear that the founders
had a hard time taking themselves seriously. Instead, they simply
gave themselves over to the playfulness of the types in the texts
used to advertise outrageously bold, convoluted, or otherwise
abnormal letterforms. For example, in Philadelphia, in the mid-
1850s, condensed types were set up to read, 'SPLENDID TYPES
FOR SQUEEZING'. Shaded types were characterized by

ED FROSSARD CALLS THIS TYPE "SHADED."
A shade off – eh? but neverthless original
*
JACOB WAS SENT TO BUY AN ITALIC SHOOTING STICK
Likewise a bushel of Diamond Hair Spaces
*
HOW DO YOU LIKE IT
HOW DO YOU LIKE THE 3D SIZE.

Here, for the first time, we are casually introduced to actual characters in the print shop: the shades of Ed, the knowledegable old
hand, and young Jacob, the gullible apprentice being sent on a
fool's errand. We are soon to learn more about their lives and see
them at work and play.

FOUR-LINE PICA CONDENSED.

CHRONONHOTONTHOLOGOS
MUCH ADO ABOUT NOTHING

GREAT PRIMER TWO-LINE CONDENSED.

ALDIBORONTIPHOSCOPHORNIO, &c.
ISABELLA, OR THE FATAL MARRIAGE.

Caslon and Livermore.

6

Hermit domain

We fill up the silent vacancy that precedes our birth by associating ourselves
with the authors of our existence.
– Edward Gibbon, *Memoirs of my life and writings*

. . . and one of these weapons is the reading of light and easy books which command attention without the labour of application, and amuse the idleness of
fancy without disturbing the sleep of understanding.
–Thomas Love Peacock, *An Essay on fashionable literature*

CASTING ABOUT FOR MATTER for the content of their specimens, the founders would let their minds wander around
their lives or print shops, resulting in texts that mirrored the times.
Text from advertisements or books they were setting might make it
into the specimen books, as well as current topics the founders felt
would catch the customer's eye and give an up-to-date air to their
type samples.

For more flexibility in demonstrating a range of text types, the
founders in the early nineteenth century turned to English verse
and prose. While the material employed may have seemed inconse-
quential to them, their choices from reviewers, authors & journalists reveal the range of contemporary reading habits. A poet's love
for the impenetrably polysyllabic is manifest in Henry Carey's popular eighteenth-century drama, *Chrononhotonthologos* (advertised at
the time as 'the most tragical tragedy ever tragedised'), cited by
Caslon & Livermore in 1830 in their showing of a Condensed
Gothic (*Figure 16*). Two other plays are mentioned on this page,
Shakespeare's comedy, and Thomas Southerne's *Isabella,* written
about 1680 and successfully revived in 1784 when Sarah Siddons
'exposed her beautiful, adamantine, soft, and lovely person, for the
first time, at Smock-Alley Theatre, in the bewitching, melting, and

1. From an Irish paper, May 30, 1784, quoted at amusing length in Henry Sampson's *History of advertising* (London, 1874), pp. 245–6.

2. Konrad Bauer, 'A Brief history of the Bauer type foundry Frankfort on Main', *Typography* 5 (London, 1938), p. 18. That the London reviewers were just as illiberal as their Scottish counterparts is noted by W.H. Ireland in his hilarious *Scribbleomania* (London, 1815), p. 3n.

all-tearful character of *Isabella*'.[1] Here the Caslon compositor was demonstrating the usefulness of Caslon's bold condensed types for playbills, particularly those with long titles.

The type specimens of the highly competitive Scottish founders in the first half of the century were especially literary. In the century after Dr Alexander Wilson cut transitional types for the Foulis brothers' press at the University of Glasgow, Scottish printing exhibited a high level of competence and competition. That Byron & later Peacock took the 'Edinburgh Reviewers' to task, is an indication of the literary power wielded in that metropolis. The German founder, Johann Christian Bauer, worked in Edinburgh from 1839 to 1847. According to his descendant, Konrad Bauer, 'There is no doubt that Bauer went to Edinburgh because it offered him the opportunity of perfecting his knowledge of punch-cutting. At that time, Great Britain, and Scotland in particular, were regarded by typefounders as the Promised Land; to them it meant the same perhaps as Venice to the painter'.[2]

Before Scotland became such a mecca for typefounders, it was the butt of jokes like those of Dr Johnson (perhaps merely attempts to get a rise out of his sycophantic Scots sidekick). In his Anglo-chauvinistic *Dissertation upon English typographical founders and founderies* (London, 1778), Rowe Mores, concluding the list of working founders in Britain, questions the existence of one particular non-Englishman in his study:

> Our history now approacheth the converging point, which centers in a Caledonian whose name is M'Phail. it is said that he hath cut two full faced founts one of Two-l. Engl. the other of Two-l. sm. pic. hath made the moulds, and casts the letter hisself. if this be true (and we have reason to believe that it is not altogether false) he must travel like the circumforanean printers of names from door to door soon after the invention of the art, with all the apparatus in a pack upon his shoulders; for he is a nullibiquarian, and we cannot find his founding-house.
>
> So much for The Founders.

Textually, Alexander Wilson & Sons' *Specimen of modern printing types* (Glasgow, 1826) may be considered typical. After the usual liberal dose of 'Quousque', the reader is treated to Biblical excerpts to show the roman types; for the exotics we find the Lord's Prayer in Anglo-Saxon, in addition to Hebrew (the opening of Genesis) and Wilson's much-praised Glasgow Homer Greek, set in Homer's opening lines. For poetry setting, there's Sir Walter Scott's 'Breathes there the man, with soul so dead...' from *The Lay of the last minstrel*. Extracts from Hume's *History*, a life of Alexander Pope, a review of a history of Spain, a discussion of Descartes and Newton, and an excerpt from Gibbon's *The Decline and fall of the Roman empire* in large script enliven the volume. There is also an essay on style, a news item on the Prussian army (that displays a large-faced letter on a minion body), and page 44 of a dictionary that runs from 'COM to Com'.

Duncan Sinclair, another active founder, started under the guidance of Wilson, the star-gazing Scot. Just prior to dissolving their partnership with the Wilson foundry, Duncan Sinclair and Sons issued a *Specimen of modern printing types* (Edinburgh, 1839), printed by Ballantine & Hughes, which employed Cicero, Bible extracts, poems, and sections of Scott's *Guy Mannering* (1815).

A varied range of book types might be typically set out, as in Ferguson Brothers' braw specimen (Edinburgh, 1846), in sample page spreads from Scott, Burns, Byron, Johnson, Dickens, the Bible, Shakespeare, Taylor's *Holy living*, and a peculiar work of the time, Samuel G. Goodrich's *Anecdotes of ants*.[3]

Clearly there is a strong connection between the selected texts & the bread-and-butter work done by the printers of the specimen books. It is conceivable that, to save time, they simply pulled standing pages from jobs set in the various types to be displayed in the specimen. The 1843 specimen book from the leading Edinburgh foundry, that of Miller & Richard, has facing-page spreads from different chapters of *The Edinburgh cabinet library*. It's a provocative but unlikely notion that the original was composed in slightly differing sizes of type, but they may have been set as samples for the customer.[4] We learn about 'The Social state of the Arabs', 'A Summer tour round Ireland', 'Dr Buckland's Bridgewater treatise', 'Hannibal to his soldiers', 'Six hours in Iceland', 'The History of Scotland', 'Discovery and adventure in Africa', 'The History of the Hebrew Commonwealth', 'Ancient kings of Arabia', 'Duty and advantage of early rising', 'Remarks on the savages of North America', 'On the formation of language', 'The Personal appearance of Linnæus', 'The Personal appearance of Aristotle', 'The Labours of

3. This text comes from *Illustrative anecdotes of the animal kingdom* by Samuel Griswold Goodrich who, writing under the pseudonym Peter Parley, became the 'most prodigious literary hack of his day,' according to the *Cambridge history of American literature*. Goodrich's Parley books generated spurious imitations on both sides of the Atlantic. 'In these books,' according to the *Dictionary of American biography*, 'a kindly and omniscient old gentleman is represented as talking to a group of priggishly inquiring children and instruction is given a thin sugar-coating of fiction. They met the educational needs of the time and sold by the million.' This work appeared as volume 15 of *Parley's cabinet library* (Boston, 1844). In 1823, on the Grand Tour, Goodrich 'met the literary celebrities of Edinburgh' (*DAB*) which would explain his connection to the publishers of that metropolis.

4. *The Edinburgh cabinet library* by Oliver & Boyd, 1830 (complete in 36 volumes at 5 shillings each), applied the formula of Scott's Waverley novels, Lardner's *Cabinet cyclopedia* (1829), written by Sir Walter Scott, and Constable's *Miscellany* (1829). See Michael Sadleir, *Nineteenth century fiction. A Bibliographical record* (New York, 1951), ii:92.

5. 'Wm Caxton was born in the Weald of Kent, as he himself tells us...'. *Cf.* Johnson's *Typographia* I:79; Lewis's *Life of Caxton*, 1736:1; Dibdin's edition of *Typographical antiquities*, 1810:I:lxxv; *The English cyclopedia conducted by Charles Knight* (London, 1856), II: 132–3. Caxton's biography was also the subject of a text by the Boston Type Foundry in 1861.
6. A revival of Caslon & Austin types preceded this, see above: chapter 3 footnotes 16 & 17.
7. From the opening of Charles Knight's biography (London, 1844), p. 9.

Real awareness of Caxton's life and printing did not jell until the Great Exhibition of 1851, for which examples of early British printing were sought out. William Blades, whose biography of Caxton appeared in 1861, organized a Caxton Celebration in 1877. See Blades, *The Biography & typography of William Caxton, England's first printer* (London, 1861; volume 2, 1863) and *How to tell a Caxton with some hints where and how the same might be found* (London, 1870). See also Rowland Hill Blades, *Who was Caxton?* (London, 1877).

the ancient Egyptians', and other topics. These are interspersed with extracts from the Bible, segments of poetry from Campbell's *Poetical works*, & a random collation from Sir Walter Scott's popular novels. A latinate litany, beginning 'Quousque tandem', cuts in occasionally.

Soon after, the dwindling type sizes of a specimen were artfully organized on Clydeside. *Specimens of type cast at the Glasgow Letter Foundry by MacBrayne & Stirling* (1847) serves an historical smörgåsbord of two-page excerpts from lives of Newton, Galileo, Petrarch, and Hutton. These are followed with extracts from a book about the battles of Agincourt, Bannockburn, and Poitiers. With canny Scots' aplomb, the histories of each nation are set out in diminishing sizes, ending with the History of England, for which the very smallest type is reserved.

Many of the Scottish founders, however, had a thriving business in London and would not so blatantly alienate potential customers, even if they were secretly Anglo-saxophobes. James Marr, who claimed to be the successor to the Wilson foundry (which had been well established with branches throughout Britain & Ireland before its dissolution around 1850), devoted sample text pages to a life of Caxton, England's first printer.[5] Marr also absorbed the foundries of Bauer, Ferguson and Huie, as well as Neill & Co. An undated *Specimen of modern & ancient printing etc.* (circa 1866) has segments on 'Early printing in England'. Dr Wilson's economical recutting of the 'Baskerville celebrated ancient type' (*Figure 17*)[6] is revived.

G. McCorquodale & Co.'s *Specimen of book work* (Newton, 1849) lays out several pages of a Caxton biography,[7] alternating with *The Character of Napoleon*.

Also in 1849, R. Stewart & Co. issued an independent specimen book in Edinburgh (Stewart started cutting type for Miller & Richard in 1838), composed of Gray's *Elegy* and bits of Gibbon.

Thorowgood laid out his script type in 1842 in paragraphs discussing punctuation, & in 1849, Neill & Co. of Edinburgh included two pages of proofreaders' marks as a 'Guide to authors in correcting the press' in their *Specimens of printing types* followed by their publication of a *Typographic guide: a series of specimen pages forming a reference book for authors and publishers*, which shows type in different leading with varying margins.

FOUR-LINE PICA ANCIENT.

ANCIENT TYPE,
Cut in the *middle* of the last century.
1234567890

TWO-LINE GREAT PRIMER ANCIENT.

It has often been a subject of wonder with thofe learned per-fons who have written concerning the arts of the *Ancient Romans*, and CELEBRATED TYPE.
£1234567890

TWO-LINE ENGLISH ANCIENT.

It has often been a subject of wonder with those learned persons who have written concerning the arts of the *Romans*, CELEBRATED ANCIENT TYPE.
£1234567890

JAMES MARR & Co., Type Founders, Succeffors to the Meffrs WILSON, Edinburgh, London, and Dublin.

8. Gibbon himself made a typographic breakthrough in restricting the use of italic in *Decline & fall*, which established the subsequently prevailing standard. See V. Ridler, 'On composition', *Bulletin* 16 of the Printing Historical Society (London, 1986).

Figgins may have noticed the precedent in Fournier's landmark 1742 *Modèles des caracteres de l'imprimerie*, which also employed texts about the ancient Romans.

9. Nikolaus Pevsner, *Studies in art, architecture & design* (London & New York, 1968).

10. The 5th edition, and the title page of a French edition, are illustrated by M. Twyman in *The Landscape alphabet* (Hurtwood, Kent, 1987), figs. 10, 11. See also Uvedale Price, *The Distinct characters of the picturesque & beautiful* (1801), and Mario Praz, *The Romantic agony* (Oxford, 1933), p. 21: 'It was in garden-designs, that the new "picturesque" sensibility eventually ran riot. The efforts of those barbers of Nature, the celebrated designers of parks – "Capability" Brown with his special type of idealized garden, and Humphrey Repton, with the "impressionist" garden – continually border on the ridiculous, and already in 1779 Richard Graves in his *Columella, or the Distrest Anchoret*, gives a delicious caricature of the picturesque *chinoiseries* indulged in by owners of parks.'

11. Mary Moorman, editor, *The Journals of Dorothy Wordsworth* (London, 1971).

The pioneering Figgins foundry made a bold move when issuing their *Specimens of new book founts* of 1862, composed solely in extracts from Gibbon's *Decline and fall*.[8] The eccentricity of Figgins in casting their vote over the Bible or other historical speculation may be a result of the foundry setting up samples for an actual edition, but also reflects the ongoing popularity of Gibbon's work.

Hermits & quaint ruins

BRITONS have always had an eccentric bias. In the height of their folly (at least, in this case, the late eighteenth and early nineteenth centuries), they thought they could improve on Nature, and many stately homes and gardens were redesigned with a touch of *Sharrawaggi* or 'controlled chaos' in the landscaping.[9]

The Tour of Doctor Syntax, in search of the picturesque, by William Coombe, was illustrated, like the other popular Dr Syntax books, with hand-coloured aquatints by Thomas Rowlandson. For the title page, Rowlandson drew a crumbling gothic ruin that spelled out part of the word 'Picturesque'.[10] Rudolph Ackermann, the art publisher, issued the book in 1812. Within a year it had gone into five editions. The Reverend Gilpin (the Doctor of the title) had no trouble finding the picturesque, and his recounting of it influenced a generation of painters and poets, not to mention landscape gardeners, who rerouted rivers and demolished hills to improve vistas and walks.

Thomas Love Peacock's more jaundiced account of the remaking of nature can be found in *Headlong Hall* (London, 1816), documenting the style of Capability Brown, who rivalled Humphrey Repton after the Creator. In her *Alfoxden journal*,[11] Dorothy Wordsworth comments:

> [15th April 1798] ... A fine cloudy morning. Walked about the squire's grounds. Quaint waterfalls abound, about which Nature was very successfully striving to make beautiful what art had deformed – ruins, hermitages, etc. etc. In spite of all these things, the dell romantic and beautiful, though everywhere planted with unnaturalised trees. Happily we cannot shape the huge hills, or carve out the valleys, according to our fancy.

Since Vaughan in the seventeenth century, English poets had located the hermit as a figure of austere contemplation in their

EIGHT LINES PICA ANTIQUE.

EIGHT
hermits.
£145!

work. From the success of eighteenth-century poems like Thomas Parnell's *The Hermit*, and Thomas Warton's *The Pleasures of melancholy*, to works by Pope and Wordsworth, where he moved from asceticism to the picturesque, the hermit endured in the popular fancy. Some gentlemen went so far as to advertise for would-be hermits in the press. In exchange for daily meals, the applicant would have to cultivate a pensive mien and refrain from shaving. Dame Edith Sitwell discusses some of these 'Ancient and ornamental hermits' in her *English eccentrics* (London and Boston, 1933; revised and enlarged, New York, 1957): 'Nothing, it was felt, could give such delight to the eye, as the spectacle of an aged person with a long grey beard, and a goatish rough robe, doddering about amongst the discomforts and pleasures of Nature'.

On 3 July 1872, the Victorian diarist Francis Kilvert visited a solitary anchorite who 'had he lived a thousand years ago would have been revered as a hermit and perhaps canonized as a Saint.' Kilvert was touched that the hermit had spent his time devising new systems of shorthand, but was appalled at the condition of the hermit's abode[12]:

12. *Kilvert's diary 1870–79*, edited by William Plomer (London, 1961) II:226–7.

> 'The house' was a sight when once seen never to be forgotten. I sat in amazement taking mental notes of the strangest interior I ever saw. Inside the hut there was a wild confusion of litter & rubbish almost choking and filling up all available space. ... The hearth foul with cold peat ashes, broken bricks and dust, under the great wide open chimney through which stole down a faint ghastly sickly light. In heaps and piles upon the floor were old books, large Bibles, commentaries, old-fashioned religious disputations, C.M.S. Reports and odd books of all sorts, Luther on the Galatians, etc.'

It is no surprise to see 'advertised' in Thorowgood (*Figure 18*):

**EIGHT
hermits.
£145!**

(The manuscript note reads: 'Another 8 Line Antique nearly ready'.) In his 1837 book, Thorowgood sees the figure fulfilling his role in the landscape:

HERMIT
Ministration

Slater, Bacon & Co. (Sheffield, 1810) juggle the idylls of a quiet Hermitage (one imagines it on the Thames near Pope's grotto) and the realities of making a living in the industrial North):

REMIT | Medium
BRITON | Machine
MUSICK | Machine
HERMIT | Richmond
SHEFFIELD | Munitissimus
HERMIT | Summerhouse

In 1863, Reed & Fox issued a specimen from the Fann Street Foundry (which had passed from Thorne to Thorowgood to Besley), stating, in Canon Clarendon extended:

HERMIT | domain

and in Eight Line pica condensed Clarendon:

HERMIT | mount

and also clearing their throats (in extended Clarendon) with

SIN | him | HUM | hem

Miller & Richard (1843) offer a long-standing position to a man of learning:

HERMIT
quamdiu
$1234567

As if to say, it's not much, but it adds up over time. It must be assumed that few were driven to such extremes for a living: there was always the dream of winning the lottery, or alternately drowning one's sorrows in bitter waters. In 'The Country Mouse', his popular translation of Horace's *Satire* (II, 6), Alexander Pope commented:

The veriest Hermit in the Nation
May yield, God knows, to strong Temptation.

Lotts & chances

See here ye Causes why in London
So many Men are made and undone,
That Arts, and honest trading drop,
To Swarm about ye Devils Shop,
Who cuts out Fortune's Golden Haunches
Trapping their Souls with Lotts & Chances ...

THE ENGRAVINGS of Hogarth and Gravelot depict the full horrors of contemporary middle– and working-class existence realistically and unsentimentally, from drinking to gambling and other obsessions and consolations of the age.

Lottery notices provided reliable formats for the introduction of new typefaces: such bills would have been an obvious venue for a printer to employ his latest, most eye-catching types. The National Lottery was re-established in 1753 to finance the building of the British Museum. In 14-line Pica, Caslon lauds 'Bish!' a popular dealer of lottery tickets: 'Chief among the office-keepers of the period was a Thomas Bish who showered millions of bills and miles of doggerel verse upon London just before the final draw took place. He had been a considerable adept in the art of puffing by means of the mock news-paragraph,' says Henry Sampson in *A History of advertising from the earliest times, illustrated by anecdotes, curious specimens, & biographical notes* (London, 1874). Bish's name appears in many of the new types of the period announcing lotteries.[13]

Surprisingly, in 1826, the last of all lotteries languished and only half the tickets were sold. Neverthless, Bish and his rivals, such as Hazard, Swift & Co, generated a vast supply of waste paper. A handbill for the last lottery proclaimed:

BY PURCHASING A QUARTER,
Your affairs need never be in Crooked-lane, nor your legs in Fetter-lane; you may avoid Paper-buildings, steer clear of the King's Bench, and defy the Marshalsea; if your heart is in Love-lane you may soon get into Sweeting's Alley, obtain your lover's consent for Matrimony-place, and always live in a High-street.
[...]
BY PURCHASING A SIXTEENTH,
You may live frugal in Cheapside; get merry in Liquorpond-street; soak your hide in Leather-lane; be a wet sole in Shoe-lane; turn maltster in Beer-lane, or hammer away in Smithfield.

13. James Mosley, *Ornamented types*, 1993, fig. 6a. An early fat face is seen in a poster for Bish, dated June 1810, illustrated in A.F. Johnson, 'Fat faces: their history, forms, & use', in *Alphabet & Image* 5 (1947, p. 47), reprinted in *Selected essays on books & printing* (Amsterdam, 1970), p. 412.

> In short, life must indeed be a Long-lane if it's without a turning.
> Therefore, if you are wise, without Mincing the matter, go Pall-mall to
> Cornhill or Charing-cross, & enroll your name in the Temple of Fortune,
> BISH'S.

The scene surrounding the drawing of the lottery was akin to the
situation, described by Hogarth above, when the South Sea Bubble
had burst ruining many gullible and greedy investors.

By 1817 there was an anti-lottery movement, promoted by the
likes of William Wilberforce, and in 1826 the lottery had to be dis-
continued because swindles, murders, and suicides had begun to
follow the outcome of each drawing. In addition, declining returns
(partly due to mismanagement) as well as the economic slump of
1819–22, led to its abolition. Increased revenue from taxation and
no further crucial financial needs (like the Revolutionary War) also
played a part.[14]

When there are gaps in the dating of founders' specimen books,
some of the new display types of the period can be dated by their
appearance in lottery notices and handbills.[15] Lottery advertisements continued to serve as specimen texts even after the end of
the lottery, either due to the lethargy of the founders or to serve a
talismanic function. As late as 1857, Besley whimsically suggested:

> No influence could control the disposition for display of
> Riches. Corresponding reduction in Prices.

Thorowgood kept the forme standing (in Four line pica Egyptian)
for

THE LOTTERY
DRAWS
Numidian time
£123456789

The above stanza (which may have been composed by Thorne,
Thorowgood's predecessor) could be interpreted as an allusion to
the new collections of African antiquities being acquired by the
British Museum thanks to the funds generated by the lottery, while
also alluding to the darkness of the new slab serif typefaces.

Thorowgood was particularly keen in promoting the lottery in
his specimen showings, for he is said to have bought Thorne's Fann
Street foundry with his winnings (Reed 1952:294). Not unexpect-

14. James Raven, 'The abolition of the English State lotteries', in *Historical Journal*
(Cambridge, England, 1991)
XXXIV: 2: 371–89.
15. Johnson, *op. cit.* Other
early decorated types used in
lottery bills are shown in facsimiles in John Ashton's *A
History of English lotteries*,
published by the Leadenhall
Press in 1893; see also my
'Looking at lottery ephemera',
in *The Ampersand*, XV:3/4,
1996, pp. 19–25; and M.
Twyman, *John Soulby, printer, Ulverston* (Reading,
England, 1966).

edly, therefore, he refers with glee to 'the lucky numbers always found in great variety in the Grand State Lotteries'. His display of Four Lines Pica Black Open is so excited that a 'typo' creeps in:

In the Grand State
Lottery, there is al-
ways great Variety
of lucky Nmbers &

Caslon & Catherwood clearly had the pulse of the nation when they composed their 1821 specimen (printed by Bensley & Sons):

BEG £12
mansion

At the height of the craze, they liken the lottery to kidnapping (in that it had captured the people's senses) in their seven-line Pica:

MANIA | ransom

Their ten-line Pica Antique states most succinctly

WIN
sums

Optimistically, they bestow on themselves

£72, 530
CASLON
thousand

The details are filled in by their two-line English Antique:[16]

Fortunate adventurers displaying magnificent mansions and splendid equipages the riches acquired by successful speculations in the State Lottery excite emulation in the spectators who gaze and sigh for the gifts of the blind Goddess which she never confers but on the bold, enter

Later, in the 1830 specimen, Caslon & Livermore (*Figure 19*) recall

Fortunatus
LOTTERY
£1234567£[17]

16. This and the preceding example are illustrated in Mosley, *op. cit*, figs 6b & 6c.
17. Fortunatus is a German nursery-tale character with a wishing-cap. The punches for this handsome letter are preserved at the St Bride Institute Library, London.

FIVE-LINE PICA ANTIQUE OPEN.

Fortunatus
Lottery
£1234567

showing the rapidly flashing numerals riffling by on the Wheel of Fortune. But a postscript, in the same book, explains the diminishing returns for the speculative investor:

> In the State Lotteries, now wisely abolished by the Legislature, the chances were so greatly against the adventurers, that, according to the Schemes, the purchaser of the whole Lottery would lose half his money. Few, therefore, but the imprudent, the inconsiderate, and the desperate, became buyers of Tickets and Shares. Should the exigencies of the Nation render the revival of Lotteries necessary, it is suggested, that by making the chances more equitable, that if the Government, instead of a profit of one half, would be contented with a sixth or an eighth, the sale of Tickets would be so much increased among the prudent and respectable classes

As consolation the founders offer the losers

FINE
PORT

in eight-line Pica Antique Shaded, and in sixteen-line Pica Antique Shaded:

Gin

while Messrs Wood & Sharwoods of the Austin Letter-Foundry express their condolences with 'Rum' in Fifteen Line Ornamented, No. 1, and the obnoxious concoction, in intoxicating Ten Line Ornamented, No. 2:

WINE
RUM

The obvious preference of the masses is expressed in a rare specimen book which makes a crystal clear minimalist statement. This is the 1809 *Specimen of improved types cast by Slater, Bacon and Co. printers and letter founders, Sheffield.* The single leaf of this specimen (following the title-page) in the Columbia University collection consists of one word in 22 lines Pica:

Gin.

Gold fever

AFTER MID-CENTURY, especially in America, the same impulse that spurred the founders to cry 'WIN SUMS' now led them to show-case another get-rich-quick scheme:

GOLD
MINE

The Boston Type Foundry in their exquisite 1820 specimen book urge the reader (in an early display type called 8-line pica Oak Leaf) to

MINT!
GOLD.

Next to printing, the profession most frequently cited in the speci-men books is mining, and many itinerant printers had turned their hand to this occupation hoping to improve their fortunes. Among others, Edward Pelouze, Sr (the inventor of matrix electrotyping), and two of his sons tried their luck unsuccessfully in California in 1849.[18] Many found that:

MINERS
Toil Hard
❉
DEEP MINES
Treasures Concealed
❉
GOLD MINES
EXPENSIVE 34 MINERALS
SILVER CERTIFICATE
❉
PRATE Miners

This is from Benton-Waldo (1893), and from Marder, Luse (1876):

MINERS.
Rare Ease. 2

From the 1896 *Pacific Coast blue book*:

MINE | Gamp
❉
MINER
Diamond 1

18. 'Typefounders and type-founding in America – Edward Pelouze' by William F. Loy, *Inland Printer*, v. 32 #4, p. 591, January 1904. See also Annenberg (1975: 211–3). William S. Pelouze hand-cast type in San Francisco in 1854, becoming the first person to make type on the West Coast. (*Inland Printer*, v. 31 #1, p. 95)

You wouldn't need an umbrella in a mine. (Before Dickens's memorable nurse in *Martin Chuzzlewit* gave her name to the umbrella, 'gamp' was an adjective for 'sporty' and a verb for 'chew' in Scots.) The last configuration appeared in more than one founder's book. Palmer and Rey had characterized him as 'MINER | Commander', and the Caslon *Epitome specimen* had referred to him as 'Miner Superior to Rector'. As a piece of typographical surloin, MINER goes back to the earliest showings of display types in the 1830s, before the California gold rush, as in the obtuse near-anagram

MINERS | SEMINE

Thorowgood saw him as everything from 'MINER | minions' to 'MINERS | EMINENT MEN'.

Philip Heinrich, a German immigrant who settled in New York and specialized in marketing German faces to the local printers, mentioned, in 1876

234 New Diggings of Gold Fields

Cincinnati in 1888 mapped out the territory in French Ionic:

PRINTERS | Reservations 39
MINERS | Dominions 2

Palmer & Rey in 1892 recalled the Gold Rush with nostalgia:

38 CALIFORNIA 47
America's Golden Wealth
Inexhaustable
4 FORTY-NINE 9
Memoirs and Letters
Good Old Days
2 GOLD ORE 3
Mountlovers Mine
Richness

but, a few pages later, in a typeface called Caxtonian, they ridicule the latecomers to the gold fields around Sutter's Creek:

GOLD MINE
Follies of Fashion
Sucker Creek

When the Civil War ended in 1865, the political and social economy of the United States was dominated by the railroad, which only reached as far as Atchison, Kansas, but was about to strike out to conquer the remaining two thousand miles to the West Coast. Many miners, disenchanted by the meagre pickings and heavy competition in the gold fields, went to work building the railroads. This theme ranks after mining in citations in the specimen books.

Discouraged by their failure in the gold fields and the collapse of their last hope for riches, the miners turned gandy dancers were dispirited and returned to the composing stand. Benton-Waldo comment

SUBSIDIZED RAILROAD COMPANIES PETITIONING GOVERNMENT
FOR IMMENSE LAND GRANTS
246 DIVIDENDS NOT A SURE THING 980

The *Pacific Coast Blue Book* has a

PROJECTED RAIL ROAD ENTERPRISE
Popular (Road to Ruin) Company

MacKellar, in Two-Line Great Primer Medieval Text, mentions

Lightning Trains over Rugged Mountain-Range

and describes the nightmares and attrition attendant on long trips:

EXCURSIONIST'S DILEMMA
Baggage Exchanged; Everything Wrong
Female Tourist's Wardrobe
SLEEPER'S TRIBULATION
Emerges with Shirt Over Head
Finds Himself Too Late
GENERAL LAUGHING STOCK
Passengers Roll Over Quickly and Tumble off the Platform
RESUMPTION OF TRAVEL
78 Wrecked Locomotives Thoroughly Removed
BRIDGE UNDERMINED
Train Submerged, 95 Passengers Lost
DANGER PASSED
45 Travellers Arrive in Safety

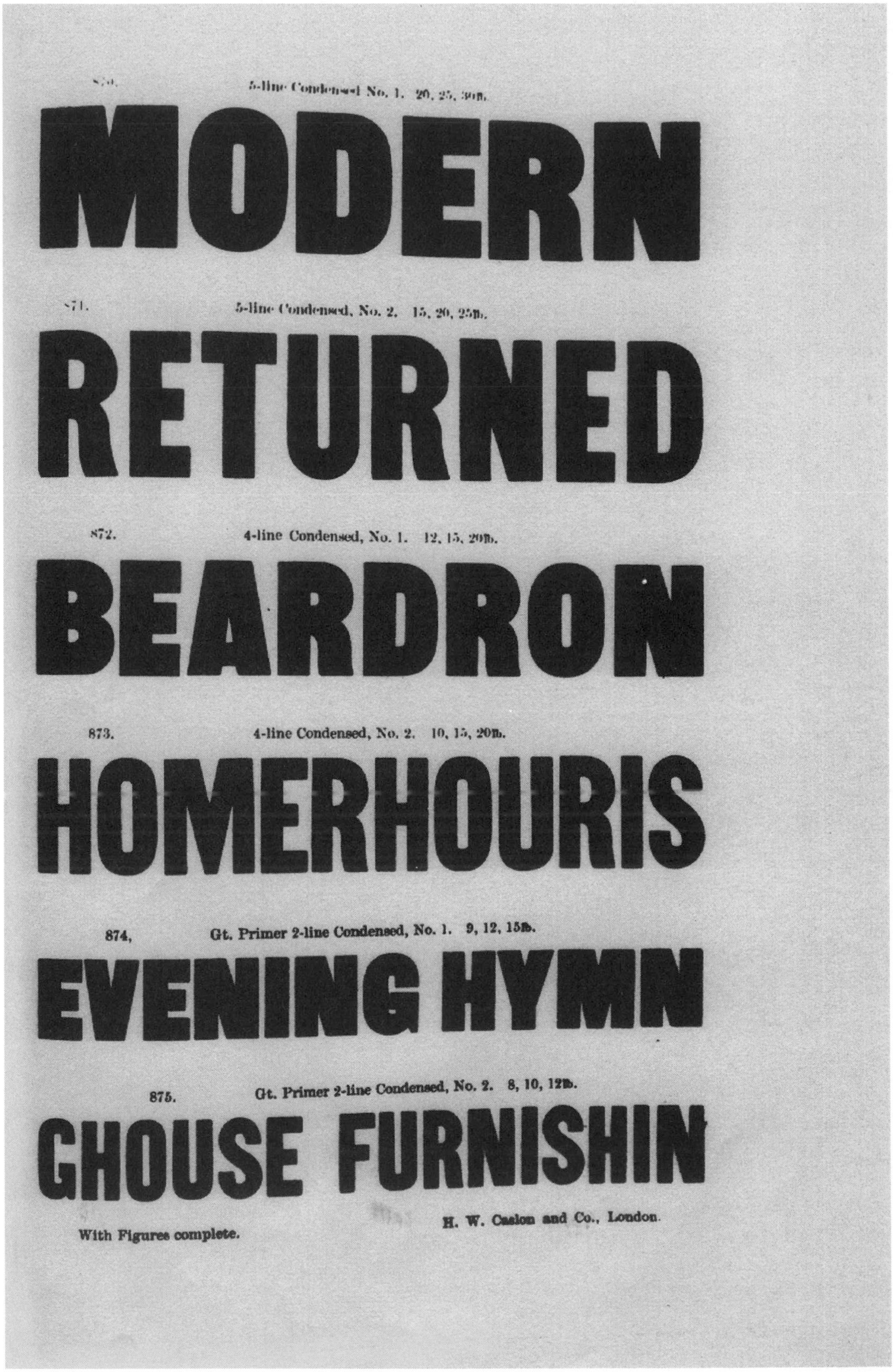

870. 5-line Condensed No. 1. 20, 25, 30℔.

MODERN

871. 5-line Condensed, No. 2. 15, 20, 25℔.

RETURNED

872. 4-line Condensed, No. 1. 12, 15, 20℔.

BEARDRON

873. 4-line Condensed, No. 2. 10, 15, 20℔.

HOMERHOURIS

874, Gt. Primer 2-line Condensed, No. 1. 9, 12, 15℔.

EVENING HYMN

875. Gt. Primer 2-line Condensed, No. 2. 8, 10, 12℔.

GHOUSE FURNISHIN

With Figures complete.

H. W. Caslon and Co., London.

7

Beardron & the Homer-houris

If the man made a Blunder, who can help it?
But mayhaps 'twas a Fault of the Printer.
– Cervantes

BY MID-CENTURY, the Caslon Foundry, which had inaugurated the Catiline tradition, finally adopted the typical modes of showing display types. Destination place names were used for large types where there was only room to show one word; for smaller types, sample headlines or a description of the face appear:

DURABILITY AND ELEGANCE COMBINED

By 1850 Caslon had absorbed the rival Wilson foundry, and in 1865, issued the *Epitome specimen book of the Caslon & Glasgow letter foundry*, a compendium of typical literary specimen styles to that point, and a classic of self-conscious – or unconscious – type-sticking. The *Epitome specimen* has a vision of text and layout: the way you look at a page and understand the words support each other, but are determined by reading. More than fifty years before Hugo Ball was carried onstage at the Cabaret Voltaire to intone his litany of nonsense, this book epitomized Dadaist phonetic poetry (*Figures 20–24*). The Dadaists rediscovered the appeal of fragments as attempts to communicate on a paraverbal level. Romance languages share certain root words & sounds; limited sounds are possible in speech (not to mention with the restricted range of letters in the roman alphabet), and chance occurences strike the neophyte poet as profound as the 'meaning' of things take on new dimensions (giving credence to Raoul Duke's homily, 'When the going gets weird, the weird turn pro').

The uncredited compositor first shows his hand in the page of condensed sans serif types (*Figure 20*). 'BEARDRON' may be his modest self-portrait. He conjurs up 'HOMERHOURIS' in the next line, and, by moving the last letter to the front of the last line, gives us 'GHOUSE FURNISHIN'. Then we are treated to five pages of Jabberwocked English, 'sane' flashes (A WOMAN IN WHITE BY WILKIE COLLINS), semi-coherent 'prantings' ('uninterrupted preliminary expense') and quadrivial Joycean puns that defied a former MI5 cryptographer to whom I submitted them.[1]

The disjunctive one-word-per-page poems of the early display type specimen books and the surreal juxtapositions of Thorowgood show up as well. The spirit of Thorowgood's

IMPORTANT TO COACHMASTERS.
BRIGHTON IN 40 SECONDS

attain a new level of poetic expression here, from the imagistic poetry of 'Crystal Refreshment Rooms' to the revisionist 'Cremantile for Measures', which vies with the racing form for telegraphic concision and hermetic soothsaying. It may be no more than *pi* with a thin crust of the compositor's favourite typographical errors, but clearly this work can hold its own against contemporary experimental poetry. Any attempt to interpret it can only be subjective and limited to the number of languages one can bring to the text.

The page shown as Figure 21 posits 'REND' instead of our old standby 'MEND', and 'HUNEM' instead of 'HUME', or his superior, 'HUMER' (all of them choice surloin). The 'nase' (German nose) of Figure 24 has become 'nuson'; 'tompier' has an air of French deception to it, like 'trompeur'. The 'moderatoh' and the fine typographical error 'dermonstate' hint at a North-country accent, and, on another page, 'Birmingham' is established. This breakthrough indicates it could concern a railway excursion to the North: 'REAN BIRMINEH | THORNEAR TUSMIN' (*Figure 23*) might be translated as 'Are we in Birmingham? They're near to us, man'. 'SHURENOD hermione' could be 'Sharing out her money'; 'unepothcumon': 'one or both, come on'. Hours of fun can be had trying to decipher these pages – 'Unsdem emodan': 'Once them were modern.'

1. Because he has sworn to observe the Official Secrets Act, I am not at liberty to disclose the paternal relationship of this individual to myself.

521   5-line Pica, No. 3. 40, 50 60℔.

BUR sane

522.   Canon No. 4. 40, 50, 60℔.

REND nuson

523.   2-line Gt. Primer, No. 4. 35, 45, 60℔.

HUNEM tompier

524.   2-line English, No. 5. 35, 45, 60℔.

DEHSLER prantings

525.   2-line Pica, No. 5. 30, 40, 50℔.

MODERATE moderatoh

526.   Double Pica, No. 8. 30, 40, 50℔.

REIGHORNE demepodern

527.   Gt. Primer, No. 9. 30, 40, 50℔.

TELEGRAPHIC communicated

With Figures and *Italics*. No Italic to 5-line.   H. W. Caslon and Co., London.

530. 6-line Pica Compressed No. 3. 30, 40, 50b.

BRIG ment

531. 5-line Pica Compressed No. 3. 30, 40, 50b.

NICER tadser

532. Canon Compressed No. 3. 30, 35, 40b.

TRIGLED shamed

533. 2-line Gt. Primer Compressed No. 3. 30, 35, 40b.

MONCRISE hemichud

534. 2-line English Compressed No 3. 25, 30, 35b.

TRENTURED dermonstate

535. Double Pica Compressed No. 3. 20, 25, 30b.

WESTMINSTER astonish many

536. Gt. Primer Compressed No. 3. 15, 20, 25b.

THE DEPUTATION published cent per

With Figures complete.   H. W. Caslon and Co., London.

551.   5-line Ionic Compressed, No. 2.   30, 35, 40lb.

HENDS shorm

552.   Canon Ionic Compressed, No. 2.   25, 30, 35lb.

MITHEB persona

553.   2-line Gt. Primer Ionic Comp. No. 2.   25, 30, 35lb.

SHURENOD hermione

554.   2-line English Ionic Compressed, No. 2.   20, 25, 30lb.

REDINBURGH present form

555.   Double Pica Ionic Compressed, No. 2.   15, 20, 25lb.

REAN BIRMINEH unsdem emodan

556.   Great Primer Ionic Compressed, No. 2.   12, 15, 20lb.

THORNEAR TUSMIN retarded changers

557.   Pica Ionic Compressed, No. 2.   10, 12, 15lb.

MANCHESTER EXCURSIONS   cremantile for measures

558.   Long Primer Ionic Compressed, No. 2.   10, 12, 15lb.

CRYSTAL REFRESHMENT ROOMS   mentions these arrangements

With Figures complete.   H. W. Caslon and Co., London.

5-line Antique 43, 60b.

HI ma

802.   4-line Antique. 30, 40, 55b.

EH dim

803.   2-line Great Primer Antique. 30, 40, 50b.

NER nase

804.   2-line English Antique, No. 2. 20, 30, 40b.

MEAN money

805.   2-line English Antique. 20, 30, 40b.

MINER bonheam

806.   Double Pica Antique. 20, 25, 30b.

SUPERIOR massorients

807.   Great Primer Antique. 15, 20, 25b.

TORECTOR conflagrator

808.   Pica Antique. 12, 16, 20b.

DIUNOTANIEN collected amount

809.   Long Primer Antique, No. 2. 10, 12, 15b.

HOUSEKEEPERISM appropriated transactions

810.   Brevier Antique, No. 2. 6, 8, 10b.

IMPROVES PORTABLE superior mahogany mantel

811.   Nonpareil Antique, No. 2. 4, 6, 8b.

MAHOGANY COROMANDELS the most improved manufactures

With Figures complete.   H. W. Caslon and Co., London.

Like a particularly nasty acrostic puzzle, you feel you almost have the meaning, then it slips away or doesn't quite fit. 'PORTANTEM SEREALOS' seems eminently decipherable. 'Porta' is a door, or it could be 'portentum,' an omen or unnatural happening. If the comp misremembered 'Cerealis' it might refer to Ceres, Earth Goddess of corn, but what do omens of corn portend? And if his schoolboy Latin is as rusty as mine, it might just as well be the Daughters of Night who carry men off to Hades. *Ah!* The Ceres are coming to take you away!

The page of stout Antiques beginning 'HI ma | EH dim' (*Figure 24*) in diminishing sizes suggests a rapidly derailing conversation with a hard-of-hearing grandmother. The 'son' (reading vertically in the left column) blurts out 'Miner superior to rector', perhaps indicating a choice of vocation not to his relative's liking, before stumbling into the polyglot block at 'Diunotanien' ('Do you know Danny then?'; 'God sees nothing?'; A Unitarian with a split personality?!) The granny's replies might concern an oriental masseur who is actually an arsonist collecting protection money. On the other hand, 'massorients' could be an arcane reference to what Rabelais calls 'the Massoretic gloss', the mediæval controversy surrounding Hebrew punctuation. Given the exegetical problem faced here, Caslon's polymath comp is pointing to the endless speculative possibilities.

After this solitary outburst, however, English type specimens become predictable as the prosperous mid-Victorians settled into their long peace, while the American founders pick up steam. The pantograph, stereo caster, electrotyping, and other innovations created a great opportunity for American enterprise in the arena of type design and casting. Similar spurts of neologistic poetry could be detected appearing in American books of the first half-century (particularly among the wood type manufacturers), such as Wells & Webb (New York, 1840) who tell us:

BRUCE | demain | MET | FOUNTINEL

or G.F. Nesbitt & Co.'s (New York, 1838):

LEBANON | huminstc | cant | rite | doan | hide

('huminste' is an interesting rearrangement of 'Hume' & 'Minister'.) As in this Caslon book, American specimens typically waver between clear suggestion and misty opacity, for example Nesbitt's

PHIUDE | corvant | RAMAGE | introduce | ART | ZADOC

As Ludwig Wittgenstein said, in his *Philosophical investigations,* 'In the end when one is doing philosophy one gets to the point where one would like just to emit an inarticulate sound.'

Dialect novels were particularly popular in America at the end of the nineteenth century. Those written by Charles Bertrand Lewis, Charles G. Leland, or Mark Twain covered a range of dialects from African-American to Chinese pidgin. In Scotland, William Alexander's *Johnny Gibb of Gushetneuk*, containing the 'pure Doric of Aberdeenshire', went through eight editions between its publication in January 1871 and October 1884 (the crucial glossary was added to the third edition).

Edward Rowe Mores treated of imaginary languages, but most comps stick with English, to which they apply metastasis, favourite transpositions, anagrams and failed palindromes.

For the closing decades of the century, we'll cross the Atlantic to wander with the peripatetic printers in the country that (in the words of Oscar Wilde) passed from barbarism to decadence without going through a period of civilization.

Mons. Noodle's
peeps at good society

He that readeth a Face at Sight hath the Gift of Kings; And verily for him
that is of the Craft it is a Dower-Royal so to tell Face from Face,
for some be Right-Rogues and offend in any Forme.
–*Mirrour of pryntyng*

AMERICAN HUMOUR in the nineteenth century was based on a familiar masculine persona, according to Alfred Habegger:[1]

> Many humorists got their laughs by wearing a mask that represented an ideal male type, the nonchalant, no-account, countrified loafer. American humor, written by men and circulating in male-dominated media – *The Spirit of the Times*, newspapers, the early variety stage – was in a very real sense the secret of American male society.

The visual substitution of object for object, or the aural or verbal play with words, dominated not only literary humour in the nineteenth century, but also the marketing of goods. As advertisements moved from being merely slight enlargements of newspaper ads to full pictorial posters, the textual and visual pun was gradually incorporated into the poster. Already by the 1830s display types developed for poster work had absorbed the puns, taking on the texture of brick for announcing solid value or the components of old orchards, replete with stray fruiting vines, to advertise nostalgic locations.[2] It is appropriate, then, that the new visually punning letterforms were used for verbal and visual sleights of hand in the typefounders' catalogues that advertised them, especially those of Thomas W. MacKellar (1812–99).

MacKellar was a poet and printer. His books of poetry included *Droppings from the heart, Tam's fortnight ramble* (1847), and

1. Alfred Habegger, *Gender, fantasy, and realism in American literature* (New York, 1982),p. 297; see also Mikhail Bakhtin, 'The Language of the marketplace in Rabelais', in *Rabelais and his world* (Cambridge, MA, 1968).
2. See, for example, Wood & Sharwoods, *The Specimen book of types cast at the Austin foundry* (London, 1838). Apart from obvious visual puns, the title page of this book is a complex of Masonic symbology, from the hidden 'Eye in the Pyramid' device to the two pillars (representing Jachin and Boaz, the right and left pillars of the Eastern Gateway, that divide the zodiac), to the mathematical progressions apparent in the deployment of ornaments (see further Eliphas Levi, *Transcendental magic its doctrine and ritual* [trans. Arthur E. Waite, Paris, 1896;

London, 1968], *passim*, and C.C. Zain, *Ancient Masonry* [Los Angeles, 1994]). The title page is shown by Gray at page 36. See also Gray, 'Chart of ornamented typefaces', nos. 58 (Litho, Caslon, 1835); 61 (Perspective, Thorowgood, 1837); 72 (Blake & Stephenson, ca. 1838); 75, 76, 86–91 (Wood & Sharwoods, ca. 1841). The earliest pictorially decorated types may be found in the work of Pouchée. See Mosley, *Ornamented types*.

3. The oldest established type foundry in the United States, it had been started by Binny & Ronaldson in Philadelphia in 1796. 'Thomas MacKellar, Ph.D., senior member of the American Type Founders' Company,' obituary in the *Inland Printer*, v. 24 #5, February 1900.

4. Current 'Gonzo' journalism is a free-associative rambling scream of consciousness where everything and anything is brought to bear on the composition as long as it occurs concurrently with the writing. The most subjective contemporary exponent, hence the best, is Dr H.S. Thompson.

Rhymes atween times (1879). He apprenticed on the New York *Spy* at fourteen, was promoted to proofreader at seventeen and, after becoming a journeyman, left New York for Philadelphia where he laboured in the printing department of Johnson and Smith's typefoundry in 1833.[3] He rose to manager of the composing room, then foreman of the entire shop, including the stereotyping division. In 1845 he was made a partner. He was the founding editor of the *Typographic Advertiser* (1855–97), of which H.L. Bullen, in the *ATF duplicate sale catalogue* (Jersey City, 1936), said:

> It is the first house organ of a type foundry ever published. Its editor from the first to last issue, covering a period of 38 years [actually 42], was Thomas W. MacKellar, who became the most famous of American type makers, and by the abilities displayed in this house organ – a combination of thorough technical knowledge, with literary and poetical genius, and the intuitiveness of the historian – made his type foundry the most famous and most extensive in the world. MacKellar was famous in his day as a writer of verse, of which some have been published in book formats, and many appear in this house organ. …There is wit and humor in his specimen lines which evoke smiles as they are read – an unusual permanent quality in such compositions quite different from the usual inanities.

MacKellar wrote and published *The American printer*, in 1866, to compete with Thomas Adams' *Typographia* (Philadelphia, 1845) and Thomas Lynch's *Printer's manual* (Cincinnati, 1859). After the death of Lawrence Johnson, in April 1860, MacKellar took over the Johnson firm, with the other junior partners, and Peter Jordan. Under his guidance the foundry would become the parent company of the conglomerate American Type Founders (ATF), consolidated in 1892. In the *ATF duplicate sale catalogue* quoted above, H.L. Bullen continues about MacKellar:

> From 1867 to 1890 he was not only the author of the texts, but also the composer of the lines of type – a composer in two senses of that word – by which his types were advertised.
>
> These lines are famous for their appropriateness and wit and humor. The books thus edited by him are the only type specimen books which may be read with pleasure. (Here are examples of the MacKellar specimen texts: Demisemi Quickstep, Grace in Her Step and Heaven in her Eye; and Life's Dream: Dimple to Wrinkle; and Coatings: Ladies' Patent Blushes.)

(The examples Bullen gives are from the 1859 book of L. Johnson & Co.) Within twenty years, MacKellar's style – today called 'Gonzo'[4]–

was widely imitated, and each American foundry had its resident
wag at the composing stand parodying headlines and advertising
claims, free-associating on the firm's faces. A few stanzas of
MacKellar's 'poetical gems' (*Figs. 25, 26*) – choice morsels from the
'want ads', circulars and flyers that make up much of the Johnson
books – will convey a sense of this peculiar humour:

TENEMENT-HOUSE SUTTEE DIVERSIONS.
Caravanserais suitable for Fifty Families in Reduced Circumstances.
Burning, Roasting, or Maiming for Life, Gratis.
Forty Per Cent. covers Crime.
For Terms and Conditions, apply to Mancurse Grindsoul, Esq.

*

FASHIONABLE EVENING PASTIMES.
Lambskin & Wolfsnap's Social Hypocritical Delineations.
Admission Restricted.
Character Systematically Dissected.

*

DISTINGUISHED DISINTERESTEDNESS
Skimpole Mundivagant, Esq.
Devotes his Undivided Energies to the Friendless
Enclose Three Stamps to his Address

Although Bullen says MacKellar started writing the specimens in
1867, his debut was surely the mid-1850s when he edited the house
journal and the modestly titled *Minor book of specimens* was issued
by L. Johnson and Co. In this book poems are set out as prose, so
that the rhyme and metre are disguised at first glance; for example,
this in Scribe Text (in an edition of the 1853 *Minor book* with the
date 1855):

> *Mirth's Delicious Morsels*
> *Negroes and Boys may whistle in the street: the Boys because they're void of*
> *better sense; and Afric's Sons because kind Providence has gifted them with*
> *whistling-pipes complete: Yea, oft I listen with a sort of pleasure when they*
> *perform in harmony and measure, and beat the time with swiftly moving*
> *feet; But still I think most sensible men, with me, that Whistling is a bore*
> *will heartily agree.*

To while away the boredom of setting a sample text repeatedly,
the comp would relieve himself with whatever came to mind for
sticking the display types. If one brilliant idea didn't fit the measure
the brainwave could mutate into goofing on current events or paro-

dies of popular culture, circulars, and other humble jobwork. If the comps were a little slow-witted some mornings, they'd look to the typeface for inspiration. The founder faced the eternal dichotomy of a need to sell his types and the urge to wisecrack. The above-cited 1853 *Minor book* of Johnson has a small pica italic Gothic Condensed reading *CUSTOMARY BENT OF HIS INCLINATIONS*, and a backsloping two-line nonpareil Gothic Shaded that is RECLINING ON DOWNY CUSHIONS.

A page of fancy types appears in which each line of text comments on the face: for the two-line diamond Light Face Condensed we read, SUCH EXCESSIVE COMPRESSING EXTREMELY DISTRESSING; for a double shaded, INGENIOUS TRIPLICITY; for an outline, HOLLOWNESS OF MERE PROFESSIONS; and the apropos description of a baroque face with median lozenge: ROPE ONIONS! A two-colour Chromatic type reads HYMEN'S SILKEN BANDS, and a range of hairline shaded faces called Phantom reads

DARKNESS VISIBLE
GLOOMINESS
PHANTOMS
FADING

A page of scripts and secretaries from this 1853 *Minor book* introduces MacKellar's cast of characters: Mr Justice Hogg, Mr & Mrs Billetdoux Turtledove, Sam. Growler, John Barbecue, Mordecai Discount, P. Nipping Fyle, J. Censor Mentor, and the happy honeymooners Jedediah Dumpling Honeyheart and Amarilla Lambkin Tendersoul.

The 1859 book from the Johnson foundry is firmly in MacKellar's hands. Here he advertises Miss Kansas Hobbyhorse's Dissertation on Pandoraboxical Phantasmagoria, and gives us two examples of his poetry:

Laughing Infancy toddles, and grave Obesity waddles;
but Grace escheweth queer models!
✱
Thou Long-tailed, Ebon-eyed, Nocturnal Ranger!
What led thee hither 'mong the types and cases? Didst thou not know that
running midnight races
O'er standing type is fraught with imminent danger?

More of MacKellar's jocular word play appears in 1868:

RUMINANTIA'S REFLECTIONS ON CUD-CHEWING
MULTITUDINOUS MONOSYLLABLES
INCOMPRESSIBLE MEGALOSAURIANS
UNBEDIZENED FEMININITIES

The success of the MacKellar foundry was the 'permission' the other typefounders needed to turn loose their own streams-of-consciousness, and late nineteenth-century specimen books are the perfect playground for market humour. In the words of MacKellar the other founders might be seen as

EXCRESCENCES | 98 Professional Imitators

The rare books of Benton-Gove of Milwaukee are among the earliest to display the waggings of loosetongued gabblespeak. Their 1873 book (many of the leaves have dates of 1876 but these may be in anticipation of the Centennial rather than after the fact) presents a fractured version of the tale of Goldilocks and the three bears in Title and Boldface types (One of the bears even manages to utter 'Now is the winter of our discontent'). In Antique Condensed No 4 they quote a Hillbilly proverb:

"LAFF AND GRO PHAT"
"Phun" for the Boys in Oshkosh 123

For their Spencerian Script they update the gigolo from the Elizabethan tradition of the *siquis* personified by Ben Jonson's Shift:

Squintie Glintie, Petit Maitre
Professor of Lady Ogling and Agreeable Nothings in Elite Circles
Antics Performed equalling Improved Puppets
Good Looks Essential, Common Sense a Hindrance

In Centennial Script they admit their methodology:

Hallucinations of a Disordered Intellect.

Describing a condensed typeface they state

CONDENSATIONS OF CELTICS
DEMANDS AND NECESSITIES OF THE ART PRESERVATIVE

The senior partner in the firm was Linn Boyd Benton (1844–1932), the inventor who adapted the pantograph to punch-cutting and thereby made possible the mass-production of different sizes of type from one master pattern. His technique was crucial to the development of Linotype and Monotype in the manufacture of their matrices. He also invented 'self-spacing type,' reducing the set widths of type to nine possibilities, divisible in an em space. His many patents were the result, he claimed, of having purchased 'the worst equipped type foundry in the United States' (Annenberg 1975:63). Frank Gove, a retired naval officer, was the salesman whose drive ensured the company's success. He was replaced by Robert Waldo, a former wholesale grocer (Annenberg 1975:62).

Bento-Waldo's book (Milwaukee, 1893) offers us

MONSTROUS MELONS
ROTUND PERSONS ROLLING MERRILY ALONG

Sticking relatively close to the bounds of good taste and propriety, the compositor can parody the traditional fodder of the typesticker.

A hint of the MacKellar style is detected in 1856, creeping into *The General specimen book* of the Dickinson Type Foundry of Phelps and Dalton, issued in Boston, where one italic is 'Slant-wise', but the wise guy at the stand was suppressed, for the bulk of the book is set in a modest piece of oratory, beginning, 'We hold these truths to be self-evident'. The text of the Declaration of Independence was a natural for American compositors, & a popular choice for setting samples of blackletter (Seen for example in Bruce, 1821, Hagar's book of 1827, Lucas Brothers' Specimen from the Baltimore Type & Stereotype Foundry, 1854, and the Buffalo Type & Electrotype Foundry specimen of N. Lyman's Sons, 1873.). The opening lines of an essay on Virginia by Jefferson appear in several books.

Many typefaces in themselves suggest comment, but the script above all others demanded a farcical approach. Partly because the connecting letters, special characters and possible swash additives made composition laborious, the script type was reserved for specialty printing such as wedding announcements. Phelps and Dalton remained lighthearted in showing their scripts:

NONPAREIL LATIN ANTIQUE.
25 A, 52 a. $2.90

DECIDEDLY Slim Bank CREDIT
1234567890

BREVIER LATIN ANTIQUE.
22 A, 42 a. $2.95

DEVASTATING Hurricanes
1234567890

20 A, 32 a.   LONG PRIMER LATIN ANTIQUE. $2.95

Ruling the Market, Bulldozing 34 SPECULATORS

14 A, 27 a.   PICA LATIN ANTIQUE. $2.95

52 RAILROAD Mishaps, Wholesale Maiming

12 A, 18 a.   GREAT PRIMER LATIN ANTIQUE. $3.80

Ingenious Flying MACHINES 78

8 A, 14 a.   TWO-LINE PICA LATIN ANTIQUE. $4.70

56 LESSONS in Smoking

25 A, 42 a.   PICA FANTAIL. $3.40

Miniature Bank BALANCES
1234567890

22 A, 27 a.   GREAT PRIMER FANTAIL. $4.30

TURNIP Sprout Salad
12345678

14 A, 20 a.   TWO-LINE SMALL PICA FANTAIL. $4.40

GOBETWEEN, Lobby Buttonholer 843

14 A, 20 a.   TWO-LINE ENGLISH FANTAIL. $7.00

294 Tightlaced DIVINITIES

7 A, 12 a.   DOUBLE PARAGON FANTAIL. $7.30

CENSUS Statistics 80

5 A, 7 a.   FOUR-LINE PICA FANTAIL. $8.65

31 Poetical GEMS

MacKellar, Smiths & Jordan,   *Sansom Street, Philadelphia.*

Let this Certify, That on the 26th day of
May 1856, F. Schoeffer Guttenberg was Elected
a Member of the New England Typographical
Society. A. Compositor, President

Phelps and Dalton also adapt a wedding announcement of MacKellar's, copied from the 1853 Johnson book:

This is to Certify, That Jedediah Dumpling Honeyheart,
of Deerfield, and Amarilla Lambkin Tendersoul, of Lowell, were
by me United in the Bands of Matrimony...

(The original Honeyheart and Tendersoul came from Manayunk and Wissahickon.) An anonymous comp setting the Payson Script for the Cleveland foundry in 1880 came up with a lugubrious solicitation 74 years in advance of the event:

Mr & Miss Sardine Fish,
Present their oleaginous regards, and respectfully solicit your presence at a
Can Opening Soiré
On Wednesday Afternoon, May 24, 1954

Another far-seeing millienialist, J. Wesley Barber, in *The Printer's text book*, published in Boston in 1875, asks

SHOULD AULD ACQUAINTANCE BE FORGOT?
"Oh, no,"'s the answer, "It should not, previous to 1999."

At the end of the nineteenth century, the tongue-in-cheek aspect of the text perfectly reflects the overwrought character of the types (if not corsetry).
CURVING LOVELINESS
Quaint Conceits of Modern Design

is how the Cleveland Type Foundry put it in 1880.

The glory of the lush Gonzo in full bore is portrayed by MacKellar (& aped by the obscure Philip Heinrich of New York) in this poetic gem for the personal column set out in Great Primer Centennial Script from the 1876 Centennial edition of the *Typographic Advertiser*:

22 A, 32 a.   Long Primer American. $3.00

COLOURING BY ARTISTIC ACCOMMODATORS
Doubtful Reports Ingeniously Manufactured for Speculative Mining Companies
Close Stock Jobbing Operations Beautifully Illustrated
1234567890

20 A, 24 a.   Pica American. $3.15

MESSIEURS HURRYUP AND WEDMEQUICK
Matrimonial Managers of Refractory, Dilatory or Inconsistent Lovers
Regulators of Domestic Infelicities
1234567890

14 A, 18 a.   Great Primer American. $3.65

SOUVENIRS MADE OF NOAH'S ARK
Walking Canes, Picture Frames, Neck Charms and Boxes
1234567890

10 A, 14 a.   Two-Line Pica American. $4.90

GOOD NUTRITIOUS FOOD
75 Cans Crusoe's Condensed Goat Milk

6 A, 8 a.   Two-Line Great Primer American. $5.60

CHIROGRAPHY
Unconsciously Written 649

PATENTED JULY 18, 1876.

MacKellar, Smiths & Jordan,   *Sansom Street, Philadelphia.*

To Women of Means, of any Pedigree!
Charles Harry Augustus Mellowtongue, Esquire, Bachelor and Gentleman,
The Pride of Fashionable Tailors,
Offers Himself to the Highest Bidder, Spinster or Widow, under Fifty Years of Age.
His Accomplishments are Billiards and Dancing.
Ten Thousand a Year Indispensable.

Platitudes and pert aphorisms, interlarded with snatches of the MacKellar style, make up the text of Collins & M'Leester's specimen (Philadelphia, 1866):

VERSICLES AND APOTHEGMS
Condensed, Extended, or deftly Emasculated,
By Outis Blanque, Esquire.
Specimens Are Herewith Submitted.

Comparing two books from the foundry of Marder, Luse (Chicago and San Francisco), we find that in 1862 their specimen is pretty straightforward, but in their *Specimen book of printing types* issued in October 1874, scattershot scat nonsense thickens the verbiage. A theme of licentiousness is manifest, with a subtext of decrepitude, secret societies, and wordplay:

PROPER STUDY OF
MANKIND IS WOMAN
✻
Men and Mules Thread the Muddy Way
Jocular Jehus a Rarity. 56
✻
NEW & NOBBY
DRUIDIC RIGHT TO ENAMEL
✻
Shinplaster Certificates of Indebtedness

Other than woad, the connection between Druids and enameling is probably a reference to masons on a bender. A Jehu was a fast or furious cab-driver: an allusion to the Israelite king who had Jezebel killed in accordance with Elijah's prophecy (*Kings* IX. 20). For not only was our comp

GENUS GIFTOGAB.
Hypnologistic Lecturer
Tadpoleist. 67

(in the words of Marder, Luse) but he was equally MacKellar's

GABBLE LOOSESPEECH
349 Interminable Scandal Yarn Spinners

and by the 1880s we are quite at home with MacKellar's fractured
view of the world:

MONS. Noodle's
Peeps at Good Society 78
✳
ACCUSATIONS
49 Chiding Lectures
✳
HUMPTIDUMPTINESS
Araminta's Waddling Lessons 43
✳
MYSTIC WINDINGS
Paths Made By Brandied Pedestrians 765
✳
SEEKING REPOSE
146 Troubled Bacchanal Slumbers

No. 5. Price. $1.50 For One Block.—Without Rule.

COUGH

COUGH   COUGH

COUGH

COUGH   COUGH

COUGH

COUGH   COUGH

COUGH

COUGH   COUGH

COUGH

COUGH   COUGH

COUGH

COUGH   COUGH

COUGH

COUGH   COUGH

MARDER, LUSE & CO., Chicago.

9

Concrete evidence

Philosophical problems arise when language goes on vacation.
– Ludwig Wittgenstein

MANY BUSINESSES were rebuilt from the ground up after the October 1871 Great Fire of Chicago. Before retooling, one typefoundry, Marder, Luse and Company, considered standardizing their body sizes but in the end reverted to the old, haphazard system. But then, after six years of experiment, & further consideration, they introduced the standard American point system still in use in England and the United States today. Although the idea had been conceived by P.S. Fournier before 1764, Nelson Hawks was the first to convince an American founder to adopt the standardization of type bodies on Pica units of approximately one-sixth of an inch. In a pamphlet 'Progress of American typefounding!' from his Tamalpais Press in Berkeley in 1958, Roger Levenson wrote

> Concerning the American Point System
> Although Marder, Luse & Co., typefounders of Chicago, had lost all their punches and matrices in the Great Fire of 1871, and as a result had to reconstitute their equipment completely, John Marder would not take the advice of Nelson C. Hawks in the following year to standardize the company's system of body measurements. However, when Hawks became San Francisco representative for the foundry in 1874, he again pressed Marder on the matter and Marder then reluctantly consented to adopt the idea, using the pica that he was already casting as the standard from which to work.
>
> Marder made a shrewd choice in deciding to use his own pica in adopting the plan, as it was identical to that of MacKellar, Smiths & Jordan of Philadelphia, the largest type foundry in the United States at that time. Despite the convenience of having their pica as the standard adopted in the

new system, the MacKellar, Smiths & Jordan firm kept delaying all-out support by offering types on both the old and the new body measurement systems. Marder's victory was complete by 1887, however, when MacKellar announced they 'unhesitatingly recommend the adoption' of the new standard. Only the year before, the United States Typefounders Association, a notorious group of wranglers, had accepted the Marder system as the standard. Once the huge MacKellar foundry supported the plan by all-out compliance, the other foundries went into full production too.

Chicago in 1880 was then the second most important newspaper city in the United States, with 28 dailies and 355 other periodical publications issued there. In addition, according to Howard Lockwood's *American dictionary of printing and bookmaking* (New York, 1894), the largest bookbinderies in the country were found there; the city boasted 300 printing offices and 'four or five type foundries.' The Marder, Luse foundry printed two dozen specimens between 1862 and the formation of ATF (though it continued to operate under its own name after the consolidation in 1892). This important foundry, which had branches throughout the United States, including the Pacific Type Foundry in San Francisco, issued, in 1883, a *Specimen of candy stamps*, which survives in only two recorded copies.[1] This specimen differed from regular type specimens published by American founders in that it did not offer fonts of type for sale, but whole page blocks, stereocast from formes in the foundry. Each of the 187 pages is numbered and priced at $1.50. These blocks were intended for imprinting text on cough drops and, in particular, confectionery of the kind that survives to this day in the form of 'Love Hearts,' the 'will you/won't you' messages swallowed by children. It is hard to tell what medium acted between the lead plates & the confectionery: perhaps red dye, sugar and water – with a dash of benzine. We do know from a journalistic account by Lafcadio Hearn that unscrupulous candy manufacturers added earth to their chocolate, lampblack to their licorice, and adulterated their confectioners' sugar with white clay:[2]

> Candy-vats and candy-pans are too often repositories of ingredients scarcely less noxious than the drugs and unmentionable articles used by legendary witches in the decoction of hell broth; and like the rites of the weird brewers, the mysteries of the confectioner's shop are awful and inscrutable.

1. The ATF copy at Columbia University, with Bullen's shelf number 'Branch Twelve No. 107', was not included in Dr James Eckman's checklist 'Chicago Type Foundry specimen books', in *Printing & Graphic Arts* (Lunenberg, VT, December 1959), nor by Maurice Annenberg in *Type foundries of America & their catalogs* (Baltimore, 1975). The late Roger Levenson found it at Columbia 'stuck to the back of another specimen' and had a photostat made, from which my illustrations have been taken. A second copy is in the collection of David Peat.
2. 'Cunning confectioners. Some light upon the mysteries of candy manufacture,' in *The Cincinnati Commercial*, September 12, 1875, reprinted in *Lafcadio Hearn selected writings 1872-7*, edited by Wm. S, Johnson, Indianapolis, 1979, pp. 60-4.

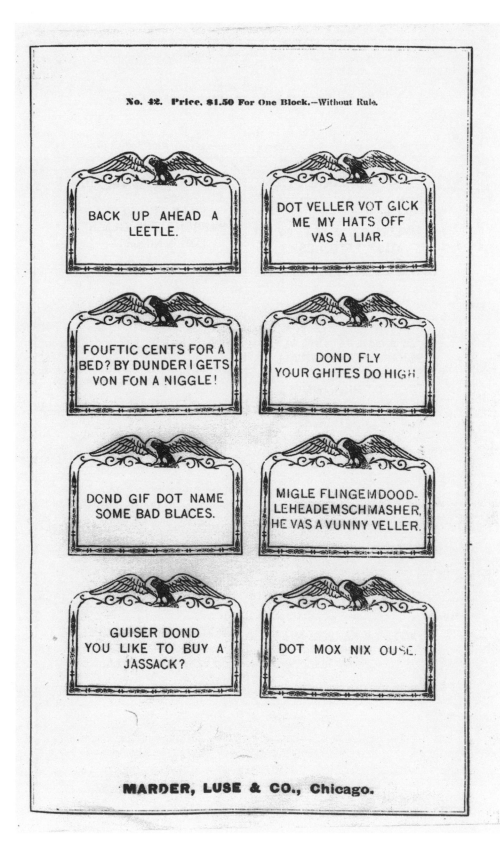

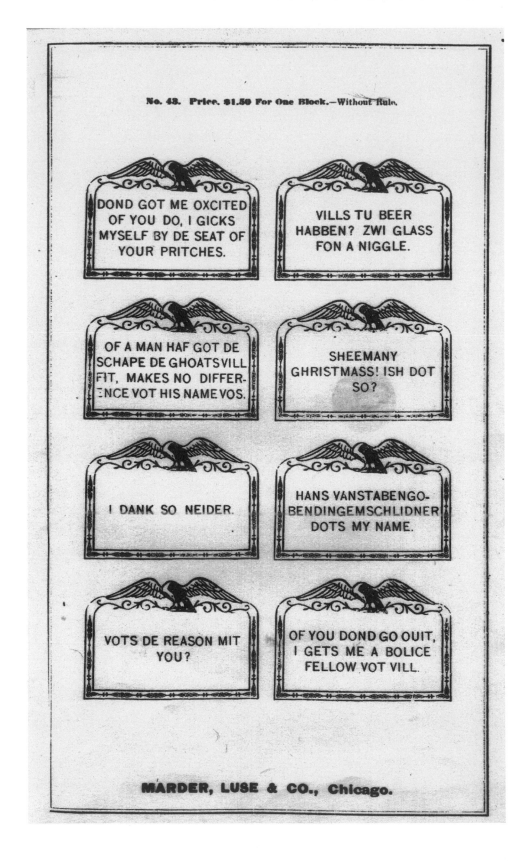

Although badly composed – the types are neither distinguished nor in great shape – the work is interesting for several reasons. It is a pioneer of the type of literature known today as 'concrete poetry,' and it is a wonderful fount of the attitudes prevalent a century ago in the vernacular of the time. There are jokes about 'Chermans' and other forms of 'Dutchmen,' who speak in the 'Katzenjammer' dialect. (*Figs. 28, 29*)

In 1837 Chicago had received a large influx of Irish and German immigrants to build the canal. After the European revolutions of 1848 more German-speaking immigrants arrived. They developed unique ways of speaking English, which are parodied in the Candy Stamps, e.g. 'Dot mox nix ouse' is literally 'It makes no difference,' taken from the German 'Das macht nichts aus.' Each notion is set apart in a frame, or on a separate line so that, after the blocks of sugar-paste or dough are imprinted, they can be cut apart and bagged to offer a variety of surprises to the consumer, much in the way that fortune cookies are still keenly scrutinized for oracular truth today. As a typical collection of the jokes & sentiments of the 1880s, Marder, Luse's specimen is a treasury of the *lingua franca* of the nineteenth century, making fun of the newer immigrants to America, and documenting the courting rituals of the time, though comments such as 'Kiss me quick' still haven't lost their flavour.

In this respect, the Marder, Luse book shows a marked resemblance to the work of Charles G. Leland, a poet and translator of the Victorian era, who focused on poems in dialect, whether those he collected or translated from the Romany gipsy language, or the very popular satirical works he composed in 'German-English' and Pidgin (or *Beche-la-Mar*: the barter-language used in Chinese and Melanesian seaports). He doffed his scholarly cap as translator of Heine to crank out the ballads of Hans Breitmann, beginning with 'Hans Breitmann gife a barty,' first printed in *Graham's Magazine* in Philadelphia in 1857. After the collected ballads appeared in 1871, they were reprinted many times and the fame of the 'bummer' (i.e. looter) and demobbed Uhlan who was proficient in 'swearing, fighting and drinking lager beer,' spread over America and back to Europe. A full understanding of the poems requires fluency in several languages and the perseverance of a *Finnegans wake* scholar, as well as frequent reference to the glossary to decipher German-

looking words that turn out to be English ('Allegader' = All together). Reviewing the one-volume *Breitmann ballads* that appeared in
1869, the *Proof-Sheet* (house organ of the Collins & M'Leester typefoundry) noted, 'A complete glossary has been added, which will
prove useful to those who may hesitate to laugh at such little things
as "Gottsdonnerkreuzschockschwerenoth" until they know what is
meant, and whether they have law and reason on their side.'

A veteran of the revolution of 1848 that sent him to the New
World, Breitmann became so popular that his earlier career in the
Napoleonic Wars was back-plotted by the author until Breitmann
ultimately became as much a symbol of the German as John Bull of
the Englishman. Leland sees no problem in reconciling a sound
classical education with an adult thirst for rowdiness: 'Breitmann is
one of the battered types of the men of '48 – a person whose education more than his heart has in every way led him to entire scepti-
cism and indifference – and one whose Lutheranism does not go
beyond "Wein, Weib, und Gesang." Beneath his unlimited faith in
pleasure lie natural shrewdness, an excellent early education, and
certain principles of honesty and good fellowship, which are all the
more clearly defined from his moral looseness in details which are
identified in the Anglo-Saxon mind with total depravity.' A peace-
time Bohemian, drunk with the New World as with new wine, he
terrorizes the hapless citizenry:

> I stoompled oud ov a dafern,
>   Berauscht mit a gallon of wein,
> Und I rooshed along de strassen,
>   Like a derriple Eberschwein.
>
> Und like a lordly boar-big,
>   I doomplet de soper folk;
> Und I trowed a shtone droo a shdreed lamp
>   Und bot' of de classes I proke.
>
> Und a gal vent roonin' bast me,
>   Like a vild coose on de vings,
> Boot I gatch her for all her skreechin',
>   Und giss her like efery dings.

The bummer was equally chauvinistic about his mother tongue and
lager beer, and Marder, Luse catered to nationalism also. The first

two pages of their book (probably cast as lead stereo plates) offer blocks in German, set in Schwabacher type, with small spot illustrations. The sentiments are predictable: 'Mein Herz,' 'Leibe Mich,' 'Sei Freundlich.' (Nos. 55 & 57 are similar treatments in German; the latter is translated on block 63; Nos. 79 & 80 have heart-shaped frames for German texts.) Nos. 10 & 11 are the English translations of the first two blocks. Nos. 12 & 13 offer more of the same banalities, apart from 'Honest John from China,' which surrounds a nasty moustachioed face.

Then we experience a change, graphically, from the small spot images surrounded by type, to more evolved compositions of type within borders or elaborate shaped frames. Nos. 14 & 15 offer the same messages as today's 'Love Hearts':'Kiss Me,' 'I'll Tell,' 'Be Mine,' 'Hope On.' The eight blocks on No. 16 constitute quite a mouthful: all are large, 1 x 2 inch blocks, with an eagle above and arrows below. The typo-riddled blocks are arranged to compose a poem:

IF YOU INTEND TO MARRY	DO NOT LONGER TARRY
I FAIN WOULD BLEIVE	THAT YO WILL DECEIVE
O HOW DELIGHTFUL	TO HAVE A LITTLE HOME
O DO NOT FAIL TO SPEND	AN EVNING WITH A FRIEND

Nos. 18 & 19 are larger still, a couple of inches square, and have a cupid sounding a trumpet with a banner bearing the messages to be read in any order:

YES, WHEN SOBER	BEWARE WIDOWS
YOU'RE A BEAUTY	CAN YOU BEHAVE?

Nos. 26 & 27 are pages of blarney & blather in appropriate brogue (*Figure 30*):

KISS ME SWATE ONE.
HOWLY MURTHER! WHAT DO YEES MANE?
WHACK! PADDY'S THE BOY.
YER A FRISKY LASS.
HURRAH FOR THE FINNEGINS.
I'M KILT INTIRELY.
WILL YE KAPE ME SHANTY FOR ME?
AH! YER A BROTH IV A B'Y.
WAS YEES IVER IN CORK?
QUIT YER THRICKS AN' GO AN.

No. 26. Price, $1.50 For One Block.—Without Rule.

KISS ME
SWATE ONE.

YER A
RALE BEAUTY
SO YE ARE.

WHACK! PADDY'S
THE BOY.

ME HEART IS
BROKE INTIRELY.

WHO STHRUCK
BILLY PATTER-
SON?

HOW LONG
ARE YEES OVER.

HOWLY MURTHER!
WHAT DO YEES
MANE?

WILL ANY GINTIL-
MIN STIP ON ME
COAT TAIL.

HURRAH FOR THE
FINNEGINS.

OULD IRELAND'S
THE COUNTHRY.

AH! NIVER YE
FEAR.

YER A SWATE
DARLIN
SO YE ARE.

NIVER A WORD.

WAS YEES
AT FINNIGAN'S
WAKE?

MARDER, LUSE & CO., Chicago.

No. 68. Price. $1.50 For One Block.—Without Rub.

SPANK IZ THE
KURE 4 TU MUCH
SPUNK.

DON'T B SASSI.

LEED ON, I
AM THI KAPTIV.

DEW ES UDE
BE DUN BI.

SCUTE WEST
YUNG MAN·

CUM
SIT BI MI SIDE
SWEET 1.

B SURE URE AHED
THEN GO RIGHT.

LARPH
AND GRO PHAT.

B WARY URCHIN,
OR U'LL KETCH IT

U TORK ME TU
DEATH.

SKRATCH 4 HOME
U CHICKEN.

U SEAM 2
GO IT BLIND.

AX THE OLD
FOLKS EF I KIN
KUM.

TWO LIP MEETS
KURE HART AKE.

MARDER, LUSE & CO., Chicago.

YER A RALE BEAUTY SO YE ARE.
ME HEART IS BROKE INTIRELY.
WILL YE BE AISY?
WILL YER HAVE A DHROP.
WAS YEES AT FINNIGAN'S WAKE?

The work was clearly thrown together. Typographical errors and hodgepodge layout indicate that not much effort was expended in its production, however this amplifies the literal content and forces the reader, perhaps used to examining fine points and typographical niceties, to focus on the language.

The Marder, Luse candy stamps carry on with more pages of pidgin English, and two in a Hillbilly dialect (Nos. 68 & 69) with the pertinence & telegraphic righteousness of today's bumper-stickers. Numbers are used instead of words wherever possible and 'You' naturally becomes 'U'. (*Figure 31*)

Block No. 78 is a page of clocks, set at 10:18; there is a page of coins; two pages of wooden-looking children; No. 72 is an unusual block of silhouetted baseball players, not unlike the racist 'Darktown Nine' offered in smaller scale as type ornaments by other founders (and seen in the first cooperative Chicago and Minnesota books published by ATF in 1892), in which the 'pitcher' is drinking a pitcher of beer while the 'Fly catcher' is asleep with a swarm of buzzing flies.

Another aspect of the Marder, Luse book is its graphic layout. While simply a product of the regularization of separate statements laid out (as slugs of type and furniture) for ease of manufacturing identical-sized candies, it does have the visual appearance of a work of concrete poetry. Although 'concrete poetry' is a relatively modern term, we see examples of it in any self-conscious typographical layout. The preface to Stéphane Mallarmé's epic final poem *Un Coup de dés jamais n'abolira le hasard* (Paris, 1897) draws attention to white space ('Les blancs, en éffet, assument l'importance, frappent d'abord.') – this is an important realization for a poet to make, though in the eighteenth century Laurence Sterne, notably, had also played with the invisible in typography.

The term concrete poetry – or *poesia concreta* – was first used by the Noigandres group in São Paulo, Brazil, in 1952. This group was founded by Augusto and Haroldo de Campos and Décio Pignatari, motivated by an awareness of the typography of their printed work. Their *pilot plan for concrete poetry* (São Paulo, 1958) begins by discussing graphic space as a structural agent. In addition to Mallarmé's pivotal work in the integration of text and typography (which Kenneth Rexroth referred to as a 'hieratic metaphysical ritual'), the early concretists also summon up the spirits of Ezra Pound, James Joyce and e.e. cummings (and Apollinaire, for what they term 'vision rather than praxis') in their telegrammatic manifesto, which is set *sans* capitals.

Such highly contrived typographic pictures as the Noigandres group created have been meticulously produced since moveable type was first cast in the 1440s. Before that there was an established manuscript tradition of *Carmina figurata* (as pictorially laid-out poems are called). They have the same charming thrill as cross-stitched samplers. When these verses became fashionable among minor seventeenth-century poets like George Wither, they were ridiculed by Addison and Dryden. Periodically this kind of eye-chart typography resurfaces as a novelty in advertising or when a fine press tries to be *au courant*, but, as Holbrook Jackson says: 'Ideographic printing is inelastic, and limited by mechanical difficulties. The media, that is typeface and ornament, can only be taught a limited number of tricks, from which, like Dr Johnson's performing dog, they cannot deviate.'[3]

This finite bag of tricks generally consists of iteration, either in blocks of text, or in staggered lines, so that visually pleasing or rhythmic patterns occur. But 'the enjoyment of patterns is not the reader's aim,' wrote Stanley Morison in *First principles of typography* (Cambridge, 1936), and, typically, the visual effect of concrete poetry reduces language to ornament.

The use of type as shading to construct elaborate pictures is naïve and betrays the lack of education of workers in this overwrought field.[4] Good examples, showing an artistic understanding of the graphic qualities of typewriter forms, were made by H.N. Werkman in the 1930s and '40s in Holland and Dom Sylvester Houédard in England in the 1960s. The laborious type pictures seen in the oeuvres of Reinhard Dohl, Ferdinand Kriwet, and Robert Lax[5] were prefigured in the great and sloppy work published over a century ago by Marder, Luse in Chicago, 1883.

3. Holbrook Jackson, 'Patterns in print', *The Dolphin*, IV:3 (New York, 1941).
4. Alastair Johnston, 'Type as picture', in *The Ampersand*, IX:1 (San Francisco, Winter 1989).
5. For a bibliography, see the footnotes to my article, cited in the note above.

Nos. 5 & 6 are the words 'COUGH' (*Figure 27*) and 'EXTRA STRONG' set out in a powder pattern and making a strong visual statement. No. 8 has a fly surrounded by the legend: 'Shoo fly don't bodder me'. The compositors cannot have been entirely unaware of the decorative effect of their page of cough drops, where the word 'COUGH' forms a powder pattern, or the more abstract concrete poem created by the field of 'XXX's as No. 83.

A fallback for concrete poets is pattern-making through repeating words in columns or powder patterns on the page. Mathematical combinations of spacing material, based on ems, are a convenient and foolproof aid to patterned typography. Such 'iteration' was an established tool of the newspaper compositor.[6] At mid-century, newspaper typography lagged behind poster and handbill printing. To prevent an inflationary war of typographic complexity by their advertisers (and spare their compositors the extra effort), the proprietors of newspapers limited the choice of type to 'Agate only'. Ads were uniformly set with a two-line initial, and lengthy copy was highly priced, so advertisers would repeat their ad for the effect of display. Illustrations were discouraged as the newspapermen didn't like the extra makeready required, and the small cuts would fill in or break down through poor impression.

Robert Bonner, a compositor noted for his good typography, took over the *New York Ledger* and, changing the focus to women's interests, drove the circulation up to 40,000 copies per day with display ads and a Barnum-like appetite for news sensations.[7] Bonner not only rose through the ranks, but made his mark on the way as a 'Swift,' or quick compositor. He is commemorated in Luther Ringwalt's *American encyclopedia of printing* (Philadelphia, 1871:168) in the article on 'Fast typesetting,' a craze that swept America before the advent of the Linotype: 'Mr. Robert Bonner – now the mighty man of the *New York Ledger* – was employed on the *American Republican* also, and is said to have set up 25,000 ems in twenty hours and twenty-eight minutes, without a moment's rest.'[8]

One of Bonner's ploys was to advertise his paper in other papers, buying a full page of small ads, all repeating the same message over and over. Thus the iteration style quickly caught on. Sometimes he would start each column with a different word so that the display letters running across the columns spelled an acrostic. Though he

6. For a fuller discussion see my articles 'The Poet as typographer' and 'Literary parlor games' in *The Ampersand* XI:2, and XI:4 (San Francisco, 1991–2).

7. Frank Presbrey, *The History and development of advertising* (New York, 1929).

8. On Bonner's career as a 'Swift' see Walker Rumble, 'A Time of giants: speed composition in nineteenth-century America', in *Printing History* 28, 1992.

9. Presbrey, *op. cit.* Up to that time, American newspaper founts didn't include large sizes, so one inch high letters would be composed out of the same letter repeated over and over in Agate. French papers of the period had full-page ads, often featuring three inch high 'Stud horse' type.

British considerations in the newspapers' change in attitude towards their customers were the introduction of the Penny Post in 1850 and the repeal of the advertising tax in 1853. Rotary perfecting presses (in general use by the late 1870s)

spent a fortune on this, it paid off, and the eventual philanthropist & race-horse owner caused a revolution by breaking the sacrosanct column rules so that ads could go to two columns and be set in larger type. Department stores like Macy's and Lord & Taylor were heralded in 30 point type.[9]

The newspaper compositors were adept at creating display advertisements using blank space and repetitious patterning to great effect. Typefounders also profited from selling spacing material with their founts, enjoying the 'fat of quads' (to use Edward Rowe Mores' felicitous expression). This is identical to the Taoist 'nothing, that gives one use of the vehicle,' expressed by Lao Tsu, for blank spaces were as assiduously composed by the typesetter as textual matter, leading to the expression 'a fat take,' meaning copy with a lot of blank space to set. Today's concrete poets can't hold a candle to the complexes of pyramids & inverted pyramids set in the 1860s.

The *trompe l'oeil* effect of the fly on the page, seen in Marder, Luse's *Specimen*, has also attracted poets and marginal book artists over the last century.

The Marder, Luse foundry was the first of the American founders to adopt the point system and patented the first type cast on it – Parallel Shaded – on 22 May 1877.[10] Although Fournier *le jeune* and Firmin Ambroise Didot (who replaced the old type names with size numbers) had standardized sizes in France in the eighteenth century,[11] the American system was independently invented by Nelson C. Hawks of Milwaukee, the Chicago foundry's representative in San Francisco, who operated the Pacific Type Foundry.

In his retirement, Hawks published a pamphlet at the Island City Press, *Explanation of the point system of printing type, with specimens* (Alameda, California, 1918), where he states that he invented the point system in 1878.

> Previous to this there was no uniformity among the makers of Type, each foundry having its own scale of Bodies, or Sizes, and differing from all the others. All haphazard, without relative value to each other.
>
> As this point system has been adopted by all the type foundries of the United States and England, it may safely be said to have revolutionized the manufacture of Printing Type. The full accomplishment of this has taken many years, and has cost an immense amount of money. In an address by Mr. Bright, of the St. Louis Type Foundry, before the American Type Founders Association, in New York City, in Dec. 1892, he estimated the loss

made 8-page newspapers possible, as well as increasing productivity six-fold. See the profile of Walter Scott, *The Inland Printer*, March 1890, VII:564–6.

10. James Eckman, 'The Chicago Type Foundry of Marder, Luse & Company 1863–1892', in *Printing & Graphic Arts* (September 1959), pp. 72–3, 77.

11. Fournier first published his proposal in 1737, and fixed the point system in 1764. Updike, *Printing types*, I, chap. 2; The Sheffield typefoundry of the Bower Brothers, and later that of Caslon, claimed to have introduced the modern point system to England in 1841, but lack of support by other founders caused the abandonment of the effort. (News item from *The Inland Printer*, June 1898, quoted by Annenberg, p. 192.) On comparative names of types, see Reed, chapter 1, Timperley *Printer's manual*, and De Vinne, *Plain printing types*, chaps. 2–3. For a comparison of English, French, German and Dutch sizes, see Smith, *Printer's grammar*, chapter VI. On the relative scale of sizes, see John Richardson Jr, 'Correlated type sizes and names for the fifteenth through twentieth century', in *Studies in Bibliography* 43 (Charlottesville, VA, 1990).

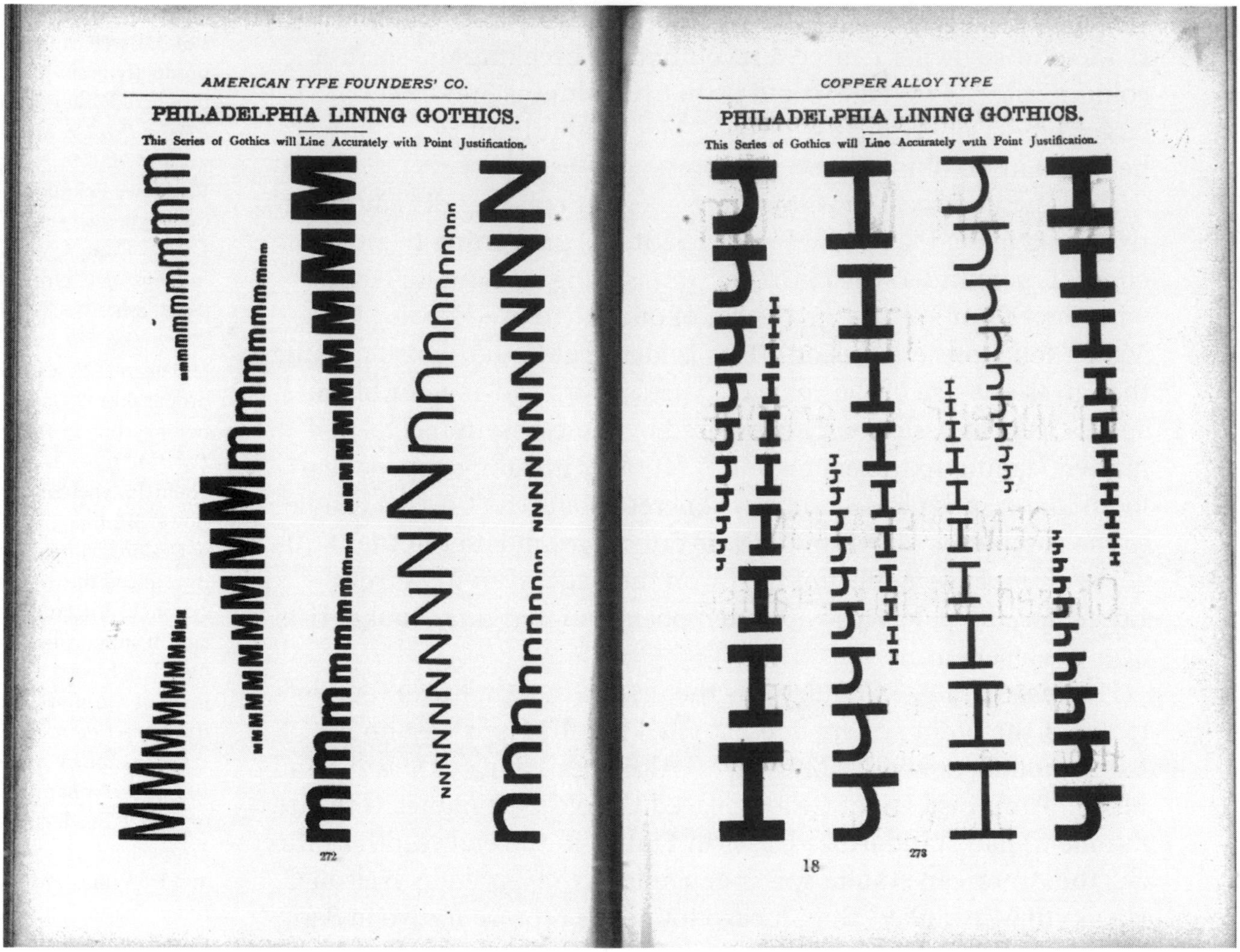
AMERICAN TYPE FOUNDERS' CO.
PHILADELPHIA LINING GOTHICS.
This Series of Gothics will Line Accurately with Point Justification.
272
COPPER ALLOY TYPE
PHILADELPHIA LINING GOTHICS.
This Series of Gothics will Line Accurately with Point Justification.
18
273

in discarding the old body molds alone, in this country, at $9,000,000. Added to this came the revision of matrices and the changing of a lot of small tools and machinery. 'But', said he, 'It marks a New Era in the History of Typography, and is the most important improvement in type making since the days of Gutenberg. After nearly 400 years of working without any system or uniformity, it has remained for a printer from the far off shores of the Pacific to come across the continent and show us old fellows how to make type'. And pointing to me, he concluded: 'As Nathan said unto David, Thou art the man.'[12]

The 'American System of Interchangeable Type Bodies' was adopted on 17 September 1886 by the United States Type Founders' Association[13], and the 'Standard Lining System' for types was introduced by American Type Founders in 1894. The compositors had a field day creating pages of abstract patterns to demonstrate the new ease with which types cast on different bodies would align at the base.[14] Two pages of 'Philadelphia Lining Gothics' (*Figure 32*)[15] demonstrate the abstract massed strength of repeated forms which still attracts artists to letterforms.

12. Roby Wentz, *Western printing. A Selective and descriptive bibliography of books & other materials on the history of printing in the Western States 1822–1975* (Los Angeles, 1975), No. 66, illustrated on p. 39.
13. 'Uniformity of type bodies', *The Inland Printer*, March 1887, p. 395; *The Inland Printer*, May 1889, p. 702; cited in James Eckman, 'The Chicago Type Foundry of Marder, Luse & Company 1863–1892', in *Printing & Graphic Arts* (September 1959), p. 77; see also 'American Interchangeable Type Bodies' by A Truth Seeker, *The Inland Printer*, April 1887, reprinted in M. Annenberg, *A Typographical journey through the Inland Printer* (Baltimore, 1977), p. 177.

14. In France the technique was known as 'Parangonage' and led to the wild mixed-type compositions of the Dadaists which were facilitated by the lining system. See above, p.4, n.2.
15. Cut by William W. Jackson. 'While Mr. Jackson was looked upon as the leader in cutting scripts, his activities were also directed in other channels. He it was who designed and cut the wonderful series of Philadelphia Lining Gothics, ninety faces in all, so proportioned and graduated as to leave nothing to be desired.'–William E. Loy, 'Designers & engravers of type, no. ix—William W. Jackson,' in *Inland Printer* (October 1898, v. 22, #1.)

8A, 16a.   Three-Line Nonpareil Alpine. $3.65

CRICKET & SPECKLED SPIDER
What's this Bug Traveling up My Coat-sleeve
$ 1234567890 ?

6A, 12a.   Double Pica Alpine. $4.35

CURVING LOVELINESS
Quaint Conceits of Modern Designs
* 1234567890 *

4A, 8a.   Three-Line Pica Alpine. $5.80

BRONTE & CO.
Makers of Fictitous Men
* 1234567890 *

HAVE ADDED THREE-LINE NONPAREIL SIZE NOT SHOWN IN FORMER ISSUES

10

Most artistic printers;
Queer artistic notions

I'd as soon have them taught the black art as their alphabet.
– Sheridan, *The Rivals*, 1775

Aⁿᵈʳᵉʷ W. Tᵘᵉʳ (1838–1900) escaped from his family-
intended career as a clergyman and became a publisher at the
Leadenhall Press in London where he revived the 'quaint cut' and
chapbook style of coarse printing which had existed in seventeenth-
century England. As a result, there was a resurgence of handbill
hawkers and street balladeers in the metropolis. Among his many
remarkable publications is a collection of printers' jokes, *Quads
within quads*, which has a miniature version of itself hidden in a
hollowed-out cavity in the back of the book, impeccably printed in
tiny type on banknote paper. He pioneered the mixing of swash italic caps with plain roman lowercase for setting verse in a fanciful
manner while retaining legibility, and designed a peculiar one-story
alphabet without ascenders or descenders.[1]

From his *Paper and Printing Trades Journal*, established in 1877,
Tuer launched the annual *Printers' international specimen exchange*. During the 1880s, printers in Europe and the United States
submitted multiple copies of their best work which were then
bound together and a copy of the compilation returned to every
participant. Each volume is an anthology of the finest ephemeral
printing and, taken together, they chronicle the rise of the Artistic
Printing movement. In *Modern printing*, John Southward credits
the individual who originated the style in Britain, where it was
known as 'Leicester Freestyle' (1899, II:76):

1. From John Millington's *Are
we to read backwards?*
(London, 1883), credited to
Tuer by Herbert Spencer in
The Visible word.

Tuer was also the inventor of
the commercially successful
'Stickphast' adhesive paste.

The grouped style, which is now being adopted in all offices in which work of a modern character is produced, was, if not actually, invented, certainly first developed by Mr. Robert Grayson, manager of the printing department of the De Montfort Press, Leicester (Raithby, Lawrence & Co., Ltd).

2. The Wrinkler is illustrated by Vivian Ridler, who is generally contemptuous of the movement, referring to 'some of the most unpleasant and the most skilful work ever forced through a stick or squeezed from a press,' in 'Artistic Printing', *Alphabet & Image* 6 (London, 1948), p. 17.
3. Quoted in Elizabeth Aslin, *The Æsthetic movement* (London, 1969), p. 79.

The founders, in a quest for novelty, had broken all the rules of legibility, so a new approach was required of the printers to lay out the overwrought decorative typefaces. Rule-bending gadgets, such as 'The Wrinkler,' invented by John Earhart (who wrote an important text on colour printing), caused the breakdown of standard boxed compositions.[2] Seeking *trompe l'œil* and other innovative effects, the printers used many colours and complex layouts which were imposed with the aid of plaster of Paris. New pictorial combination ornaments flooded the market in a variety of styles: Egyptian, Assyrian, Greek and Japanese. The *International specimen exchange* is also a treasure-trove of ideas containing each printer's most intricate jobs – usually self-promotion – guaranteed to fire the imagination of his competitors. Tuer's own submissions are curiously out of synch as he sticks to the old Caslon types & seventeenth-century style of the *aesthetique ruinée* that he had popularized.

Other printers readily adopted motifs and an asymmetric layout from what *The Inland Printer* called 'the Japanesque-Medieval style' as their springboard. After Japan was opened up to foreign commerce in 1853, the flow of goods increased steadily. Lasenby Liberty's store in London catered to the new taste in Japanese furnishings from 1875. In America, the 1876 World's Fair stimulated the first wave of *Japonism*. On January 7, 1879, the sons of George Bruce, the New York type founders, patented their type number 1,063, an odd blend of cross-hatching and cuneiform-like strokes, which they intended as a graphic representation of Chinese pictographs. By 1880, motifs from Japanese export ceramics, then seeping into wallpaper and furniture design, found their way into Bruce's sons' ornament specimens in New York. These pictorial building blocks became the playground of the ephemeral jobbing designer. According to *The Cabinet Maker and Art Furnisher*, a British trade periodical, 'Japanese art has taught the advantages of asymmetrical arrangments so that one need not always have pairs.'[3]

Ben Hur Lampman (1934:15) recalled one of the 'priests to beauty' who was an adept at this kind of composition:

Tom Ford was of the orbital persuasion – lean, frail, bent-shouldered Tom, with a feminine gentleness of blue gaze and a rare gift for the composition of letterheads and display advertisements. Those of his own craft used to style poor Tom a most 'artistic' printer, which was to say that he was one who was priest to beauty in his daily work, and sorrowed for his own unworthiness, it may well have been, and found the deceitful anodyne of drink.

Alcoholic perhaps, but above all 'artistic.' The founders' texts of the 1880s are riddled with

Artistic Effects
Artistic Novelties 2475 Newest Accepted Designs
ARTISTIC PRINTING
&
Artistic Printer

The effects of the 'Artistic' movement in design lingered in packaging from companies who retained their designs for the next century. The Jacob's Cream Cracker box and the Wild Woodbines cigarette package are good examples. That the whole of Western culture was swept with an Asian fever is apparent from literature and the art world. By the 1880s, French poets were showing the influence of Japanese literature as the *Pillow books* and other early classics were translated. Gauguin, Van Gogh, Bonnard, Toulouse-Lautrec and others acquired Ukiyo-ë prints and copied them in their work.

The first bold step towards asymmetric layout in book typography was made by the painter James McNeill Whistler who studied the way Hokusai and other Japanese printmakers incorporated short texts into their artworks. In a series of pamphlets published in the 1880s, Whistler opted for austere typography, adorned solely by his monogram butterfly that mutated throughout as a decorative element. His *Gentle art of making enemies* (1890) is considered the first modern book design in its non-symmetrical arrangement, though it was preceded by several others such as *Whistler v. Ruskin – art and art critics* (1878), and *Mr. Whistler's 'ten o'clock'* (1888). The oddly exaggerated margins were the reverse of the traditional classical imposition, where the foot margin is largest, the fore-edge next, and the gutter smallest.[4] Whistler's head margin was largest and the gutter second, foreshadowing some of the layout grids formalized in the 1930s. But to be completely idiosyncratic, he placed

4. John R. Taylor, *The Art nouveau book in Britain* (London, 1966), pp. 52–3.

marginal notes at the top of the page and wrapped them round the side of the text. The delicate placement of the type block achieved a balanced imbalance via an inscrutable logic. Through his early friendship with Oscar Wilde, Whistler indirectly influenced Charles Ricketts who propounded the asymmetric style and achieved clean, harmonious, and trend-setting results.

At this time in America, Theodore L. De Vinne was campaigning for 'virile' typography. The license of the late-Victorian type designers had led to an overabundance of novelty types that were florid and spineless (a situation akin to that of today and the explosion of 'desktop fonts'). A survey of the output of Edward Prince (before the private presses monopolized his time) or Hermann Ihlenberg, who worked for MacKellar, shows feeble letterforms that have strayed far from the fold of legibility. William Morris's desire for a return to the ideals of the Renaissance, abetted by Emery Walker, did not emerge in a vacuum. According to De Vinne, in his lecture, *Historic printing types*, read to the Grolier Club (1886:99*n*),

> Not long ago Mr. Henry O. Houghton of the "Riverside Press," solicited a foreign type-founder to make for him a series of firm faced types, flat enough to take generous color, and firm enough to withstand strong impression, for which he furnished as models the types of an old Venetian book. The founder declined, saying that the taste of the time was for light-faced types, and that he would cast no other. Mr. Houghton has since had the types made in Boston. Their popularity shows the soundness of his judgment.

Shortly thereafter, William Morris bestowed his chunky ideology on the world. This was not an isolated event but the culmination of a longing for a lost ideal that the late Victorians thought had been attained by the earliest printers in Venice. After the successful Caslon revival, the Chiswick Press had the Basle Roman cut in the early 1850s, setting the stage for Morris and Emery Walker, who based the Golden type on a roman of Rubeus. But even as Morris's publications began to send shockwaves through the world of books, contemporary critics, such as John Southward, stood fast (*Modern printing*, 1899, II:12):

> The *Kelmscott Press* style of book printing – introduced by the late William Morris – has attracted so much attention that reference to it becomes unavoidable, although few printers think that there is much likelihood

4A, Plain Caps, $2.85.   36 Point Mikado.
4A, Ornamental Caps, $3.30.   Complete Font, $10.65
8a, Lower Case, $2.25.   Ornaments, $2.25.

···This·Type
≡is Hereby Dedicated to
His Majesty, Mikado, ❀
≡≡ ···423 Onion Street

3A, Plain Caps, $3.45.   48 Point Mikado.
3A, Ornamental Caps, $3.60.   Complete Font, $12.50
6a, Lower Case, $2.70.   Ornaments, $2.75.

Only a Loving··
≡ Couple, only a
Swinging Gate ◉
❀ 12:30 O'clock

that what they regard as its peculiar characteristics will permanently influence present styles of book printing.

Southward, like De Vinne, thundered against 'effeminacy' in types (*ibid*, 16):

> Much of the favour shewn towards the Morris style of printing is due to the fact that to a large extent it may be regarded as a protest against the prevalent "feminine" printing which Mr. De Vinne has so vigorously denounced.

The breakthrough in typography after Morris was more than matched by the revolution in decoration brought on by the Arts & Crafts movement he also spurred. As far as typographic design went, however, the Japanese motifs quickly became confused with Greek and other elements, and so a hodge-podge 'artistic style' of no certain cultural derivation arose.

Visualising the separate formes (in modern parlance the individual colour separations) for a typically complex work of the artistic printing era, one can see how the underpinnings of asymmetric layout were anchored in the typographers' minds. Though in general every square inch of paper was filled – even overprinted – the imposition of type shows an assurance and understanding of visual balance not based on traditional axial composition. However, this confident spatial deployment was to lie dormant until Jan Tschichold's 'New Typography' arrived in the late 1920s to clear away the clutter of Victorian overornamentation.

In 1885, W.S. Gilbert and Arthur Sullivan's comic opera *The Mikado* swept the 'willow pattern' plate into popular consciousness. The effects of this vogue were even felt in type design, as some of the least-structured letterforms ever created soon appeared. The Cleveland type foundry version of 'Mikado' is virtually unreadable (*Figure 34*). Designed by Henry Schuenemann and released about 1887, it was the first completely undisciplined type. Many other artless faces followed, for example, Hermann Ihlenburg's Spiral (patented October 14, 1890), released by MacKellar, Smiths and Jordan. A completely different face called Mikado was released about the same time by Miller & Richard.[5]

Ernest Fenellosa and Arthur Dow lectured widely in America on Japanese design. Although the effect of Fenellosa's writing was not

5. Information on Mikado kindly supplied by Dave Norton.

really felt until Ezra Pound discovered his essay on 'The Chinese written character as a medium for poetry' in 1912, books such as Percival Lowell's *Soul of the Far East* (1888) attracted spirits like Lafcadio Hearn's to Buddhism. Hearn was another typesetter turned journalist turned author. He moved to Japan and recast old folk tales (in the style of Edgar Poe) in his book, *Kwaidan.*

By the 1880s, MacKellar gave us classic *renga*-like vignettes. (Renga is the Japanese linked verse form where each short poem of two or three lines creates an image that in turn suggests the next couplet.) The syllabic restraint on the eighteenth-century Japanese *haiku* poets like Issa and Bashō – who composed lines of five, seven, and five syllables – is here imposed by the relation of the type size to the measure.

Like the designs referred to as 'artistic', the poetry of the specimen books in the 1880s, though clearly tossed-off, has a kinship to Japanese verse forms such as *haikai, tanka,* and *renga (Figure 33)*:

CRICKET & SPECKLED SPIDER
What's this bug travelling up my coat sleeve?

is a haiku from MacKellar. Here's one of Cleveland's *tanka*:

ALWAYS WRONG
He Sighed. Then Whispered
FIFTY YEARS
*
Tear   IDLE   Tear

Pacific Coast offers this specimen of *renga*:

HOT Rolls
Gone BANK
HARD Times
Walks CHARM
SUMMER Shower
Paramount SECRETS

Wildly disparate thoughts swirl through the Marder, Luse compositor's mind:

CHINESE
Heathens. 46
*
EXPLANATIONS
Drunk and Disorderly!

July 5th, 1872.
✽
FOUGHT NOBLY
Hunkidori on the Jump.
For a Dime. 12

The dainty Japanese æsthetics in the ornaments gives way to raucous humour in these 'American' *renga* from MacKellar in 1882:

MOONSHINE SEEKERS
ZEALOUS WORKERS IN SEARCH OF
QUEER SHOVERS
✽
GRASSHOPPER SUICIDES
SWALLOWING COLORADO BEETLES
✽
CREMATED
Japanese Moguls 23

or these from Cleveland in 1893 in 'Chinese' type (*Figure 35*):

ELECTROTYPE FOUNDRY
COURSE TAKEN BY MOUNTAIN MOONSHINERS
EXPOUNDING UPON BOSSISM
✽
EXCELSIOR
STRAYED AND STOLEN
LOST HISTORY
✽
SAINT VINE ALLEY
FLOWING

6. See my article, 'Racism by design', in *Ampersand* VIII:1 (San Francisco, 1988). Even today racism can be detected in such 'official' literature as the U.S. Parks Department brochure describing the Chiracahua Mountains in New Mexico as 'once infested by Apache Indians.'
7. Escaped slaves often joined Indian tribes for security. A remnant of this tradition can be seen in the tribes of African-Americans who celebrate in fanciful feathered regalia every year during Mardi Gras in New Orleans.

But while foreign arts were influencing æsthetic ideas in the design of ephemeral printing, and a widening awareness of Asian culture spread as Chinese and Japanese ports opened up to trade, the jobbing printer looked with suspicion on the 'joss worshippers'. The dark side of American culture is pervasively racist. Such stereotypes had long been a feature of the founders' stock blocks.[6] The Chinese (though often a Westerner in Chinese garb and surroundings) complacently smokes a pipe amid crates of tea; the negro, also smoking, is depicted in grass skirt *and* Indian feathered headdress with the monstrous bales of tobacco he totes.[7] The kitsch appeal of the cuts issued by the various founders now provokes catharsis in our recognition of easy stereotyping and intractable attitudes born of ignorance.

12A.   9 POINT CHINESE. $1.20

ELECTROTYPE FOUNDRY
COURSE TAKEN BY MOUNTAIN MOONSHINERS
EXPOUNDING UPON BOSSISM.

10A.   12 POINT CHINESE. $1.60

MESSOPOTAMIA
THE QUARRY WHERE GIANTS GREW
WESTERN CONTINENT.

8A.   18 POINT CHINESE. $2.25

EXCELSIOR
STRAYED AND STOLEN
LOST HISTORY

6A.   24 POINT CHINESE. $2.40

SAINT VINE ALLEY
FLOWING

Cleveland Type Foundry,   202   *Cleveland, Ohio.*

Nevertheless, racism permeates typography to this day. Unthinkingly and invariably, typographers specify Koch's Neuland when the topic is Africa, or assign Schneidler's Legenda to Arab subjects. This is the most superficial form of 'allusive' typography. The naïve & childish scripts cut in the 'Japanese' vein in the 1880s are at best amusing: the product of jocular condescension to an ill-understood syllabary. But the obverse of the coin was overt persecution of the Chinese, who were viewed as both exotic and sinister.

Charles G. Leland, the scholar-poet and editor of *Vanity Fair* we met in the last chapter, followed the success of *The Breitmann ballads* with a linguistic switcheroo. In 1876 he turned out the equally researched, if still largely tongue-in-cheek, *Pidgin-English singsong*. This time the Coolie-man is his target, with another dense glossary appended:

> S'posey you go make all-samee,
> Den you blong five dolla' betta.
> Sing-song finish. How you likee?

Clearly, the public likee velly much, for this book also went through the press many times, even though the Chinese in America were still largely confined to California, and their conversation was largely a matter of conjecture projected from the music-hall stage. Leland's hapless characters, Wang the Snob, Ping-Wing, and Slang-Whang, dream of going to 'golo land' – California, the land of Gold:

fan-kwei = ⎫
'foreign devil' ⎭

> My hearee one tim China-side f*l*om ve*ll*y olo witch,
> Supposey my go fan-kwei land, my gettee plenty *l*ich

8. Mary Roberts Coolidge, *Chinese immigration* (1909: 504).

Between 1880 and 1890 there were 100,000 Chinese in the U.S., three-quarters of them in California. Ninety-seven percent of the U.S. population was of European or British North-American ancestry; the Chinese constituted about 1% of the total.[8] The 'melting pot' might more accurately be called a 'salad bowl'. 'Anti-Coolie' clubs, white Protestant forerunners of the KKK, believed in their manifest destiny and chose the 'Heathen Chinee' (as Bret Harte styled him) as their scapegoat.

In Oscar Harpel's compendious anthology *Poems and poetry of printerdom* (Cincinnati, 1875:278) we find Lou Hoding's admonitory poem 'John Chinaman is coming.'

The racism towards the Chinese, like most other hatreds, had economic roots. When the blacks were nominally freed from subjugation in the British Empire by the Emancipation Act of 1833, they were replaced by Chinese labourers, causing a rift between bosses & workers. The ousted workers wanted their jobs back at any wage.

A Chinese Exclusion Act was passed in Congress in 1882 to keep Chinese workers out of the United States. This was supplemented by the inhumane Scott Act of 1888 which extended the proscription to all Chinese women. The Cleveland specimen states, with finality, 'Chinese Emigration Prohibited.' The specimen book of the Cincinnati Type Foundry presents a shabby misspelled sage:

BRETHREN OF CONFUSCIUS
A Special Meeting will be held on
Jossday, to confer the Washeewashee
degree on 218 Squirter, or first degree
members of the above noble fraternity

The 1876 book of Marder, Luse, a little more insightfully, refers to

ECSTATIC INFLUENCES OF OPIUM
That which shocks One Part will Edify the Rest.
Economic Chinese Happiness. 123

The Palmer & Rey book from San Francisco (where most of the urban Chinese were restricted to a ten-block ghetto behind the Barbary Coast) insinuates:

The Smile of the Chinese so
Childlike and Bland

The *Pacific Coast blue book* of American Type Founders describes

EIGHTEEN HUNDRED PRETTY CHINAMEN
Within Those Limits Only Bounded

Our 'Necromantic' typesetter considers:

Ancient Learning Dark
Chinese Devotion
Joss Worship

Benton-Gove & Co. (Milwaukee, ca. 1876) point out the indigenous natives with trophy scalps in their Treasury Open showing:

Lo, the Poor Indian, Whose Untutored Mind
A Large Assortment of Full Heads of Hair Always on Hand.
Sioux Reservation. 1875.

The specimen books' ethnographic commentary ranged further afield as well. Light is shed on the condescension of early anthropologists towards primitive peoples in Cincinnati's 1888 book:

AUSTRALIAN ABORIGINES
Mild and Harmless Denizens of the Forests
Sarcastic Biographers
*
INDIAN RAVAGE

Though it's unclear who's doing the ravaging, the Whites, even in adversity, ultimately appear as bosses:

WARD STRIKERS VOTED
THREE CAUCASIAN SUPERVISORS
BROKEN HEADS

Yet there is no doubt of the heritage of our man, the effects of which he feels down to his boots:

OLD TIME.
Scotch Reel. 12
MILESIAN BENDERS

But other Europeans come under suspicion:

TWO MAIDS of Venice sailing in their GONDOLAS
Each with her trusted Dago armed with Stilleto.

and he doesn't forget to slander the Jews:

KRAMP, KOLIC & GRYPE,
Israelitish Venders of green Fruits.
Summer Complaints. 13

The African-American gets a roasting in this vile joke[9] from Barnhart Brothers & Spindler's 1883 Specimen book:

WELL DONE GOOD AND FAITHFUL SERVANT

9. This joke was published by Artemus Ward in 1860. Mark Twain appropriated it for the punchline of his story 'Riley – Newspaper Correspondent' & made the servant a Negress, in his *Sketches new and old*, 1917, p. 204. See Pullen, *Comic relief* (1983: 91–2, n.10).

Text at the Funeral of a Darkey
24 Who Had Been Burned to a Crisp in Texas 38

The Pacific Coast blue book of 1896 has this suspect couplet:

DARKEST HOURS OF NIGHT
Development of 1225 Baboons on Coon Heights

The Union Type Foundry of Chicago, in a September 1892 ad in *The
Inland Printer,* advertise their American Old Style No. 2 thus:

THE INDIAN AND HIS HUNTING GROUNDS
Are fast disappearing, the one by various paleface refreshments,
the other by civilized landgrabbers.
*
AMERICAN TWO-LEGGED COONS
Plenty south of Mason and Dixon Line. 92

Harrild & Sons characterize types with

ETHIOPIAN SERENADERS
OBEDNIGO

James Conner's Sons of New York (in June 1886), displaying their
new Nubian type, jealously refer to

Our Renowned African Lake Explorers.
Insipid Pinguidinous Southern Maidens of Rich Mahogany Complexion
75 HAPPY BRIDES 43
Excruciating Agonies of American Wedded Existence
*
Dusky Pugilistic Nubian Warriors.
Uncompromising Cannibals, Less Black Than We're Painted.
74 DRAGOMAN 39
Airily Garmented Heathens Striking for Short Clothes!

For all his liberal attitudes, Democratic politics, whimsical humour,
and lip service to emancipation, our tired tramp printer shows that
deep-down he's as suspicious, nasty, and racist as the next blue-
blooded American male.

Another good contemporary description of the strife in the print-
shop, that extends to regionalism as much as to nationalism, is
recorded by C.G. Leland in a ballad appended to the collected tales
of Hans Breitmann, published in London in 1876. The publisher,

Trübner, sets the scene thus:

> The explanation of the poem entitled, "The First Edition of Breitmann," is as follows:— It was not long after the war that a friend of the writer's to whom "The Breitmann Ballads" had been sent in MSS., and who had frequently urged the former to have them published, resolved to secure, at least, a small private edition, though at his own expense. Unfortunately the printers quarreled about the MSS., and, as the writer understood, the entire concern broke up in a row in consequence. And, in fact, when we reflect on the amount of fierce attack and recrimination which this unpretending and peaceful little volume elicited after the appearance of the fifth English edition, and the injury which it sustained from garbled & falsified editions, in not less than three unauthorised reprints, it would really seem as if this first edition, which "died a borning," had been typical of the stormy path to which the work was predestined.

The ballad, 'showing how and why it was that it never appeared', is in Breitmann's characteristic brogue:

Dere vent to Sout Carolina
  A shentleman who dinked,
Dat te pallads of der Breitmann
  Should paper pe und inked.
Und dat he vouldt fixed de brintin
  Before de writer know:
Dis make to many a brinter,
  Fool many a bitter woe.

All in de down of Charleston,
  A druckerei he found,
Where dey cut de copy into *takes*
  Und sorted it all around.
Und all vas goot peginnen,
  For no man heeded mooch,
Dat half de jours[10] vas Mericans
  Und half of dem vas Dutch.

Und vorser shtill, another half
  Had vorn de Federal plue,
Vhile de anti-half in Davis grey
  Had peen Confederates true.
Great Himmel! vot a shindy
  Vas shdarted in de crowd,
Vhen some von read Hans Breitmann,
  His Barty all aloud!

Und von goot-nadured Yankee,
  He schwear id vos a shame,
To dell soosh lies on Dutchmen,
  Und make of dem a game.
Boot dis make mad Fritz Luder,
  Und he schwear dis treat of Hans,
Vos shoost so goot a barty
  Ash any oder man's.

Und dat nodings vas so looscious
  In all dis eartly shpeer,
Ash a quart mug fool of sauer-kraut,
  Mit a plate of lager-bier.
Dat de Yankee might pe tam mit himself
For he, Fritz, hafe peen,
In many soosh a barty
  Und all dose dings hafe seen.

All mad oopsproong de Yankee,
  Mit all his passion ripe;
Und vired at Fritz de shootin-shtick,
  Vheremit he vas fixin type.
It hit him on de occiput,
  Und laid him on de floor;
For many a long day afder
  I ween his het was sore.

10. 'Jour' (French for day) is short for journeyman, has echoes of Scots' 'dour' (sullen), but is also a phonetic spelling of 'giaour', a Persian word for infidel, applied by the Turks to Christians and understood as 'dog' by Beckford and Byron.

Dis roused Piet Weiser der Pfaelzer,
  Who vas quick to act und dink;
He helt in hand a roller
  Vheremit he vas rollin ink.
Und he dake his broof py shtrikin
  Der Merican top of his het,
Und make soosh a vine impression,
  Dat he left de veller for deat.

Allaweil dese dings oonfolded,
  Dere vas rows of anoder kind,
Und drople in de wigwam
  Enough to trife dem plind.
Und a crate six-vooted Soudern man
  Vot hafe vorked on a Refiew,
Schvear he hope to Gott he mighd pie de forms
  If de Breitmann's book warn't true.

For a few stanzas, personal quarrels are sorted out violently between this southerner and a Yorker, and between a Bostonian and a Londoner. Other comments include that of a 'Proof Sheet' who says it's all like the lady who went to hear Artemus Ward lecture and said it was a shame the people laughed so much when the poor young man didn't know what he was saying. For his trouble he is clobbered with an ink keg as

> Fool many a vighten brinter
>   got well ge-gooked his goose.

But all ends well, as the murdered printers find a friendly host awaiting them at the Pearly Gates:

> De souls of ancient brinters
>   From himmel look down oopon,
> Und allowed dat in a *chapel*
>   Dere was nefer soosh carryins on.
> Dere was Lorenz Coster mit Gutemberg,
>   Und Scheffer mit der Fust,
> Und Sweynheim mit Pannartz trop deers,
>   Oopon dis teufel's dust.
>
> Dere vas Yankee jours extincted
>   Who lay upon the vloor,
> Dere vas Soudern rebs destructed,
>   Who vouldt nefer Jeff[11] no more.
> Ash deir souls rise oop to Heafen,
>   Dey heardt de oldt brinters' calls,
> Und Gutemberg gifed dem all a kick
>   Ash he histed dem ofer de walls.

    By the 1880s, however, the founders in following the trends in the marketplace were clearly appalled at some of the developments. James Conner's Sons pronounced 'All freak faces barred', in the

11. A printshop ritual, 'Jeffing' is a form of dice, regularly played to see who will buy the beer or get a fat take. The number of nicks that land face up constitute each player's score. As 'Quadrats', the game is recorded in Moxon's *Mechanick exercises*, published in 1683. An edition of Moxon, annotated by Theodore L. De Vinne, was published by the Typothetæ of New York in 1896.

Typographic Messenger, and announced in a rather folksy manner:

> There seems to be a general demand for the abolition of 'crazy' type, and a return to the more substantial and readable faces that are now being shown by the tip-top founders of the country. It is a well-known fact that general job-work executed with 'crazy' faces will not [*sic*] bear inspection only for a short time, when they not only become tiresome to the eye but a source of mystery to the printer why he did it.... It actually gives an artistic and common-sense printer a pain to look at some of the tomato can printing that is met with every day called artistic typography. Ugh!

At the end of the nineteenth century, Theodore L. De Vinne published his magisterial four volume work *The Practice of typography*. In *Plain printing types*, his treatise which brings elements of taste to the history of type design, he rails against the recent fads for decorative types (1899:359–60):

> The old craving for highly ornamented letters seems to be dead; it receives no encouragement from type-founders. Printers have been surfeited with ornamented letters that did not ornament and did degrade composition, and that have been found, after many years of use, frail, expensive, and not attractive to buyers. ... More changes have been made in the direction of eccentricity than in that of simplicity. Fantastic letters were never in greater request, but they rarely appear as types in books. To see the wildest freaks of fancy one must seek them not in the specimen books of type-founders, but in the photo-engraved lettering made for displayed advertisements and tradesmen's pamphlets. In a treatise on printing-types further remark on engraved lettering is not needed.

11

Typographical tourism

Allons! The road is before us! It is safe — I have tried it — my own feet have
tried it well — be not detained!
–Walt Whitman

THE PERIPATETIC FRINGE has broadened the horizons of the
press from the first. As settlers opened the American continent
in the mid-nineteenth century, itinerant printers rode along with
prospectors and hustlers in boxcars to steel's end all over the
American West. A union card was admission to work as a 'sub' in
almost any small-town newspaper office. The post filled by the
tramp would have been recently vacated by one of his brethren,
described by Walt Whitman:[1]

> the jour printer with gray head and gaunt jaws works at his case,
> He turns his quid of tobacco while his eyes blur with the manuscript.

The tramp printer flourished over a century ago before the advent
of Ottmar Mergenthaler's successful type-composing machine, the
Linotype, in 1893. Those 'of the orbital persuasion', travelling slightly ahead of invisible pursuers, could be counted on to reappear in
outlying print shops at fixed intervals, though some were propelled
by more sombre tragedies than drink or debt in a straight trajecto-
ry. Each was a master of 'the art preservative', able to stick upwards
of a thousand ems of agate or nonpareil type in an hour, his wage
determined by the number of pasted proofs in his 'string' at the end
of the shift.[2] With the added incentive of a half pint of whisky, some
could overhaul or refurbish presses.

These characters, with nicknames like 'Thin Space', or referred to
anonymously as 'Slug Five', lived the carefree moment-to-moment

1. *Song of myself,* xv, 1855.
2. In 1869 the average wage
was 22 cents per thousand
ems. Topnotchers like 'Dirty
Shirt' Smith could net $3 in a
ten-hour shift. John E. Hicks,
*Adventures of a tramp printer
1880–1890* (Kansas City,
1950). Wages were higher in
New York. In 1853, Mark
Twain wrote to his mother
that he received 23 cents per
thousand ems. This was a
starting salary which could
increase up to 35 cents per
thousand (Samuel L. Clemens,
'I do set a clean proof.' [Berk-
eley, 1984]).

existence of 'gay cats' in worn-out stovepipe hats & black sateen 'thousand-mile' shirts. Their lifestyle was celebrated in doggerel poems in the many typographical journals of the 1880s. Whatever they made subbing was usually quickly dissipated in gaming parlors, bars, bordellos and similar dens of ubiquity. It may have been a respite between the saloons and cribs, but even in the printing office the beer bucket was regularly sent out to be replenished. And however and whenever the wanderlust struck there was no holding the tramp back. If he was at the case, he might, like the 'Old John' of legend (recalled by Lampman), resign with a pontifical sweep of his left hand, scattering a quarter column of type while declaiming, 'Get you to your respective places!' Behind him stood the print-shop's coven of horseflies, the office Towel (an institution more venerable than the imposing stone), and its companion soapy washbasin; before him, no certain door, with the wolf never far from that conjectural spot.

Yet the printers were no ordinary hobos; they were educated men who could recite Shakespeare and the Bible. They formed a brotherhood that valued its traditions. They could recall a vast repertoire of questionable poems and songs, which were invariably attributed to James Whitcomb Riley or the journeyman poet Eugene Field.[3]

The tramp who tarried long enough to make an impression was revered by the apprentices and others in the shop. He was a man of the world and unusually erudite, in addition to being a crack comp. Some rose from the ranks to become journalists, editors and well-known writers, signing their work with 'M. Quad' (Charles Bertrand Lewis) or other clues to their typesticking origins. As the Palmer & Rey specimen (1892) put it:

GRADUATES OF PRINTING OFFICES
Among Journalists many have received their
early training at the Printer's Case

Among such literateurists can be numbered Charles F. Brown ('Artemus Ward'), Horace Greeley, Bret Harte, Lafcadio Hearn, W.D. Howells, Bayard Taylor, and Walt Whitman. Brigham Young himself worked the press in Utah. But the most renowned printer-turned-author of the century was Samuel Clemens ('Mark Twain').

3. Eugene Field was a printer & newspaper editor who published several books of verse. His erudition is apparent in his *Echoes from the Sabine farm*, his translations from German, Latin and Greek, and the general tone that pervades his works, such as *The Love affairs of a bibliomaniac* (New York, 1897). His parodies of Chaucer and other medieval poets belong with the non-sense of Edward Lear and the parodies of Lewis Carroll. Like Mark Twain, he often wrote in American dialects. In his 'Ballad of Slug Fourteen', Field recalls the occasion dreaded by the tramp printer:

One night we all remember well
He pied a market galley all to hell;
Again, spaced out agate with non-
pareil.

One of Twain's speeches, delivered to the United Typothetæ of America in 1890, characterizing the tramp in his milieu, was published in *The Inland Printer*, a journal founded in 1883 in the wake of MacKellar's *Typographic Advertiser*:[4]

> I can see that printing-office of prehistoric times yet, with its horse bills on the walls; its 'd' boxes clogged with tallow, because we always stood the candle in the 'k' box at night; its towel which was not considered soiled until it could stand alone, and other signs and symbols that marked the establishment of that kind in the Mississippi Valley. I can see also the tramping journeyman, who fitted up in the summer and tarried a day, with his wallet stuffed with one shirt and a hatful of handbills; for if he couldn't get any type to set, he would do a temperance lecture. His way of life was simple, his needs not complex; all he wanted was a plate and bed and money enough to get drunk on and he was satisfied.

Twain was well qualified to depict the scene, having learned the craft at age 12 in the composing room of Joseph P. Ament's Hannibal weekly *Courier*. By 18 he had worked in St Louis, Cincinnati, Philadelphia and New York; he retired from tramping at 20. His autobiographical writings record some exploits of America's tramping printers, among whom Twain's fellow-apprentice Wales McCormick was one of the most colourful. In his autobiography, Twain recalled that he and McCormick, who boarded with Ament's family, were not paid wages, but were promised two suits a year. Instead they received hand-me-down clothes. Cast-off shirts gave Clemens 'the uncomfortable sense of living in a circus-tent' and were so snug on the giant McCormick as to nearly suffocate him, particularly in the summertime. Twain characterized Wales as 'a reckless, hilarious, admirable creature; he had no principles, and was delightful company'.[5]

By 1850 McCormick had left Hannibal, eventually settling in Quincy, Illinois, where Twain saw him while on a lecture tour in 1885. (After this reunion, Twain regularly gave McCormick financial assistance.) McCormick was the inspiration for the handsome and flirtatious printer named Doangivadam in *No. 44, the mysterious stranger*: 'Hamper him as you might, obstruct him as you might, make things as desperate for him as you pleased, he didn't give a damn, and said so. He was always careless and wasteful, and couldn't keep a copper, and never tried'.[6]

4. Reprinted in *The Inland Printer*, August, 1974, p. 96.
5. Robert Pack Browning, Michael B. Frank and Lin Salamo, *Mark Twain's notebooks & journals, volume 3* (Berkeley, 1979), from Notebook 27, August 1887–July 1888, p. 305.
6. 'Autobiographical dictation, 29 March 1906,' in Mark Twain's *Autobiography*, edited by Albert Bigelow Paine (New York, 1924).

7. Manuscript of one page beginning 'injun Joe's death ...', possibly written in 1897, in The Mark Twain Papers, U.C. Berkeley. McCormick also appears on page 98 of the story 'Villagers' in *Huck Finn and Tom Sawyer among the Indians*.
8. *Mark Twain's mysterious stranger manuscripts*, edited by William M. Gibson (The Mark Twain Papers, Berkeley, 1969).

The irreverent character of the tramp is illustrated by some of Twain's best anecdotes, which unveil the otherwise mysterious origin of phrases that have entered popular mythology:[7]

Rev. Alex Campbell, founder of the Campbellites, gently reproved our apprentice, Wales McCormick, on separate occasions for saying Great God! when Great Scott would have done as well, & for committing the Unforgiven Sin when any other form of expression would have been a million times better. Weeks afterwards, that inveterate light-head had his turn, and corrected the Reverend. In correcting the pamphlet-proof of one of Campbell's great sermons, Wales changed 'Great God!' to 'Great Scott', and changed Father, Son and Holy Ghost to Father, Son and Caesar's Ghost. In overrunning, he reduced it to Father, Son & Co., to keep from overrunning.

On another occasion, McCormick abbreviated Jesus Christ to 'J.C.' When told by Campbell never to diminish the Saviour's name, 'he enlarged the offending J.C. into Jesus H. Christ'. In a further reminiscence, Twain wrote that 'Wales inserted five names between the Savior's first and last names, said he reckoned Rev. Campbell will be satisfied now'.[8]

By the 1880s, the tramp winds up shoulder-to-shoulder in the type specimens with the HERMITS, CRANKS, 567 LUCKY MEN and assorted 8 Cent CHAPS:

Remarkable Tramp Printers. July 3d.

*

STORIES OF A TRAMP TOO STEEP TO CREDIT

*

SHADOW STEW
110 Cents with Hambones
Served for Tramps

*

SEE THE TRAMP
Winks his Eye and hies East

*

EXERCISE IN PUNCTUATION
TRAMP! TRAMP 1863

*

COMMONPLACE AND MEDIOCRE
Facetious Attempts to Besmirch Poor Tramp Travelers

But the *Specimen* book of the Central Type Foundry of St Louis (1886), which includes 'Specimens of Desirable styles of Modern Faces manufactured by other foundries' (Boston Type Foundry,

Dickinson Type Foundry of Boston, and borders from Cincinnati), cautions in Long Primer Pen Italic:

> *Advice to the young Printers: Don't tramp as long*
> *as you can avoid it. That is to say, do not throw up a*
> *situation when you are making a good living, and start*
> *out in search of more lucrative or agreeable employ-*
> *ment. There is no place where you are not likely to*
> *find Printers in abundance, with every advantage on*

and in Great Primer Pen Italic:

> *When seedy Printers come your way*
> *telling of Fat Takes and Big Pay they*
> *would have, if they could only manage*
> *to get to some place where they formerly*
> *worked, don't believe half they say, for*
> *probably the whole is untrue; $678.90*

Cincinnati (1888) suggest

> 234 COMICAL JOKES
> WINTER 56 WIND
> WALKERS 890
> 24 TRAMPS
> TRIPS 34
> 78 CARS
> MEN 5

Cleveland's compositor expresses himself thus:

> COMMANDING THE ROAD TO RICHMOND
> CAN ANYTHING BE MORE EASY AND YET TEDIOUS
> THAN EATING RATS AND MICE EATING CHEESE

Diet, or the lack of it, motivates his cry:

> TASTELESS
> SMEARED
> BANANA

His ideal floats before him in Palmer & Rey's Nymphic:

> HOT COAL BEDS
> Delicious Toothsome Dinners
> Free Cigars
> Fat-Witted Jests on Cooks

The goal of many a tramp was San Francisco's Barbary Coast, as conjured by Palmer & Rey in their 1892 book:

Boyhood's Dream: Freedom, Money and Adventure
Blushing Maidens of Barbary Coast

The specimen book of Palmer & Rey gives a rich sampling of the gamut of the job printer's experience, as in this text:

AS YOU PENETRATE INTO THE LABYRINTHINE RECESSES OF SOME FOSSILIZED PRINTING OFFICES NOT SITUATED IN SOUTHERN AFRICA, NO WHITEWASH BUSINESS OF ANY KIND LIGHTENS THE SCENE, BUT THE MIDNIGHT FEATURES OF THE OFFICE TOWEL[9]

The Benton-Gove compositor (1873), lingering in the Veld, provides this surreal fantasy:

While in the Diamond Mines of Southern Africa and Standing on the Dizzy Brink of an Awful Precipice we saw a Big Keg of Lager Beer Rolling Fiercely toward us up the Precipitous and Thickly Wooded Embankment and following closely in its wake was a Patent Duplex Back-Action Bung Starter

He returns to North America for:

MEXICAN BANDITS
Relieve the Tired Travelers

Whitman framed the wanderlust thus:

Long having wander's since, round the earth having wander'd,
Now I face home again, very pleas'd and joyous,
(But where is what I started for so long ago?
And why is it yet unfound?)

An introspective moment brings forth this (somewhat impressionistic) confession in American Type Foundry's *Pacific Coast blue book* of 1896. What did the compulsively traveling tramp seek?

I AM HUNTING THE MAN
WITH THE AGED JOKE; THE MAN WITH
THE FISHING POLE
THE MAN WHO STOPS
AND INSERTS HIS THUMB IN YOUR
OVERCOAT BUTTON

9. Why not in South Africa? The reference is to the *Specimen of book, newspaper, jobbing & ornamental types* published by Miller & Richard in 1876. Having commenced business in Edinburgh and expanded to London, Miller & Richard's empire extended as far as Palmer & Rey's foothold in San Francisco by the late nineteenth century. Their 1876 book had thirty pages, repeated over and over, of 'Scenes in South Africa', beginning, 'As you penetrate into a secluded valley in South Africa, the whitewashed farmhouses gradually unfold themselves, scattered at short intervals along the hills...'.

THE MAN WHO BLOWS
IN THE BARREL OF A GUN IS A
SUITABLE ONE FOR
THE DUDE WITH
TOOTHPICK SHOE IS MINE
MIDNIGHT HOUR

Another sample hints at other reasons to hit the road:

DEFAULTER'S ROUTE BOOK OF FOREIGN
EXCURSIONS WRITTEN BY AN ABSENTEE
SHOWING HOW TO SUCCESSFULLY AND
PLEASANTLY EVADE PURSUING OFFICERS

The tramp wasn't picky about his lodgings on the road, but he was able to maintain an amused distance from his circumstances, as shown in these sample placards (from Cleveland, 1880 & '93):

BOOMERANG HOTEL
This justly celebrated House will be open to receive a
limited number of guests between 3:35 and 3:45 a.m.,
✳
HUNGRY AND THIRSTY SOULS COME
Early and Eat and Drink Yourself to Death Without Cost
Everything Strictly First Class
And Guaranteed to Kill Anybody in Seventeen
Sittings, Don't Fail to Call

A tramp at Marder, Luse muses on his traveling life:

INTRODUCTORY OVERTURES TO HIGH-TONED AVENUE HASH FACTORIES.
Do you Dance the German, and Have You Tried the Boston Dip?
Are You a Boarding-House Novice?
Semi-Idiotic Chorus by the Young Ladies, "Oh My!" 24680
✳
RESEARCHES IN COUNTRY HOTEL BEDS.
An Opposition Based on the Ground of Inexpediency!

As a respite from the hard life of the road, the tramp dreamed of

RETREAT for the Careless Tramp[10]

The Cleveland[11] Type Foundry of Henry H. Thorp (1893) provide a

"HELL BOX RETREAT."
For the purpose of filling a long felt want,
we shall open March 23d, 1897, a Hospital

10. A retirement home for printers, much discussed in *The Inland Printer*, became a reality in May 1892, when the Childs-Drexel Home for Union Printers was opened in Colorado.

11. According to tramping lore, the name Cleveland itself is a 'typo': it was originally 'Cleaveland' until a typesetter short of space in a headline threw out the 'a'. The Cleveland Foundry was instrumental in the introduction of the platen jobbing presses, the Chandler & Price, and the Gordon.

and Asylum for the relief and cure of the mu-
tilated wrecks which mark the wake of the
average Art Preservative Works.

while dreaming of

FRENCH
Helena of Killdare
✻
18 STRICT 67
Preservation of Health
✻
8 SHADY 5
Seaside Reveries

James Marr, of Edinburgh had wistfully mentioned a

Letter-Founders Provident Retreat
near Craigmiller Castle

A comp at Marder, Luse of Chicago (1876) thinks nostalgically of

THE MARINE HOSPITAL
Sweetest Home of My Childhood
Oft Have I Strayed

How far he has strayed is hinted at in such samples as these from
Palmer & Rey (1892):

SUMMER-SOJOURN AMONG THE CYPRESSES OF MONTEREY
DEFENDING TERROR STRICKEN INHABITANTS FROM THE RAV-
AGES OF 87654 BALD-HEADED BUMMERS
EXPERIENCES OF A BEER-KEG TAPPER
✻
PRINTERS MEETING
Opium Cultivation in South America
✻
Consumption of Liquors
PROGRESS OF MEDICAL SCIENCE
Therapeutic Utilization of Hypnotic Science
Synthetic Cocaine
✻
INGENIOUS DYPSOMANIA
Singular Intoxication by Cantharides[12]
Native Grasses
✻
CHOICE BUDS

12. Commonly known as
Spanish Fly.

5 POINT ANTIQUE, No. 4.

24A, $1.15. 48a, $1.45. Complete Font, $2.60

LAUGH AND THE WORLD
Laughs With You Weep and You Weep
Alone Be Glad Your Friends
$12345 Are Many Be Sad 687901

8 POINT ANTIQUE, No. 5.

24A, 48a. $2.80

COMING REWARD
The Happy Farmers Viewing
45 their Crops 67

12 POINT ANTIQUE, No. 4.

14A, $1.45. 22a, $1.25. Complete Font, $2.70

DEATH BLOW
Dr. Jones, of Soan,
1234567890

6 POINT ANTIQUE, No. 5.

24A, 48a. $2.30

EDITORS, LABORERS
The Growth of Moral Ideas is Due
67 Economic Measures 35

10 POINT ANTIQUE, No. 4.

16A, $1.05. 22a, $0.85. Complete Font, $1.90

PROHIBITION IN
Dakota has Received its
1234567890

18 POINT ANTIQUE, No. 4.

10A, $1.60. 16a, $1.60. Complete Font, $3.20

WHISKY
Useless 4 Cure

24 POINT ANTIQUE, No. 4.

6A, $1.65. 10a, $1.75. Complete Font, $3.40

OF SNAKES as Men 45

28 POINT ANTIQUE, No. 4.

6A, $2.90. 10a, $2.80. Complete Font, $5.70

KNOW Biters 5

36 POINT ANTIQUE, No. 4.

5A, $3.75. 8a, $3.30. Complete Font, $7.05

$1 GOT While

48 POINT ANTIQUE, No. 4.

4A, $5.40. 6a, $4.35. Complete Font, $9.75

LOAded $1

Cleveland Type Foundry, 99 *Cleveland, Ohio.*

and Cleveland's comp, ruefully off the wagon, notes (*Figure 36*):

WHISKY | Useless 4 Cure
OF SNAKES as Men | KNOW Biters
GOT While | LOAded

and asks 'WHY DO BOYS DRINK?' He also mentions 'Merry Children' and wishes us 'Merry Christmas', adding 'PLEASE RE-MIT'. But alcohol alone doth not these 'MERRY BOYS,' 'MER-RY MEN,' and 'Many MEN Merry' make. It's all choice surloin.

While socially he sees himself amongst the educated classes, his way of life makes the tramp printer an intimate of burglars and outlaws. Palmer & Rey's 1892 book catalogues card games, suggesting they are as busy as Gargantua at his arithmetical studies:

OLD SLEDGE TAUGHT | Mr. Aceofspades, Professor of Pinocle
Chuck-a-Luck and Freeze-Out | Poker, non-Impartible
THREE CARD MONTE | The American School of Bunko | Double High Five
THE WIDOW | Or Improved Cut Throat, in | Five Lessons
STUD HORSE | Arizona Jack and Keno | By a Retired Sport

Benton-Waldo (in 1884) provide a whole saga of one Professor Lightfingers, who moves between the *beau monde* and the *demi-monde* attaining notoriety:

PROFESSOR LIGHTFINGERS RECOMMENDS
CARELESSNESS IN BOLTING FRONT DOORS AND GATES
SCOURING THE TOWN FOR CROOKS
HAY-FORKS AND FLAILS IN REQUISITION
POLICEMEN HUNTING NIGHT INVADERS
ANGRY HOUSEWIVES OVERHAULING BUREAU AND
MOUNTED POLICE CALLED
LIGHTFINGERS TAKEN IN CUSTODY

We learn what drives him to such escapades:

SOCIETY IS ONE POLISHED HORDE
FORMED OF THOSE MIGHTY TRIBES
THE BORES AND BORED

The Professor reappears in MacKellar's Lining Gothic in an ad in the July 1889 *Inland Printer*. By the Fall of that year, however, MacKellar in the *Typographic Advertiser*, has turned him into Professor Sneakthief.

The dandified printer sported at night, and frequent reference to the witching hour is made in the specimens. Here's one scenario from the *Pacific Coast blue book*:

MIDNIGHT EXCURSIONS

❋

MIDNIGHT CONCERT

Awoke 8 Maidens

❋

MIDNIGHT SERENADERS CRUSHED

Here's another:

BLACK BEAR
HUG HER HARD

❋

HERMANN
COMING

❋

DANGEROUSLY BRIGHT EYES
BEAMING FORTH NIGHTLY FROM BEWITCHINGLY MAIDENLY FACES
UNDER SMALL CAP COVERINGS

❋

NOTADIME & EMPTYWALLET
MATRIMONIAL BROKERS

❋

INDEPENDENT YANKEE GIRL
FOREIGN DAME

❋

HYMENTOWN ROWDIES

Figures come into play with

NEAR 2 Madre
MEANS 8 Tablets

The tramp conjurs a dream date:

OYSTERS AND CHAMPAGNE
POODLE DOG WITH SALLY LUND AT THREE
O'CLOCK IN THE MORNING

What 'poodle dog' is a euphemism for we can only guess, but the reality was more often 'MAD DOG' or 'RED DOG' and our tramp was dreaming in a ditch.

Benton-Gove (1873) set out the menu in their Gothic faces:

BIVALVULOUS GUTTA-PERCHA CLAMS
Undetonating and Non-explosive Beans with Red Onions
*
LUXURIOUS RELISHES APICIAN DAINTIES
Door Jam Pigeon Toes Smothered in Turnip Sauce Limburger Cheese
*
CHOICE VEGETABLE COURSE
Green Bean Chow-Chow with Burdock Leaves
*
CHOICE GAME TIDBITS
Boned He Fleas Stuffed with Gnats

Thomas MacKellar in his *Fourteenth specimen book* (1882) has
us contemplate an equally appetising bill of fare:

RARE DELICACY
Kidneys Rolled in Sawdust
PREPARATORY COURSE
Snail Soup
Mussel Soup, Explosive Bean Soup
PRECIOUS TIDBITS
Cock's Comb with Flea Sauce
LIQUID
17 Fine Gins
BANQUETS
Mirthful Feasts 58

In the same book, somewhat concerned, he mentions

FETICH
8 Savage Idols
Dull FUN 2

CEMETERY RECIPE
Soothing Syrups for 91 Infants

WHOLESALE INFANTICIDE
Recipes for Destroying Infantile Constitutions
Prepared Cordials and Soothing Syrups

Benton-Waldo, a little more flippantly, refer, in 17 point Bremen, to

NUMEROUS ACCIDENTS TO THREE THOUSAND CHILDREN
The Revolving Scarecrow Only 85 Dollars Each

They also revive the hermit:

STRICTEST SOLITUDE
PLAIN FOOD FOR HERMITS
*
Franklin Typographical Society's Annual Supper
All the Members Enjoy One Square Meal

We can only speculate as to what brings to the printer's mind such *disjecta membra* as these from Cincinnati (1888):

TEMPTING MORSEL
STEWED FROG
*
51 NEAT PRINTERS
FANCY DESIGNS
*
STEAMSHIP
*
CASTAWAY
*
UNEXCEPTIONAL PORTRAIT PHOTOGRAPHY
*
FOREIGN BRANDIES
IMPORTED CIGARS

We know, though, that our poetic compositor was never sure of the morrow. The steamship, instead of symbolizing a pleasure cruise, may portend disaster; the daguerreotype (or the quicker, cheaper and less-fragile tintype) doesn't interest him, for who would want an image to remember him by? In his dreams he wishes for the almost attainable: the finest liquor and tobacco. As long as he remains a neat printer, these things are within his grasp.

If the life of a tramp offers little money and less security, it has other consolations, and the tramp scoffs at attempts to reform him, as shown in this snippet from Cleveland:

When the ruinous results of reckless restrain
riotous ruffians ruthlessly romping rough roads rightly
then religious reform rigorously refined will really do

Alliteration was a product of the literary style of the times. In 1877, M. Schmidt and Co., Lithographers, Printers, Designers, published

Shadrack S. Stevens' speculations. Sallie Sparkle's serio-comic story,
an illustrated 18-page booklet about speculation in Sanfrancisco,
every word of which begins with 's'.

Our tramp is a card-carrying hack. We hear from Marder, Luse in
1874:

SONG OF THE SIERRAS.
Breezes Blowing Through Tresses
Poetical License.234

✻

Bunkoed

✻

AH! HOW GOES THE BOTTLE?
A Swallow Doesn't Make A Summer. 74

✻

UNHESITATINGLY
Told to the Marines

✻

STILL WANTED!
Maid of the Mist. 567

In the hymeneal department we note his continued frustration:

OVER THE WAY
Charlotte Rouberts Abroad
79 Dismal Swamp 39

In a type called Unique Celtic the scene at 'HYMEN'S Shady
Retreat' is sketched out:

61 MEMBERS Discouraged
SILENT Listeners 23
6 SHORT Hours
RED Lights 5

In large sizes of De Vinne, Cleveland tells us

TEACH
Fret Mind

✻

FINDS
Rich Girl

✻

Hoe Tip

The red lights and discouraged members summon the apocopated

rhyme of 'Hoe' (also the name of a press manufacturer) which
recurs in Cleveland's book, in a Latin type called Modern Antique.
He strikes it rich:

MINER
Diamond 1

Hoe at 2

We find the lure of the exotic lurking in this bed of figures:

VERY BLACK
234589

DARK DIANA
123450
3 JUMBO 6
5 DEAR 8

In yet another scenario from the *Pacific Coast blue book*:

PRETTY MOLLY PERKINS DANCES
Moonlight Excursion 21 Train
❊
ROMANTIC
Maidens 417
❊
COAL MINES
Excavating
FRENCH BOND
Judgments
FLEETING HOURS
Smiles of Hope

A similar vignette is suggested by Marder, Luse:

MODEST MAIDS.
With Little Dimpled Shin
Rogueish Sin.3
❊
JULI LOLLIPOP
Season Invigorator!
Frigidity 14
❊
VILE DRINKS!
Bibulous. 2
❊

GORGEOUSLY BEDECKED NYMPHS
Mislead the Dazed Night-Wanderers from the Way
Hospitable Thoughts Intent.23

✳

SELECTIVE SOIREE.
Quiddative.2

✳

HIGH-TONED
Historical nobody.
Aristotle.2

✳

FRUMPISH FEMININITY!
Fat and Freckled Fiery Frauleins!
Furious Fussers.135

✳

INSULTING PUPPIES IN PANTS
Queer Dissuading Capacity of Stoga Boots.
UTILITY COMBINATION. 1234

✳

ANCIENT MAIDENS
Nucleated Orbicles on Wings
Hopeless Idiocy 12

But our dear ladies of the night, who have gone from jailbait to Valkyries in the time it takes to stroll up the block, get the last word:

MALIGNANT MUMMY
Malgracious Male Make-Shift
Mulish Mome.

For talismanic purposes Cincinnati (1888) recall

HERMIT
Round Dome 7

The 'HERMIT' slowly faded from the specimen books, but there were always plenty of 'ANCIENT RUINS' to ponder. Benton-Gove & Co. (Milwaukee, ca. 1876) were the first to look sceptically at Schliemann's archaeological finds, in Long Primer Gothic No 1:

WONDERFUL DISCOVERIES IN
ANCIENT MYCENÆ AGAMEMNON'S
BONES RESTORED TO DAYLIGHT NOW
WHO COMES NEXT

TOURISM 159

With the rise of tourism, the popular study of Egyptology permeat-
ed the middle classes. MacKellar, Smiths & Jordan offer a package
for the budget-minded traveller in their Obelisk type, shown in *The
Inland Printer* for August 1891:

NORTHWEST EGYPTIAN AIRLINE RAILROAD
Luxurious equipments, Safety, Unique Scenery, Fast Time, Courteous Attendants
*
FIFTEEN MINUTES AT PYRAMID OF CHEOPS
Ancient Rivers, Sand-clad Plains, Ruined Temples and Mummy Tombs
*
MONUMENTS OF NINEVEH
Noontide Rambles amid Crumbling Buildings
*
ROMANTIC MEMORIES
Eating Dinner with Sphinx and Centaur
*
Mozambique MOUNTAINS

In 1893, the Cleveland Type Foundry of H.H. Thorp mention
'MUMMY Scholars', while Palmer & Rey of San Francisco (1887)
offer us in Obelisk:

NORTHWEST EGYPTIAN RAILROAD
Daylight Views of Ruined Temples and Tombs
Fifteen Hours at the Pyramids
*
HISTORICAL MEDITATION
Rambles Among Crumbling Ruins
Monuments of Nineveh

The Pacific Coast blue book sends us a little off-course in 1896:

PICTURESQUE AND ANIMATED DESCRIPTIONS OF EGYPT
Most Admirable Collection of Anecdotes
Illustrating Ancient and Modern Curios
From Sahara Desert 345 Miles Southward

The tramp of course is a veteran tourist:

Travels AMERICAN Walker
*
Wear OLD Shoes

LATIN ITALIC.

6-Pt.   NONPAREIL LATIN ITALIC.

THERE WAS AN OLD FELLOW, WHOSE NAME WAS DICK,

Used to Come into the Office and Pick up a Stick, and Swear any Comp. in the place he could Lick—At Setting
Type he could make 'em Sick, with his Clickety, Clickety, Bobbing and Bobbing,

8-Pt.   BREVIER LATIN ITALIC.

HE COULD SET UP A THOUSAND AN HOUR.

In Appearance this Chap was not Genteel.   He'd a large red Nose and was out at the Heel;
His Face seemed to say he could go a Square Meal.   From his general Style

10-Pt.   LONG PRIMER LATIN ITALIC.

YOU WOULD HARDLY FEEL, WITH HIS CLICKETY,

Clickety, Bobbing and Bobbing, He could Set up a Thousand an Hour.   This
Tramp would Sail in and Fill up his Case

12-Pt.   PICA LATIN ITALIC.

WITH SUCH WOND'ROUS SPEED, HE ALWAYS
Would Race, that You'd fancy the Matter Ejected from Space,
The Type dropped so Fast, each in its Place,

18-Pt.   GREAT PRIMER LATIN ITALIC.

WITH HIS CLICKETY, CLICKETY,
Bobbing and Bobbing, He Distributed a Thousand
An Hour; yes, he Did!

22-Pt.   DOUBLE SMALL PICA LATIN ITALIC.

MORAL: SO ALL YOUNG MEN
Both Great and Small, when Setting Type
Don't Bob at all.   Nor Click.

PALMER & REY, SAN FRANCISCO, CAL. AND PORTLAND, OR.

(142)

12

The Fellowship
of Bohemian Scribes

There is no great ingenuity without an admixture of dementedness.
– Seneca

NUMEROUS TEXTS in the specimen books flesh out the portrait of the Rabelaisian tramp printer. It is hardly surprising that two journeymen compositors from this world – Mark Twain and Walt Whitman – purged American literature of the genteel tradition. Twain, like Chaucer centuries before him, codified the vernacular, making possible a whole new approach to the transcription of speech.[1] Those who, for their daily bread, typeset the contents of an average paper with its fire-breathing editorials, hard and soft news, oily eulogiums & phony advertising claims, see through the veneer of a society. Such a close reading makes one a polished parodist of its style. No doubt it was his apprenticeship at the typestand, as well as the frequent calls for his epistolary talents, that led Samuel Richardson to write the first English novel, *Pamela*, in 1740.[2]

How our itinerant 'Bohemians' came to be so named is recounted by Matthew Mattox, N.P.R. (the pseudonym of Will Visscher) in his collection of sketches and rhymes, *'Vissch'* (1873:43):

> Gus. McKeat, as he is called in Ireland, and Auguste Maquet, as they spell it in France, a Franco-Irish novelist, is the man who is responsible for christening a certain class of newspaper writers 'Bohemians.' Not a very certain class, either, since I come to think, but rather, as Artemus Ward used to say, 'on the contrary, quite the reverse.' Perhaps this Gallic-Celt called these writers 'Bohemians' because they are a sort of literary gypsies, strolling from one subject to another; or, perchance, on account of their disposition to compass the universe in their peregrinations; or, he may have had no reason at all, which is often the case with novelists and poets.

1. 'It is a pity that Chawcer, who had geneyus, was so unedicated. He's the wuss speller I know of.'–*Artemus Ward in London*, 1867. Twain, like Bret Harte, was indebted to 'Artemus Ward' (Charles Farrar Brown) for indicating the humour in folksy speech & rustic ways. W.D. Howells believed that Twain fashioned his literary persona after Ward's. See *Artemus Ward's best stories* (New York, 1912), intro.

Henry Shaw ('Josh Billings') is another nineteeth-century American humorist who wrote in a bumpkin dialect that slows down the reader. The tradition was carried on by Ezra Pound. The first to transcribe black American speech in fiction was another printer, 'M. Quad' (Charles Bertrand Lewis).

2. 'It has repeatedly been remarked that the unctuous pietism of Richardson's novels succeeds in covering only in appearance their sensual, turbid background. Certainly, the art of Richardson, founded, as it was, upon accurately observed manners, could not well avoid certain contradictions in its effort to conciliate morality with the unbridled sensuality of the period.' Mario Praz, *The Romantic agony*, (Oxford, 1933), pp. 96–7.

After this promising introduction, Mattox goes on to delineate the Bohemian newspaperman's qualifications:

> Sometimes on western dailies he occupies at the same time the position of city editor, local reporter, commercial reporter, river reporter, musical and dramatic critic, telegraph and news editor and proof-reader; perhaps attends a little to the general business of the establishment, carries a route in an emergency, and often when the chief is away for a few months, distributing visiting cards in New York, he will condescend to perform the duties of that leisurely mortal.
>
> ... He may dine with a clergyman, and interview a murderer before the next refection. He may report the proceedings of a legislative body and give in the same issue of his paper an account of the tearing down by a mob of the building in which that body met. He must be able to write obituary poetry, and do it often in ten minutes, while he is overwhelmed with work and perhaps trying to think of something amusing to say about a police-court trial. ... He must combine the loquacity of a prestidigitateur with the impudence of a life insurance agent. He must be a stranger to modesty and willing to ask a widow over the mangled remains of her husband, how the thing happened. Above all things he should be able to out-puff a forty-horse-power engine. He should be enthusiastic on groceries, learned in dry goods and profound in hardware. The stars and the stock of the theatre should be his pets and the *repertoire* of every actress with all her fine points on the stage should be his chiefest study.

All the news that fits

THE TRAMP'S ASSIMILATION of all aspects of a newspaper's content and style, along with his characteristic irreverent touch, can be seen in such samples as these from Marder, Luse (1876–93):

LATE NEWS FROM THE SANDWICH ISLANDS.
Labor Market Quiet; Breadstuffs Heavy; Missionaries Steady.
Highly Important Information, if True! 89

❋

BARBECUES AT THE SOUTH SEA ISLANDS
Roast Missionary on Toast

or this daft offering from Cincinnati (1888):

TWENTY EIGHT
White Elephants Stolen

and this up-to-date bulletin from Palmer & Rey (1892):

Long Continued Crisis in the Balkans

GIGANTIC FAILURE OF COLONIZATION IN CENTRAL AFGHINASTAN
Somewhat Dubious & Unreliable Diplomatic Information

A.T.F.'s *Pacific Coast blue book* remarks the

UNAVOIDABLE BUT LAUGHABLE SITUATION
GENERAL GORDON'S VALIANT DEFENCE OF KHARTOUM
THE MAHDI'S OVERWIIELMING HORDES $345
*
THE ABSYNIAN STRUGGLE
Menelick's Big Shoans too much for the Italians

They revise Tennyson's imperialist couplet:

OF THE PAST, LILIUOKALANI
Better Half a Year of Europe than a Cycle of Cathay
Or even a Bi-Cycle in San José

A Hard sell

While poking fun at the ditties employed by advertisers, the
founders compose doggerel to promote their own printing services.
J. Wesley Barber, author of *The Printers' text book* (Boston, 1875),
tells us plainly

HE WHO BY HIS BIZ WOULD RISE,
Must either burst or advertise! 917
*
SING OF HIS START, HIS GREAT AMBITIONS SCOPE
THE CAPITAL THAT GAVE HIM
CAUSE FOR HOPE; THEN TELL
THE DOOM TO WHICH A
MAN WAS FATED WHO
NEVER ADV'D
*
THE MAN WHO LOSES ALL OF FORTUNE'S PRIZES
IN FACT THE MAN WHO NEVER ADVERTISES

A STACK OF GOODS WITHIN HIS STORE
WHICH CAN'T BE LESS OR NEVER MORE

SING BUSINESS MEWS THE DISMAL FATE
OF HIM WHO LABORS BUT TO WAIT

MOST BOUNTIFUL CUSTOM WILL BANISH
BEWAILING FAILURES IN TYPOGRAPHY

Benton-Waldo offer this ditty on the value of advertising:

LITTLE DROPS OF PRINTER'S INK A LITTLE TYPE DISPLAYED
Makes our Merchant Princes with all their big parade
Little Bits of Stinginess Discarding Printer's Ink
Busts the man of business and sees his credit sink.

Nelson Hawks, composing a page of Grant No. 2 for the Pacific States Type Foundry, circa 1893, came up with this:

EXCELLENT SERMON FOR ALL NON-ADVERTISING SINNERS.
Word or Two Upon this Page: You'd Scarce Expect One of My Age in Merchandising to Engage
AND HOPE TO GET A PAYING TRADE
Without the Local Paper's Aid. And Yet I Did That Very Thing: I Opened Up a Store
LAST SPRING. THIS MONTH THE
Sheriff Took My Stock and Sold it from an Auction Block. Don't View Me
WITH A SCORNFUL EYE BUT SIMPLY
Say As I Pass By There Goes a Fool Who Seems to Think He
HAS No Use for Printer's Ink. There is a Truth
As Broad as EARTH and Business
MEN Should Know Its Worth
It's Simply This The Public
BUYS Its Goods From
Them Who Advertise

Hawks was a controversial figure on the late nineteenth-century typographical landscape. He was criticised in *The Inland Printer* for selling complete printing outfits to amateurs who then undercut Union shops in competing for small jobs. But he was instrumental in persuading Marder, Luse to adopt the standard point system for type bodies. One of his ventures was the Pacific States Type Foundry and he composed eight pages for a specimen book that they issued around 1893. George Harding (who put together the Kemble Collection on Printing at the California Historical Society) annotated his copy and had Hawks initial the pages he had created. Two of his amusing efforts relate to the physical qualities of type:

THE SOLID AND HEAVY
Antique Types of Beauty, the Gothics and Dorics and Titles immense, fail to please the best Tastes in the full line of Duty, or endure for all Time, like the Roman Condensed. How dear to my Heart is the One I have captured; by our camp-fire she blushes and shrinks from your View; But I know that in spite of my being enraptured, She'll give it to Me when I've read this to You.

✳

THE WILLOWY GIRL

You may talk of your Darlings of Dumpling Proportions and call them the best in the Feminine World, but I'll challenge you all to withstand my assertion that the sweetest of all is the Willowy Girl. The Poets and Painters of past Generations have pictured in colors and Language most rare, and Minstrels have sung, ever since the Creation of Beauty full-statured beyond all compare.

Nickel=faced Leaders to...match...5=lb. founts, 46c per lb.

THE QUEENS OF THE EARTH

are the Exquisite Creatures whose Forms Tower Upward in Grandeur and Grace, while Nature is kind in Respect to their Features in adding the Charm of a Beautiful Face. From Ocean to Ocean she claims our Devotion, entrancing our Hearts in the Dance's mad whirl, Portraying the Essence and 7565

POETRY OF MOTION

this Venus Ideal, the Willowy Girl. No Boldface Extended was ever intended to capture the
Heart of a Sensible Man, for though doubtless
with Virtues and Usefulness blended, they stir
not the Heart as the Tall beauties can.

Hawks's heartfelt poem perfectly suits the typeface, called Venetian, that it is set in. The types themselves are often characterized or recommended by the compositors:

This Pretty Letter Kerns not and therefore Breaks not.
Very Useful and Beautiful Type Cast on Standard Pica Body no
Kerned Letters to Bother the Operator and Break and Ruin
the Fount. All complete.

✳

O, a Glorious Fame is the Fame of the Fray
For the Banner of Stars and of Stripes; But the
Mightiest Soldiers

ARE METAL TYPES

✳

TYPOGRAPHICAL MONSTROSITIES

✳

ELEGANT POSTER TYPES FOR LILIPUTIAN PRINTING ESTABLISHMENTS MAGNIFIED
TWO HUNDRED AND NINETY THOUSAND POWERS AND PERFECTLY LEGIBLE
INDISPENSABLE TO THE ART TYPOGRAPHICAL

✳

A JUMBO CASE

Where Sleepers Dwell!
For Poster Printers

✻
CHIROGRAPHY
Unconsciously Written 649
✻
INVISIBLE
13 BRIGHT IDEAS

The designer is invoked by ATF for their clownish face Grimaldi:

GROTESQUE CREATURE
Design Useful Faces

The Portable book of specimens of the Benton-Waldo Type Foundry (Milwaukee, 1893), introduces that foundry's 'self-spacing' type. This theme runs throughout the book in testimonial letters, head-lines, and a paragraph that starts:

> Perhaps in no art has there been so little progress in four centuries as in the art of typesetting. The machines, some of which are in use, are still inef-ficient, and the greater part of the enormous and increasing quantity of type used is set as type was set four hundred years ago. If Franklin could come from among the shades, and take his place before the case, he would have nothing to learn. There has been no development of the art to corre-spond with the evolution of the marvelous perfecting presses of to-day from the slow and laborious hand presses of half a century ago, or with the growth of the art of stereotyping, folding, pasting, and mailing. Increased speed in the setting of the same quantity of matter has been secured only by the multiplication of cases.

This was written on the eve of Ottmar Mergenthaler's breakthrough which was to make our tramping typesticker obsolete. Linn Boyd Benton himself hastened the comp's demise by selling his panto-graph for cutting matrices to Linotype.

In many respects, the old adage, *plus ça change, plus ç'est la même chose*, is true of the vast improvements in printing and type-setting technology. Speaking in San Francisco, George L. Harding talked about the effect of technical innovations on the state of type design:[3]

3. Talk delivered to the Rox-burghe Club of San Francisco on February 6, 1933; pub-lished as *D.B. Updike and the Merrymount Press* (San Fran-cisco, 1943), pp. 4–5.

> With greatly improved mechanical equipment at their command, type-founders set for themselves the task of producing everything their ma-chines could be made to produce without thought as to whether their products in themselves were worth producing. Their types approached mechanical perfection but with each passing year sank lower in esthetic

value. Their specimen books grew in size and pretensions with their pages filled with all the wild and weird imaginings in type-design which human ingenuity could conceive. ... Like a fortune in spend-thrift hands, the printers' glorious heritage from the past was dissipated and forgotten.

In April 1884, the *Inland Printer* editorialized about the haphazard use of the new combination ornaments to fill space 'in a reckless manner': 'Designs, unmeaning and offensive to good taste, are scattered promiscuously from a poster to a business card, and as the evil is increasing from day to day, we think the present an opportune time to call attention to the fact.' From among the samples, they single out a circular, headed 'The Fellowship of Jesus. An Hour for Simultaneous Prayer throughout the World,' and point out the inappropriateness of four pagan symbols used as corner vignettes on this flyer. After speculating on various possible reasons for the juxtaposition, they conclude that a 'little learning is a dangerous thing.' It was clearly in reference to this circular that Cincinnati set up their own artistic contribution in their specimen book for 1880 (*Frontispiece*), recasting the event in a surreal dimension, and bringing our glorious brotherhood together for an exercise in collective consciousness raising. While the types are particularly weak, the carpet effect of the border is handsome. The wily comp who conceived of 'An Hour for Simultaneous Writing Throughout the World,' was certainly a card-carrying member of 'The Fellowship of Bohemian Scribes,' and even signed the page, 'A.J.R.', and gave us his New York address.

Politics & buncombe

AS DESCRIBED in *The Inland Printer* (April 1889; 1977:273), our Existential transient is 'Certain to be pretty well up in his information touching on the leading questions of the day, & is ever ready to engage in a controversy, it making no material difference whether the subject is one of theology or politics, or on matters dramatic, musical or pugilistic'. And it was the specimens that gave him the forum to voice that controversial opinion, an opportunity he took with relish.

Judging by the specimens such as these from Palmer & Rey (1887–92), echoing similar sentiments found in Thomas MacKellar's *Typographic Advertiser* #87/88 (Winter/Spring 1877), our tramp

4. Paul Fisher, *An Uncommon gentry* (Columbia, Mo., 1952), intro, p. xvii.

was a typographical subversive, to say the least. 'Had he been more democratic he would have been an anarchist':[4]

Messrs. Make, Muchof, It & Co.— Sirs: I have shipped to you this day per agreement, a large consignment of defeated, discouraged politicians. Please do the best you can with them, and your name implies much, and fit them up for our next attempt for victory, and oblige.   Central Committee.

*

LEGISLATIVE MEASURES FOR
LENGTHENING THE TERM OF DEMOCRATIC
PRESIDENCY TO 2345678 CENTURIES

*

PATENT AUTOMATIC ELECTORAL COUNTERS
HONEST OFFICIALS CONSTRUCTED ACCORDING TO CIRCUMSTANCES
UNIVERSAL SUFFRAGE SUPERSEDED

*

WONDERFUL REPEATING APPARATUS
TEN THOUSAND MAJORITIES MANUFACTURED TO ORDER
OMNIPOTENCE OF MONEY-BAGS

*

MIDNIGHT TO MORNING
LARGE MINORITIES MADE SMALL MAJORITIES
GLORIOUS BALLOT

*

Dictionary of Orthographical Ambiguities.
Compiled for the Benefit of Phrenologists, Spiritual
Mediums, Clairvoyants, Visionaries, Political Candidates
and Loquacious Gossipers. Useful for Shallow-Pated
Pedantic Pedagogues

*

CORRUPTING Associations
Politicians REGENERATED
QUEER POLITICAL ORATIONS

*

EDITORIAL
Leading Articles
Hog Wash

The *Pacific Coast blue book* gives us an

Announcement of Gentlemen desirous of running the government
Peculiar election trickeries not despised 248

From MacKellar (1882; 1886) we learn of:

TRICKY CANDIDATES
Office Races, Smiling Faces and Kind Embraces
✳
Boodletumville Whitewashing Association
Bribed Politicians Vindicated   Assisted Canadian Tourists
Tarnished Reputations Polished Successfully

In *The Inland Printer* for April 1884, Barnhart Bros & Spindler
announce:

UPRIGHT AND HONEST AMERICAN CONGRESSMEN
Biggest And Most Stupendous Humbugs Under the Popular Political System of the United States
25134 MILWAUKEE AND PHILADELPHIA 67890
Political Bums of Every Nation From Constituencies Representing Nobody but Themselves

This useful flyer, from Marder, Luse (1876), comes set in Circular
Italic:

> *We are this day in receipt of a large invoice of American Slang Phrases, Pet
> Names, and a choice selection of pure 'Billingsgate,' imported expressly for
> this occasion, which we now offer to City and Country Stump Speakers for
> use in the present deadly struggle – to character – for political preferment.
> Extraordinary care has been taken in making selections for our trade so
> that an unusually large number of 'appropriate expressions' for use in
> either party, or any nationality, sex, age, color, or religious opinion, are
> embraced in our Political Book of Buncombe.*

They also comment on

CHICAGO THE LONG SOUGHT FOR PROMISED LAND
Home of the Confidence Operator, Bunko Steerer and Faro Dealer.
Full Protection by Officials Guaranteed. 234

And from Benton-Waldo (1893), we learn:

AMERICA THE HOME OF
THE FREE AND BRAVE CHICAGO THE ABIDING
PLACE OF THE CARPET BAGGERS

Dudes & mugwumps

THE COMPS were also quick to pick up new jargon. They adopted (and cited in the specimens) such trendy monikers as 'Dude' and 'Mugwump'.

HONOR
THE DUDE
KING

commanded the Palmer & Rey specimen of 1887.

THE DUDE
DARE 5

they tell us. According to *The Oxford English dictionary*, 'Dude' was a term coined in 1883, meaning exaggerated fastidiousness in dress, speech and deportment, even to the extent of affecting Englishness. Doubtless the fastidious tramp had mixed feelings about this fellow. Benton-Waldo (1893) tells us that the Dude is someone to reckon with, particularly when Priapus raises his head:

MAIDENS BEWARE FOR THE
Impecunious Dude Stalketh Abroad in
Tight Fitting Raiment

James Conner's (grand) Sons who operated the United States Type Foundry in New York City offer (1888):

Slender Smooth-faced Lunatics
Harmless Imbeciles 23 Raging Maniacs
3 CRUSHED DUDEISM 4
✱
Numerous Unfounded Remarks as to Professor Pedagogue A. Periwinkle's
Horrible Midnight Hallucinations
✱
5 Deacon Snowball's Lecture 7
OLD RUMBAGOISM
✱
Tactics of 6 Charmless Dude Reporters

Marder, Luse (*The Inland Printer*, March 1886), in their patented Imperial type, disdainfully speak of

CRUDE IDEAS OF DUDEISM
Transient Flickerings of Intellect 678

'Mugwump', another recent neologism, was originally a jocular term for boss or great man (occuring in Eliot's *Massachusetts Bible*), but by the 1880s was applied to undefined or non-partyline politicians. The *Oxford English dictionary* cites the *New York Evening Post*, 20 June 1884: 'We have yet to see a Blaine organ which speaks of the Independent Republicans otherwise than as Pharisees, hypocrites, dudes, mugwumps, transcendentalists, or something of that sort'.

Eugene Field celebrated the Mugwump in a verse written in 1885 in the style of Edward Lear:

> A year ago and his plumes were red
> As the deepest of cardinal hues,
> But in the year they've changed, 'tis said,
> To the bluest of bilious blues!

In the words of Benton-Waldo:

> MUGWUMPS ARE PLENTY
> Their Wants are Many and All they Require
> now is the Earth $12

Barnhart Brothers & Spindler of Chicago note, in their Cadence specimen printed in the January 1888 issue of *The Inland Printer*:

> MUGWUMPERY IN THE ASCENDENCY THIS YEAR

The same foundry's 1883 book includes some remarkable poetry in Great Primer Gothic Extra Condensed:

> Chromoplastitudes & Chloroplastidesems
> Boltesmanaz and Crossmannerism
> 234 Exaggerated Ginflingers Flopperdoesing 789

and, in Double Small Pica Lightface Gothic:

> HIFALUTIN CODFISH NABOBS

The sesquipedalian typesetters' relish of such ten-dollar words as 'MENORRHAGIA' and 'Necromancer' (Palmer & Rey, 1892), reflects their love of language (if not their care with spelling). James Conner's grandsons mention 'Oscitant Delights | After Dinner' and 'Expert Milk-Maidens. CIBARIOUS LACTESCENT COM-

POUNDS' in 1888. And if they couldn't find a savoury enough phrase, like 'RAGINGS OF THE EPIZOOTIC' (Marder, Luse, 1874), the logomaniacal comps would coin one, like *Pacific Coast's* 84-point 'Bazoo', or Cleveland's 1880 nod to Lear (whose *Fourth book of nonsense, poems, songs, botany, music, &c* – including 'The Pobble' – had appeared in 1877):

THE SCOOTINABULATION OF HIS SCOOT
And ever thus merrily sang the Pobble with a broken nose

The typographical errors ('Peacher' for 'Preacher', 'Afghinastan', 'Absynian', 'Confuscius') show that the founders were more concerned with the appearance of the type than with what it said. The ATF branch in San Francisco mislabelled one of its types as 'LAW ITLAIC'. (This style, which originated with Marder, Luse circa 1870, was based on the penmanship seen in legal briefs.) Palmer & Rey pronounce the unspeakable in Crayon:

Academy of Tyqograqhic Art

'Sci-fi' & 'lit-crit'

THE FOUNDERS' reading habits were still displayed in their books. A certain Roman insurrectionist is half-remembered in a wretched stub-pen script as

Catline & Co.

And the 'LAYS OF ANCIENT ROME' of Macaulay have become

ANCIENT TYPOGRAPHICAL ABSURDITIES.

On the other hand, Palmer & Rey (1892) elevate Jules Verne in presenting their Great Primer Skinner Script:

Pride of Byron and Satire of Swift
Brilliance of Tennyson and Poverty of Chatterton
Vituperation of Junius
Wild Imagination of De Quincey and Verne
Subscribed Capital, – – $234,567

Mentions of the telephone and other newfangled gadgets appear alongside alien sightings worthy of today's *Weekly World News*:

MOON RESIDENTS
Startling Discovery of Wondrous Creatures
Search's Theory
Plain Optical Demonstration

MacKellar (1882), clearly a fan of Dickens, finds the new age 'Pecksniffian.' He heralds the possibility of

THROUGH EXCURSIONS TO THE MOON
12345 Supper Given en Route and Books Explaining Lunar Wonders

In 1884, the far-seeing Benton-Waldo announce:

BE IT KNOWN, That on and after the 29th day of March,
1985, passengers desiring transportation on the Rapid Transit
Air Line, between the planets Jupiter and Mars, must procure
their tickets three seconds before the advertised time of flying.

Phileas Fogg, Esquire, joins Little Dorritt in the specimen books, raising Verne to the pantheon of Dickens, Byron and Burns. Farmer, Little (New York, 1880) mention Dickens & Babbage beside Catiline. Dickens was celebrated in an expensive set from the Central Type Foundry of Saint Louis

(1886) in Latin Antique:

DICKENS AMUSING NARRATIVES $20

Perhaps Peacock inspired the typesetters invention of characters such as Boston's (1861)

PROF. HO. BUMPUS FEALD, PHRENOLOGIST
Develops Talent in the Muddy Headed $1.

Ruskin is mentioned as the 'Prime Minister of Taste'; Leigh Hunt appears fleetingly, and we find this approbation of Coleridge in Benton-Waldo:

Coleridge's Religious, Poetical and Dramatic Effusions!
A Complete Literary Work on the Questionable Doctrine of Theopneusty

Edgar Poe flits through the Marder, Luse comp's mind:

FIFTEENTH
Century when Manutius
READ Nevermore
JOYOUS Thought

He also lauds

BARON MUNCHAUSEN
MOST TRUTHFUL OF ALL
HISTORIANS.

In 1882, MacKellar mentions (*Figure 33*):

BRONTE & CO.
Makers of Fictitous [*sic*] Men

Sir Walter Scott & his 'Breathes there the man, with soul so dead ...' weathered the century well, but Marder, Luse (1876) couldn't resist adding a punchline:

Breathes there a Man with Soul so Dead who never to
Himself hath said
I ought to Punch that Muttonhead?

The Great Western Type Foundry (1888) revises him thus:

BREATHES THERE A MAN WITH SOUL SO DEAD

❖OTHELLO.❖

---

12 A. 18 a.   GREAT PRIMER OTHELLO. *(St.)* $3.25

GRIEVOUS MURDER OF DESDEMONA RECORDED

Doubting Othello Deceived by Iago 30

8 A. 12 a.   DOUBLE PICA OTHELLO. $4.00

REVENGEFUL MOORISH HUSBAND

Violent Emotions Aroused

6 A. 8 a.   DOUBLE GREAT PRIMER OTHELLO. $5.00

MOURNING SHROUDS SOLD

Melancholy Raiment 12

6 A. 8 a.   CANON OTHELLO. $7.50

SHADOWS OF EREBUS

Gloomiest Abode

4 A. 5 a.   SIX-LINE PICA OTHELLO. $10.00

MODERN ROSES

Floriculture 8

Who to His Friend Has Never Said
I Would Like to Borrow Five Dollars
CURRENT FUNDS OR LEGAL TENDER ACCEPTED

The books have a share of Victorian homespun wisdom and sanctimonious homilies, but these are interlineated with the riper stuff. Shakespeare is quoted frequently: 'By the pricking of my thumbs, something wicked this way comes'; 'Put money in thy purse'; 'We are such stuff as dreams are made on', in Palmer & Rey (1892); and 'Now is the Winter of our discontent...' in Benton-Waldo. In 1874, Marder, Luse found:

Those two Gentlemen of Verona.
Drunk & Disorderly

At other times the original receives a rich interpretation, as in the Cincinnati specimen book of 1888, which shows their dark new type Othello (copied from a face originated by the Central Type Foundry of St Louis four years earlier) in a mixture of headlines and ad copy (*Figure 38*).

Blades's tantalizing study, *Shakspere and typography*, appeared in 1872. An article in the *Printers' Circular* (Philadelphia, Oct 1874, edited by R.S. Menamin) also asked 'Was Shakspeare a printer?'

The Bard's influence is seen in some stanzas of original work, as well. A glossolalist at Palmer & Rey writes (*Figure 39*):

TIS NOT IN MORTAL	FOUGHT ALL
Command success but They	Battles over again and
now deserve it 43	Thrice did 43

KIND HEART	NOTHING
More than simple	Extenuate nor
Faith are 26	Black 25

THOUGH THIS
Play to them 'tis Death to
Mormons 345

STAND NOT
Upon the order of 9

CRANKS
Nods, Becks 8

ANTIQUE EXTENDED No. 4.

6-Pt. NONPAREIL.

TIS NOT IN MORTAL
Command success but They
now deserve it 43

BREVIER. 8-Pt.

FOUGHT ALL
Battles over again and
Thrice did 43

10-Pt. LONG PRIMER.

KIND HEART
More than simple
Faith are 26

PICA. 12-Pt.

NOTHING
Extenuate nor
Black 25

16-Pt. COLUMBIAN.

THOUGH THIS
Play to them 'tis Death to
Mormons 345

22-Pt. DOUBLE SMALL PICA.

STAND NOT
Upon the order of 9

30-Pt. FIVE-LINE NONPAREIL.

CRANKS
Nods, Becks 8

40-Pt. DOUBLE PARAGON.

COME
Peacher 2

PALMER & REY, SAN FRANCISCO, CAL. AND PORTLAND, OR.

(97)

22 A 46 a   8-Point (Brevier) Apollo. $3.00

ALL DEMANDS FOR READERS FILLED

The Universal Publishers' Trust Company is hereby pleased to announce to all literary aspirants throughout the world, that it has perfected arrangements with an unlimited number of indiscriminative and uncritical "book-devourers," whereby it is enabled to unload upon them any quantity of romantic, trashy and character-slicing novels, scientific essays, notes of travel, war articles, art criticisms, personal letters and memoirs, anything, no matter how devoid of talent. This trust does not agree, however, to bring about any increase in the amount

14 A 32 a   10-Point (Long Primer) Apollo. $3.25

SOME INDESCRIBABLE LONGINGS

Though you may try ever so hard to fill this "long felt want," we despair of success crowning your efforts, since these yearners themselves find it quite impossible to furnish you with the slightest hint as to what they required in this line of literature, no two critics being able to agree in their ideas as to what would constitute a really first-class, genuine, name-blown-in-the-bottle, thoroughbred U. S. novel. $3

14 A 30 a   12-Point (Pica) Apollo. $3.50

MOURNING IN CLASSICAL CIRCLES

Writers of fiction whom this circular reaches will please take particular notice of the fact that many literary critics are shedding the bitterest tears, in the most copious quantities, because no distinctly "American" Novel has been produced as yet. That there exists the lack of such work

10 A 20 a   18-Point (Great Primer) Apollo. $4.00

SPRING POETS MEET

Notice is hereby given that the forty-eleventh yearly reunion of the Society for the Laudation of Vernal Beauty will begin on the 2d day of

COME
Peacher 2

– the cri de coeur, perhaps, of one fed too long on 'Shadow Stew'.
The same Palmer & Rey book offers the Shakespearian

Stranger Than Fiction BUT MUST BET 59
24 DEAD FOR ONE Ducat the nobler
Deep book but SHALL READ

while Cincinnati in 1878 suggest

A BANQUO'S GHOST
Was Sat Down on

Benton-Waldo (Milwaukee, 1893) composed a circular to nascent
authors in 8-point (Brevier) Apollo type (*Figure 40*):

ALL DEMANDS FOR READERS FILLED
The Universal Publishers' Trust Company is hereby pleased to announce to
all literary aspirants throughout the world, that it has perfected arrangements with an unlimited number of indiscriminative and uncritical "book-
devourers," whereby it is enabled to unload upon them any quantity of
romantic, trashy and character-slicing novels, scientific essays, notes of
travel, war articles, art criticisms, personal letters & memoirs, anything, no
matter how devoid of talent.

They go on to mourn the fact that no distinctly 'American' novel
has, as yet, been produced, but derail into the 'forty-eleventh yearly
reunion of the Society for the Laudation of Vernal Beauty.'

AMERICAN LITERATURE
Proclaimed by the Foreign Critics
Worth 645 Centimes

lamented the *Pacific Coast blue book* of American Type Founders.
The Illinois Type Foundry rejoins, in a June 1884 ad in *The Inland Printer*,

QUARTERLY AMERICAN LITERARY REVIEWS
American Literature seems to be but little understood abroad; but at
Home its biting Sarcasm and Scintillating
Wit are read with great Pleasure and keen Enjoyment 1883

Indeed, the lofty *Edinburgh Review*, analysing Ashe's *Travels in*

America, had said, 'Though all she [America] has written were obliterated from the records of learning, there would (if we except the writings of Franklin) be no positive diminution, either of the useful or the agreeable.' Marder, Luse's 1874 book demonstrates that the comp, too, holds most contemporary writing in contempt:

GLEANINGS FROM MODERN LITERATURE
Selected Stock of Slop-Shop Goods, Second-Hand Rubbish.
Questionable Æsthetics. 6789
Youthful Quibblers and Aged Punsters.

Short stories that our typeslingers would be embarrassed to hear called prose poems record the urban myths of the late nineteenth century, & foreshadow the beautifully elliptical style of Max Jacob, the Cubist author of *Le cornet à dés*. Page 73 from the May 1893 book of the Cleveland type foundry, advertising their Poster Commercial types, admirably fills the bill (*Figure 41*). This was written by Bob Burdette, associate editor of the *Burlington Hawkeye*, noted humorous lecturer, and author of *First-class snake stories*, some of which were anthologized in Mark Twain's *Library of humour* (New York, 1888), along with Burdette's wry impression of the typewriter.

Above all, the typesetter saved his poetic eulogies for his first love: his craft. In the Illinois Type Foundry ad quoted just above, we find

SHOOTINGSTICK, TWEEZER & GAUGEPIN,
Practical Delineators of the Art Preservative of all other Branches of
Like Respectable Avocations,
No. 12,345 Stoneproof Alley, State of Wornoutprinterdom

He surveys the tools of his trade in *The Pacific Coast blue book*:

SCREW, BUCKEYE,
Grover, Yankee, Albion Job
Composing Sticks 5

GOLDING'S STANDARD,
Perfect News Nos. 1, 2, 3, Boston
Newspaper Sticks

The composer of Palmer & Rey's book couldn't resist the chance to parody Adelaide Ann Proctor's 'The Lost chord' from her *Legends & lyrics* (1858):

48A, 20A, 200a.　　　12 Point Poster Commercial.　　　$11.25

A REMARKABLE SNAKE STORY

How a Mexican Reptile Defied the Lightning

$1234567890

A family in San Luis Potosi possessed a very fine rattlesnake. They had captured it by means of a forked stick when it was a baby, and had succeeded in domesticating it. In the course of years it grew to be fourteen feet long, and was tame and very playful. It became very much attached to its master and would follow him about the house like a dog. During the recent storm in San Luis many houses were struck by lightning. Nobly determined to die for its benefactor it

20A, 10A, 125a.　　　18 Point Poster Commercial.　　　$11.75

CRAWLED ON THE TOP

Of the Chimney and Stood on End.

$1234567890

The electricity attracted by this living lightning rod reduced to ashes the noble reptile and also the house. There is no use in letting the newspapers have a monopoly on these snake stories. I'm something of a liar myself.

TYPOGRAPHICAL DAMOCLES
Seated one day on a composing stool, I felt angry and hard to please
For the d's of my jobbing long primer were mixed with the
lower case p's; my eyes wandered far from the copy,

FROM WINDOW TO CEILING
They sped, till they rested at last on some plaster
that hung from the roof overhead

The compositor has also nicely disguised the rhyme at first glance by interrupting the flow with subheads, breaking the 'law of the line' a century before poet Charles Olson defined 'Projective verse'.[5]

An entire page of Latin Italic is given over to a poem celebrating the comp in 1884 (*Figure 37*):

THERE WAS AN OLD FELLOW WHOSE NAME WAS DICK,
Used to Come into the Office and Pick up a Stick, and Swear any Comp. in the Place he could Lick —
At Setting Type he could make 'em Sick, with his Clickety, Clickety, Bobbing and Bobbing,

HE COULD SET UP A THOUSAND AN HOUR.
In Appearance this Chap was not Genteel. He'd a large red Nose and was out at the Heel;
His Face seemed to say he could go a Square Meal. From his general Style

YOU WOULD HARDLY FEEL, WITH HIS CLICKETY,
Clickety, Bobbing and Bobbing, He could Set up a Thousand an Hour. This
Tramp would Sail in and Fill up his Case

WITH SUCH WOND'ROUS SPEED, HE ALWAYS
Would Race, that You'd fancy the Matter Ejected from Space,
The Type dropped so Fast, each in its Place,

WITH HIS CLICKETY, CLICKETY,
Bobbing and Bobbing. He Distributed a Thousand
An Hour; yes, he Did!

MORAL: SO ALL YOUNG MEN
Both Great and Small, when Setting Type
Don't Bob at all. Nor Click.

In a typeface called Outing we discover this sombre verse:

DEATH LOCKS MY FORM IN HIS IRON EMBRACE;
COLD ARE MY HANDS AND EMPTY MY CASE
BUT THE VISION NOW COMES OF A SIT[6] IN THE SKY,
SO I'LL LAY UP SOME TYPE AND DISTRIBUTE ON HIGH

5. 'Which brings us up, immediately, bang, against tenses, in fact against syntax, in fact against grammar generally, that is, as we have inherited it. Do not tenses, must they not also be kicked around anew, in order that time, that other governing absolute may be kept, as must the space-tensions of a poem, immediate, contemporary to the acting-on-you of the poem? I would argue that here, too, the LAW OF THE LINE, which projective verse creates, must be hewn to, obeyed, and that the conventions which logic has forced on syntax must be broken open as quietly as must the too set feet of the old line.' Charles Olson, 'Projective Verse', in *Human universe and other essays*, (New York, 1967), p. 56.

6. 'Sit' is the tramp printer abbreviation for a more or less permanent situation.

Over at Cleveland (1893) we find the deep-rooted source of his grief:

MEMORY CLINGS TO THE PAST
And the Hopes of Youth Fall in the Blast

When our doggerel poet at the typestand tramples on sentimentality, we sense his hidden bitterness:

OUR LITTLE POLLY'S DEAD AND THE FEATHERS
ON HER HEAD WILL NEVER FLUTTER UP
ABOVE THE DOOR FOR THE BLACK HEN
BELTED HER WITH HER LITTLE CROOKED SUP,
& POLL WANTS A CRACKER NO MORE

In the nineteenth-century typefounders' books there is no shadow that falls between the inspiration and the act, or the intent and the reality, of type and composition. The poem is grounded in the instant of composition, leaving no room for a complaint such as that voiced by Charles Olson in *Projective verse*:

> What we have suffered from is manuscript, press, the removal of verse from its producer and reproducer, the voice, a removal by one, by two removes from its place of origin and its destination.

Very often the text in the specimen books exists only in the act of setting the type, making a fluid connection between the thought and the appearance of the words. Armed with the full array of lead types of the last century, the founders' specimens spoke with the eloquent tongue of poet and proselytizer. A century after Dibdin's complaint of the 'heterogenous compound of fat and lean faces all crying out *Quousque...*', each type had found its own voice.

Names appear in the specimen texts that we can no longer identify, though we can almost envision Muldoon and Miginnis in their battered hats and thousand-mile shirts, but it is fitting that these manifestations of industrial art should be unsigned.

So *ave atque vale* from our anonymous compositor, as the old spirit returns and we discover that bitter cynicism masks a romantic heart. The last word comes from Benton-Gove of Milwaukee (1873), set in Antique Condensed and Gothic:

OH DON'T YOU REMEMBER THE SPOT BEN BUT
Where You and I Used to Steal a Little While Away with the Spoons

BUT THE BULL-DOZER IS THERE NOW BEN BUT
And You and I More's the Pity Must Start Two Saloons

THE POET OF THE FUTURE
Hiding His Light Under the Bushel of a Specimen-Book

Appendices

The Lineage of the British typefounders

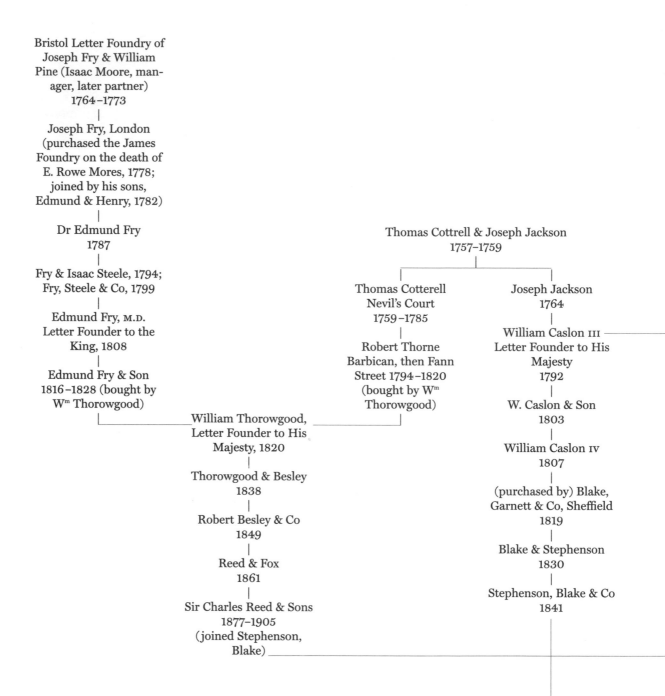

Bristol Letter Foundry of
Joseph Fry & William
Pine (Isaac Moore, man-
ager, later partner)
1764–1773
|
Joseph Fry, London
(purchased the James
Foundry on the death of
E. Rowe Mores, 1778;
joined by his sons,
Edmund & Henry, 1782)
|
Dr Edmund Fry
1787
|
Fry & Isaac Steele, 1794;
Fry, Steele & Co, 1799
|
Edmund Fry, M.D.
Letter Founder to the
King, 1808
|
Edmund Fry & Son
1816–1828 (bought by
Wᵐ Thorowgood)

Thomas Cottrell & Joseph Jackson
1757–1759

Thomas Cotterell
Nevil's Court
1759–1785
|
Robert Thorne
Barbican, then Fann
Street 1794–1820
(bought by Wᵐ
Thorowgood)

Joseph Jackson
1764
|
William Caslon III
Letter Founder to His
Majesty
1792
|
W. Caslon & Son
1803
|
William Caslon IV
1807
|
(purchased by) Blake,
Garnett & Co, Sheffield
1819
|
Blake & Stephenson
1830
|
Stephenson, Blake & Co
1841

William Thorowgood,
Letter Founder to His
Majesty, 1820
|
Thorowgood & Besley
1838
|
Robert Besley & Co
1849
|
Reed & Fox
1861
|
Sir Charles Reed & Sons
1877–1905
(joined Stephenson,
Blake)

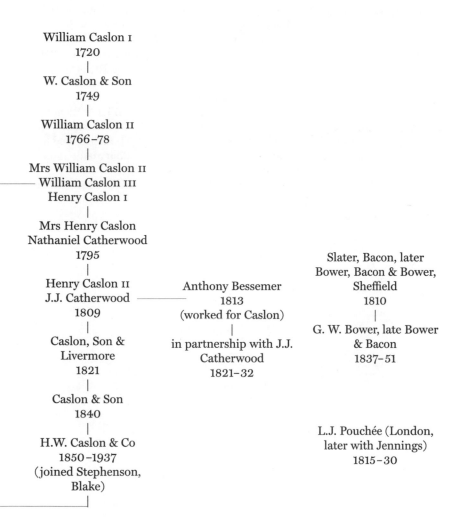

William Caslon I
1720
|
W. Caslon & Son
1749
|
William Caslon II
1766–78
|
Mrs William Caslon II
William Caslon III
Henry Caslon I
|
Mrs Henry Caslon
Nathaniel Catherwood
1795
|
Henry Caslon II
J.J. Catherwood
1809
|
Caslon, Son &
Livermore
1821
|
Caslon & Son
1840
|
H.W. Caslon & Co
1850–1937
(joined Stephenson,
Blake)

Anthony Bessemer
1813
(worked for Caslon)
|
in partnership with J.J.
Catherwood
1821–32

Slater, Bacon, later
Bower, Bacon & Bower,
Sheffield
1810
|
G. W. Bower, late Bower
& Bacon
1837–51

L.J. Pouchée (London,
later with Jennings)
1815–30

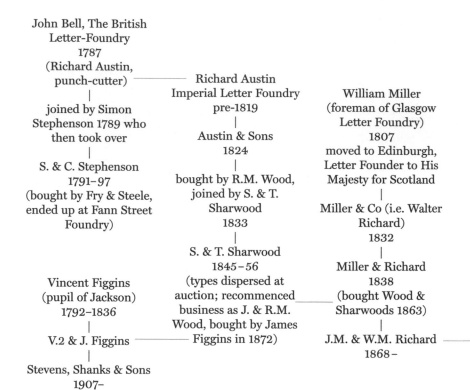

John Bell, The British
Letter-Foundry
1787
(Richard Austin,
punch-cutter) ——————— Richard Austin
| Imperial Letter Foundry
joined by Simon   pre-1819
Stephenson 1789 who |
then took over   Austin & Sons
| 1824
S. & C. Stephenson |
1791–97   bought by R.M. Wood,
(bought by Fry & Steele,   joined by S. & T.
ended up at Fann Street   Sharwood
Foundry)   1833
|
S. & T. Sharwood
1845–56
Vincent Figgins   (types dispersed at
(pupil of Jackson)   auction; recommenced
1792–1836   business as J. & R.M.
| Wood, bought by James
V.2 & J. Figgins ———————— Figgins in 1872)
|
Stevens, Shanks & Sons
1907–

William Miller
(foreman of Glasgow
Letter Foundry)
1807
moved to Edinburgh,
Letter Founder to His
Majesty for Scotland
|
Miller & Co (i.e. Walter
Richard)
1832
|
Miller & Richard
1838
(bought Wood &
Sharwoods 1863)
|
J.M. & W.M. Richard ——————
1868–

Alexander Wilson &
John Baine ———— John Baine (Dublin
(Camlachie)   branch; 1747, indepen-
1742   dent in Edinburgh;
| 1787, emigrated to
Glasgow Letter-   America) ———
Foundry of A. Wilson &
Sons
1762
(moved to London by
descendants in 1834)   Neill & Co (Edinburgh)
Alex Wilson & Sons   1838 –
(London); Dublin &
Edinburgh branches
styled A. & P. Wilson,
Wilsons & Sinclair, the   MacBrayne & Stirling
latter became indepen-   (Glasgow)
dant in 1839 ———— Duncan Sinclair & Sons 1840 – 50
| 1840 – 61
(1850 London branch (bought by John Milne
purchased by Caslon, & Co; auctioned 1870)
renamed Caslon &   Ferguson Brothers
Glasgow Letter-   (Edinburgh)
Foundry; Edinburgh &   1846
Dublin branches   (also in business with
bought by James Marr)   J.C. Bauer)
|
James Marr & Co
1853 – 74
(bought by Miller &   R. Stewart & Co
Richard)   (Edinburgh)
              1849

The Lineage of the American typefounders

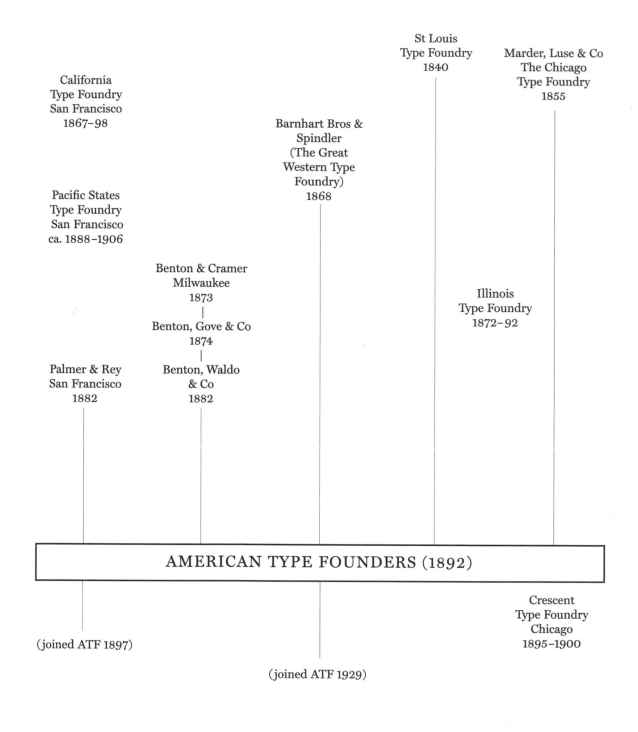

California
Type Foundry
San Francisco
1867–98

Pacific States
Type Foundry
San Francisco
ca. 1888–1906

Benton & Cramer
Milwaukee
1873

Benton, Gove & Co
1874

Palmer & Rey
San Francisco
1882

Benton, Waldo
& Co
1882

Barnhart Bros &
Spindler
(The Great
Western Type
Foundry)
1868

St Louis
Type Foundry
1840

Marder, Luse & Co
The Chicago
Type Foundry
1855

Illinois
Type Foundry
1872–92

AMERICAN TYPE FOUNDERS (1892)

Crescent
Type Foundry
Chicago
1895–1900

(joined ATF 1897)

(joined ATF 1929)

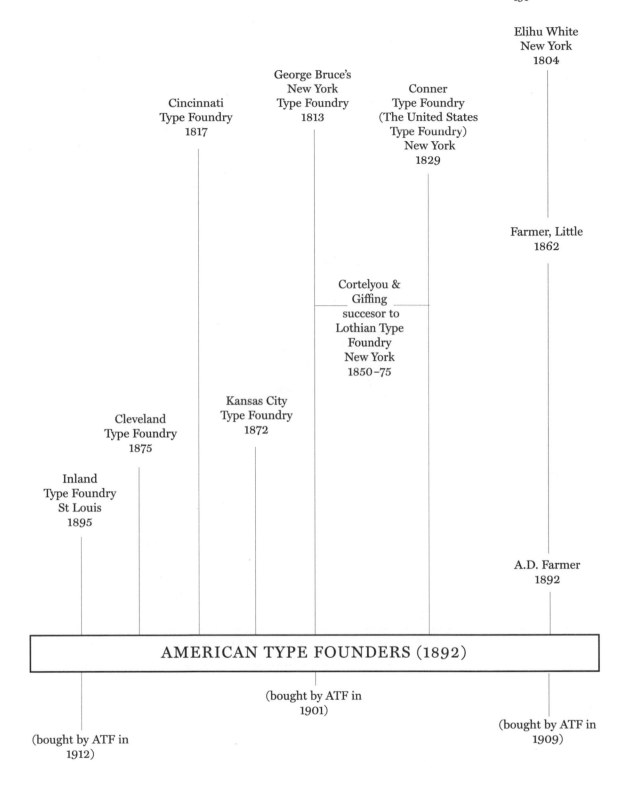

Elihu White
New York
1804

George Bruce's
New York
Type Foundry
1813

Conner
Type Foundry
(The United States
Type Foundry)
New York
1829

Cincinnati
Type Foundry
1817

Farmer, Little
1862

Cortelyou &
Giffing
succesor to
Lothian Type
Foundry
New York
1850–75

Kansas City
Type Foundry
1872

Cleveland
Type Foundry
1875

Inland
Type Foundry
St Louis
1895

A.D. Farmer
1892

AMERICAN TYPE FOUNDERS (1892)

(bought by ATF in
1901)

(bought by ATF in
1912)

(bought by ATF in
1909)

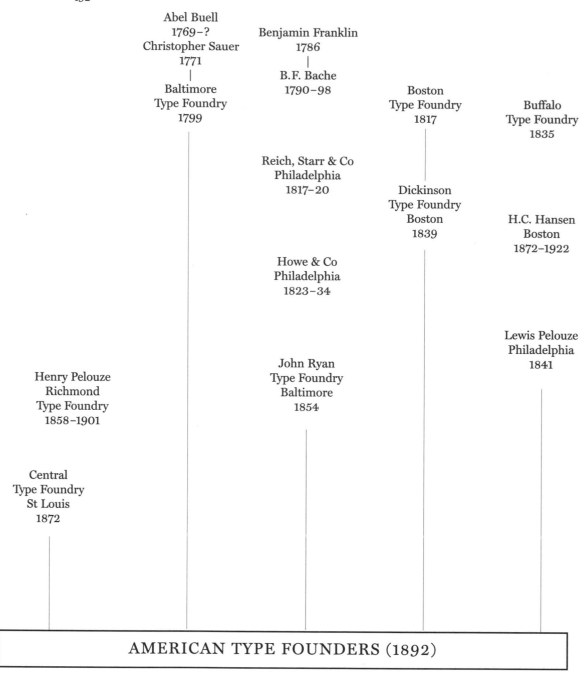

Abel Buell
1769–?
Christopher Sauer
1771
|
Baltimore
Type Foundry
1799

Benjamin Franklin
1786
|
B.F. Bache
1790–98

Boston
Type Foundry
1817

Buffalo
Type Foundry
1835

Reich, Starr & Co
Philadelphia
1817–20

Dickinson
Type Foundry
Boston
1839

H.C. Hansen
Boston
1872–1922

Howe & Co
Philadelphia
1823–34

Lewis Pelouze
Philadelphia
1841

Henry Pelouze
Richmond
Type Foundry
1858–1901

John Ryan
Type Foundry
Baltimore
1854

Central
Type Foundry
St Louis
1872

AMERICAN TYPE FOUNDERS (1892)

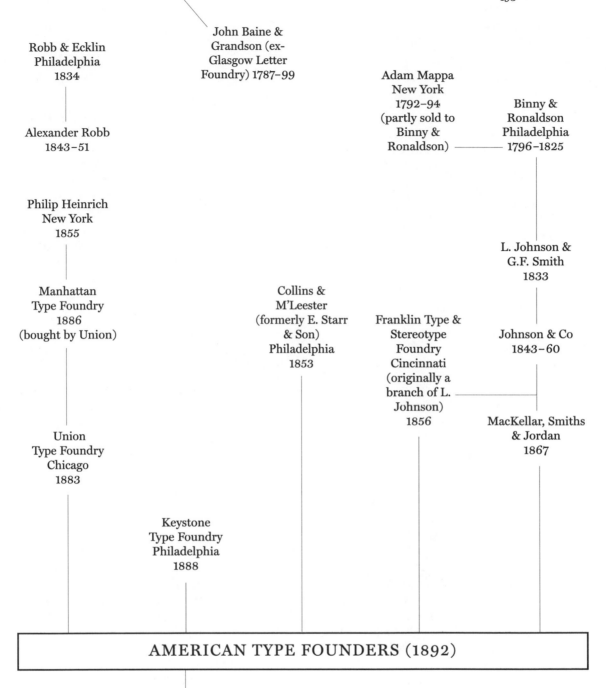

Robb & Ecklin
Philadelphia
1834

Alexander Robb
1843–51

Philip Heinrich
New York
1855

Manhattan
Type Foundry
1886
(bought by Union)

Union
Type Foundry
Chicago
1883

John Baine &
Grandson (ex-
Glasgow Letter
Foundry) 1787–99

Adam Mappa
New York
1792–94
(partly sold to
Binny &
Ronaldson)

Binny &
Ronaldson
Philadelphia
1796–1825

L. Johnson &
G.F. Smith
1833

Collins &
M'Leester
(formerly E. Starr
& Son)
Philadelphia
1853

Franklin Type &
Stereotype
Foundry
Cincinnati
(originally a
branch of L.
Johnson)
1856

Johnson & Co
1843–60

MacKellar, Smiths
& Jordan
1867

Keystone
Type Foundry
Philadelphia
1888

AMERICAN TYPE FOUNDERS (1892)

(bought by ATF in
1919)

Type Specimens Consulted

KEY:
* = has been republished in facsimile
§ = Poltroon Press collection, Berkeley
• = San Francisco Public Library
% = Kemble Collection of the California
   Historical Society, San Francisco
‡ = Columbia University Library, New
   York
œ = Rochester Institute of Technology,
   New York
= Bentinck-Smith Typographical Collec-
   tion, Houghton Library, Boston
$ = The Newberry Library Wing
   Collection, Chicago
£ = St Bride Institute Printing Library,
   London

1. British

Joseph Aston (Manchester), ca. 1808 •
Austin, Wood, Browne (London) 1867 $
   1885 $
John Bell's British Letter Foundry
   (London) 1788* £
R. Besley & Co. (Fann Street Foundry)
   (London) 1852-3 ‡ 1854 £ ca. 1857 £ $
A. Bessemer (London) 1830 £
Blake, Garnett & Co. (Sheffield) 1819 £ ‡
   ca. 1827 £
Blake & Stephenson *Select specimen*
   (Sheffield) 1830 £ ‡ 1835 ‡
Bower, Bacon & Bower (Sheffield) 1826 ‡
Bower & Bacon (Sheffield) 1830 £ 1836 ‡
British Foundry: *see S. Stephenson*
William Caslon I *Type specimen sheet*
   (London) 1734* ‡
William Caslon & Son (London) 1764 ‡
William Caslon II (London) 1766* £ $
   In Luckombe 1771*
William Caslon III *Specimen of large letters*
   (London) 1785 # *Specimen of printing
   types* (London) 1785* (Selections added
   to facsimile of 1766 Specimen, published

as *Journal of Printing Historical Society*
   #16 [1981/82]) £ • $
William Caslon ('& Son' deleted; 'Jr. & Co.'
   added) (London) 1803 • ‡
William Caslon IV (London) 1816 ‡
Caslon & Catherwood (In C. Stower,
   Printer's grammar, London, 1808)* £
H. Caslon & Catherwood (London) 1821 ‡
Henry Caslon (Catherwood deleted)
   (London) ca. 1821 £ 1825 £
Caslon & Livermore (London) ca. 1827 $
   1830 ‡ £   1832 $ 1838 £
Caslon & Glasgow *Select specimen* 1850 •
H.W. Caslon & Co. (London) 1843 $
   1857 ‡ £ $
Caslon & Glasgow *Epitome specimen*
   1865 ‡
Central Type Foundry (London) 1896 $
Fann Street Foundry of Reed & Fox (late
   Besley & Co.) (London) 1863 £ ‡
   1868 # £   ca. 1872 %   1873 #
   1879 #   1892 #
Ferguson Bros (Edinburgh) 1846 ‡
Vincent Figgins (London) 1793 £
   1801*   1815* ‡ £   1821[?] ‡ £
   1824 £   1827 £   1828 £
   1832 £ ‡   1835 œ
V. & J. Figgins (London) 1838 % £ $
   Specimen of phœnetic types 1841 ‡
   Epitome specimen 1845 £
   Specimen of new book founts 1862 ‡ £ $
   Centenary edition 1892 § $
Joseph Fry & Sons (London) 1785 $
   1786 £ ‡ •
E. Fry & Co. (London) 1788 ‡ • £
Fry & Steele (London) 1794 ‡ • $
E. Fry *Pantographia* (London) 1799 § • £
   ‡
Edmund Fry (London) 1816 ‡ • £ $
E. Fry & Son (London) 1823 ‡
Edmund Fry 1824 • £ ‡ $ 1828 £
Glasgow Letter Foundry 1833 ‡ (*See also
   A. Wilson & H.W. Caslon*)

2. North American

American Type Founders (Phila.) 1895 ‡
Pacific Coast blue book (San Francisco)
1896 § • ‡ % # $ ATF (Buffalo) 1897 §
ATF (Jersey City) 1906 § 1912 § 1923 §
Baltimore Type Foundry 1854 % ‡
1881 $ 1883 $ 1883–8 ‡
Barnhart Bros & Spindler 1881 $ 1883 # ‡
1885 # ‡   1891 #   *Pony specimen
book* (Chicago) 1889 $ # ‡ § (N.B. 'identi-
cal' book issued by five founders) 1900 §
Benton-Gove & Co. (Milwaukee) 1876 ‡
1882 ‡ Benton-Waldo (Milwaukee) 1884
‡   ca. 1886 # (*ATF duplicate copy*)
1893 ‡ § (*ATF duplicate copy*)
Binny & Ronaldson (Philadelphia)
1812* ‡ # $
Boston Type & Stereotype Foundry 1820 #‡
1826 $ 1827 %   1828 #‡   1832* # ‡ $
1835 •   1837 ‡ #   1841 # $ 1845 $
1856* # ‡ $ 1857 # ‡ 1861 #   1864 # ‡
1869#‡ $ 1871#‡$ 1874#   1876%‡#$
1877 $ 1878 $ 1880 #‡   1881$ 1883% #
‡ $ 1884 $ 1885 %   1889 %   1892 # % •
D. & G. Bruce (New York) 1818 # ‡ (in C.S.
Van Winkle, *The Printer's guide*) 1821 #
1828 ‡   1833 %   1837 ‡
1848 # ‡ $ 1853 % #   1858 • #
Bruce's New York Type Foundry 1865 # $
1869 %•#$ 1881 $ George Bruce's Son &
Co. (*Abridged specimen*) 1878 § ‡ #
1882 (+ *5 supplements to 1887*) §•‡%# $
Buffalo Type & Electrotype Foundry of
Nathan Lyman 1841 ‡   1873 %   1889 $
Central Type Foundry (St Louis) 1886 #
1889 ‡   1890 ‡ $ 1891 ‡   1892 # $
Chicago Type Foundry = Marder, Luse
Cincinnati Type Foundry (O. & H. Wells)
1827 ‡   1834 ‡   1844 ‡   1856 $
1857* $ 1868 ‡   1878 %   *Thirteenth
book* 1880 # ‡ *Fourteenth book* 1880 ‡
Fifteenth book (Compact edition) 1882 ‡
Seventeenth book 1888 § ‡ % # $
Cleveland Type Foundry (H.H. Thorp
Manufacturing Co.) 1880 ‡   1890 ‡
1892 ‡   1893 ‡ % § $ (*ATF duplicate
copy*) 1895 % # ‡ $

Collins & M'Leester (Philadelphia) 1858 ‡
$ 1866 § ‡
Conner & Cooke (New York) 1834 $
James Conner & Son (New York) 1850 $
James Conner & Sons (New York) 1852 # ‡
1854 ‡ $ 1855 #   ca. 1865 %   1869 $
ca. 1875 %   1879 $ 1888* ‡ % # $
1891 ‡ % # $
Cortelyou & Giffing (New York) 1850 ‡ #
Peter Cortelyou (New York) 1867 %
De Vinne Press (New York) 1891 § 1907 §
Dickinson (Boston) 1842 ‡ # $ 1847 % # $
(Phelphs & Dalton, Props) 1856 • ‡ % $
Minor specimen book 1859 # $ 1867 $
1868 ‡ % 1876 # $ 1883 ‡ %# 1893 # $
S. Ecklin & Co. (Philadelphia): *see A. Robb*
Farmer, Little & Co. (New York) 1862 #
(Boston) 1867 ‡ %   1874 $ 1878 #
1879 $ (New York) 1880 ‡%•$ 1881 #
1882 ‡ % # $ 1884 #   1885 # $
A.D. Farmer (Old New York) 1897 % # $
1900 § $
Franklin Type Foundry of Allison & Smith
(Cincinnati) ca. 1880 ‡ %   1883 #
1885–6 ‡ %   1890 $ 1892 % $ 1895
Franklin Letter Foundry of A.W. Kinsley
(Albany, NY) 1828 %
William Hagar & Co (New York) 1826 ‡
1827 %   1831 ‡   1841 ‡   1854 ‡ $ 1866 ‡
1869 •   (*See also White, Hagar & Co.*)
Philip Heinrich (New York) 1878 ‡   1886 $
Howe (Philadelphia) 1830 ‡
Illinois Type Foundry 1873 $
Johnson & Smith (Philadelphia) 1834 % #
‡ $ 1842 % #   1844 % ‡ $
L. Johnson & Co. (Philadelphia) 1845 ‡ #
Minor Book 1853 % ‡ #   1855 #   1857 ‡
$ 1859 % ‡ $ 1860 #   1865 % ‡
G.B. Lothian (New York) 1841 ‡ (*bought by
Cortelyou & Giffing 1850*)
Henry Ludwig's Printing Office (New York)
1847 ‡
MacKellar, Smiths & Jordan (Philadelphia)
1868 #   1871 % ‡ $ 1872 •   1873 $
1875 %   1876 #   1882, 1884, 1885,
1886, 1888, 1889, 1890, 1894 • ‡ § % # $
Marder, Luse & Co. (Chicago, San Fran-
cisco & Minneapolis) 1862 ‡   ca. 1870 $

1874 % #   1876 % ‡   1878 %   1881 ‡ $
Specimen of candy stamps 1883 ‡
1893 % § # $

Minnesota Type Foundry 1892 §

Montreal Type Foundry 1850 ‡ $

Narine & Co. *Schedule of printing types*
(New York) 1852 ‡

Nesbitt & Co. (New York) 1838 ‡

New England Type & Stereotype Foundery
(Boston) 1827 #   (Henry Willis, Agent)
1829 (Greele & Willis) *copy at North-
western Univ.* 1834 ‡ • # *Supplement* #
1851 #   1855 ‡ % *Additions* 1859 #
1880 #

Pacific States Type Foundry (San Francisco) 1889 %   1893 % *Handy book*
1899 %

Pacific Type Foundry: *see Marder, Luse*

Wᵐ H. Page & Co. (Greeneville, Cᴛ) 1867 %
1872 % • $

Painter & Co., Agents for MacKellar,
Smiths & Jordan (San Francisco) 1878 •

Palmer & Rey (San Francisco) 1889 $
1892 § ‡ •

Edward Pelouze (New York) 1840 $

Henry L. Pelouze, Richmond Type Foundry
1888 $

G.C. Rand & Avery, Printers (Boston) 1861•

Alex Robb (Philadelphia) 1846 #

James Ronaldson (Philadelphia)
1816* ‡ % #   1822 ‡ % #

Shniedewend & Lee Co. (Chicago)
*Specimen of types manufactured by
MacKellar Smiths & Jordan Co.* 1888

R. Starr & Co. (Albany, New York) 1826 %‡

John F. Trow, Printer, Stereographer (New
York) 1851 ‡ #   1853 #   1856 •

Union Type Foundry (Chicago) 1888 %
1889 $

United States Type Foundry (N.Y.) 1888 ‡

Darius Wells & Co. (New York) ca. 1839 ‡

Wells & Webb (New York) 1840 ‡   1854 $

O. & H. Wells: *see Cincinnati Type F'ndry*

Elihu White (New York) 1812 ‡   1818 ‡ #
(in C.S. Van Winkle, *The Printer's guide*)

White, Hagar & Co. (New York) 1833 ‡ %
$ 1835 ‡ $ (*see also Farmer, Little &
Co.*) 1844 $ 1849 $

3. European

G.B. Bodoni (Parma) 1818* •

Caslon et Cⁱᵉ (Paris) 1861 •

Jules Claye *Types de caractères ... anciens*
(Paris) 1875 •

Delacologne (Lyons) 1773*

Ambroise Firmin Didot (Paris) 1784

Pierre Didot l'Aíné (Paris) 1819 • ‡

Firmin Didot et Fils (Paris) 1828

Johannes Enschedé en Zonen (Haarlem)
1768*   1773*   1806 •   1841 •

Fournier *Modéles des caracteres* (Paris)
1742*

Gauthier Frère & Cⁱᵉ (Besançon) 1835 •

Claude Lamesle (Paris) 1742*

Adam G. Mappa (Rotterdam) ca. 1781 ‡

J.F. Rosart (Brussels) 1768*

C.A. Spin & Zoon (Amsterdam) 1853 ‡

Stads– en Courant-Drukkerij (Amsterdam)
1843 ‡

Fonderies E. Tarbé (successeur de Molé)
(Paris) 1836 ‡

Karl Tauchnitz (Leipzig) 1835

Vatican Press (Rome) 1628*

Thorey, Virey & Moret (Paris) 1810 ‡

Thorey, Virey (Paris) 1843 •

M. Weiss (Malta) 1845 ‡

4. Periodicals*

American Art Printer (C.E. Bartholomew, NY) 1887–93
American Bookmaker (Howard Lockwood, NY) 1885–96
American Chap-book (Will Bradley, ed., Jersey City, NJ) 1904–5
American Model Printer (Kelly & Bartholomew, NY) 1879–84
American Printers' Specimen Exchange (H. McClure, ed., Buffalo, NY) 1886–90
The British Printer (Mclean-Hunter, London) 1888–1933
Caslon's Circular (H.W. Caslon & Co., London) 1875–1928
Electrotype Journal (A. Zeese & Co., Chicago) 1874–1902
The Electrotyper (Shniedewend, Lee & Co., Chicago) 1873–90
Engraver & Printer (Boston) 1891–96
Hailing's Circular (Cheltenham)
The Inland Printer (Inland Type Foundry, St Louis) 1883–1958
Internationaler Graphischer Muster-Austausch 1880–91
The Occasional Typograph (San Francisco)
The Pacific Specimen (Marder, Luse, & Co., San Francisco) 1874–81
The Paper & Printing Trades Journal (Leadenhall Press, London) 1873–91
Paper World (C.W. Bryan, Holyoke, MA.) 1880–98
The Practical Printer (Inland Type Foundry, St Louis) 1899–1911
Press News (London)
The Printer & Bookmaker 1897–1952
The Printers' Bulletin (John K. Rogers & Co., Boston) 1858–63
The Printers' Circular (R.S. Menamin, Philadelphia) 1866–90
The Printers Friend (London)
The Printers Guide (Painter & Co., San Francisco) 1877–83
The Printers' International Specimen Exchange (Andrew Tuer, ed., London) 1880–92
The Printers Miscellany (St John, New Brunswick)
The Printers Register (London) 1863–83
The Printers Register (Central Type Foundry, St Louis) 1874–92
Printers' Review (Golding & Co, Boston) 1880?–86?
Printing (San Francisco) 1889–90
Printing & Stationery World (NY)
The Printing Press (Franklin Society, Chicago) 1875–6
The Printing Times & Lithographer (Wyman & Sons, London) 1875–1900
Printing Trade News (NY) 1882–1915
The Proof-Sheet (Collins & M'Leester, Philadelphia) 1867–80
The Quadrat (A.C. Bakewell & Co., Pittsburgh) 1873–84
The Specimen (Marder, Luse, Chicago)
The Superior Printer (Earhart & Richardson, Cincinnati) 1887–90
The Typographic Advertiser (L. Johnson/MacKellar, Smiths & Jordan, PA) 1855–93
The Typographic Advertiser (J. & R.M. Wood, London) 1862–67
The Typographic Messenger (James Conner's Sons, NY) 1865–89
Typologie Tucker (Paris)
Typothetae & Platemaker 1898–1900

*This list is based on the holdings of the California Historical Society's North Baker
Research Library in San Francisco which contains the library of William F. Loy.

Names and Sizes of Types*
in the Anglo-American point system

3 point	Minikin (*Excelsior* U.S.A.)
4 point	Brilliant
4¹/₂ pt	Diamond
5 point	Pearl
5¹/₂ pt	Ruby (*Agate* U.S.A.)
6 point	Nonpareil
6¹/₂ pt	Emerald (*Minionette* U.S.A.)
7 point	Minion
8 point	Brevier
9 point	Bourgeois
10 pt	Long Primer
11 pt	Small Pica
12 pt	Pica
14 pt	English
16 pt	2-Line Brevier (*Columbian* U.S.A.)
18 pt	Great Primer
20 pt	Paragon
22 pt	Double Small Pica
24 pt	Two-line or Double Pica
28 pt	Two-line English
36 pt	Two-line Great Primer
44 pt	2-line Double Pica (*Meridian* U.S.A.; *Trafalgar*, Caslon, 1810)
48 pt	Canon (or Four-line Pica)
60 pt	Five-line Pica
72 pt	Six-line Pica (*etcetera*)

———

*On comparative names of types, see Reed, chapter 1, Timperley *Printer's manual*, and De Vinne, *Plain printing types*, chaps. 2–3. For a comparison of English, French, German and Dutch sizes, see Smith, *Printer's grammar*, chapter VI. On the relative scale of sizes, see further John Richardson Jr, 'Correlated type sizes and names for the fifteenth through twentieth century,' in *Studies in Bibliography* 43 (Charlottesville, VA, 1990).

Glossary

Terminology used in nineteenth-century printing offices

BOURGEOIS (pronounced BURJESS, or BUR-JOYCE) = 9-point type common in newspaper setting

BREVIER = 8-point type, formerly used in books of this type

CHAPPEL = fraternal organization within a print-shop used to establish decorum and settle disputes

COMP = a compositor

COMPOSITION = set-up type; also, material used in making rollers

CUT = non-typographic material, such as an illustration, used in a forme

DEAD BANK = where printed matter sits awaiting distribution

DEVIL = printer's apprentice

DINGBAT = ornament cast in lead

DIS = to distribute type

EM = the square of a type body (thus in Pica type it's twelve points wide by twelve points high)

EN = half the above (6 points wide by 12 points high)

FAT TAKE = a typesetting job with a lot of blank space, such as poetry or display work

FLONG = laminated paper used for making a stereotype mould

FORME = pages of type held in a metal chase or frame by quoins and wooden furniture, ready for printing

FURNITURE = oblong pieces of wood used to fill up the blank space in a forme

GALLEY = A tray, usually brass or zinc, for holding composed matter

HELL BOX = container for broken or worn type waiting to be melted down

HORSES = antique name for pressmen

IMPOSING STONE = marble-topped table for locking up pages of type for printing

JEFFING = another name for 'quadrats,' often played to see who buys the beer

JOB CASE = a case for type containing all the main characters for text setting; superseded cap (for 'capital') or upper case and lower case

JOUR = journeyman printer, pronounced like French 'jour' (day)

LEAD (pronounced 'led') = *vb*: to separate lines with strips of lead; *n*: the actual piece of spacing material, often two points thick

LOCK-UP = to assemble matter in a forme to be printed

MAKE-UP = the art of breaking galleys of composition into pages

MATRIX = brass negative used for casting type; can also be made of lead or paper in stereotyping (plural: Matrices, or Mats)

MUT = an em quad

NONPAREIL = six-point type, generally the smallest type in a shop

NUT = an en quad

OFFCUT = strips of paper left over from larger sheets, useful for smaller jobs such as bookmarks or bookplates

PI = jumbled type; a page that has fallen into disarray

PI SORTS = non-roman characters such as mathematical symbols occasionally needed in composition

PICA = typographical unit, possibly derived from the medieval *picco* scale (related to the cubit), about a sixth of an inch; also 12-point type

POINT = the basic typographical unit (a twelfth of a pica), about 1/72nd of an inch

QUAD = spacing material, usually an em

QUADRATS = a game like dice, played with spacing material

QUOIN = wedge device for locking up formes

REGLET = 6– and 12-point wooden strips used with furniture

ROUNCE & COFFIN = the crank and bed of an iron handpress

SHOOTING STICK = tool for unlocking formes by knocking the wedges out

SIGS = signatures or gatherings of printed pages, once they have been folded and collated

SLING TYPE = to distribute type

SLUG = a six-point wide piece of lead used for spacing; a line of Linotype; a board for organizing subs in a large shop

SOLACE = a fine or punishment imposed by the Chappel for infractions such as swearing or leaving type on the floor beneath your case

STEREOTYPING = creating a thin lead replica of a page of composition for presswork

STEREO = the plate made by stereotyping, used for printing, which saves wear and tear on the actual type

STICK TYPE = to set type in a composing stick

STRING = the amount of matter composed in a shift (measured with a length of string) when compositors were paid by the number of ems composed

SUB = substitute compositor, a temporary worker

STUD-HORSE TYPE = large sizes of display type

TYPE-HIGH = Generally 0.918 of an inch, the height of type to paper

WAYZGOOSE = winter holiday in the Chappel

WIDOW = a solitary word at the end of a paragraph, to be avoided

WORK-UP = a piece of spacing material that rises to type-height and is printed, causing a blotch on the page

ZINC, or ZINCO = an illustrative block, now often made of magnesium

– 30 – = 'there is no more' (written at the end of copy)

— *30* —

Bibliography

Thomas F. Adams, *Typographia, or, the printer's instructor*, Philadelphia, 1845

Maurice Annenberg, compiler, *Type foundries of America and their catalogues*, Baltimore, 1975

_____, *A Typographical journey through the Inland Printer 1883–1900*, Baltimore, 1977

John Ashton, *A History of English lotteries*, London, 1893

Marius Audin, *Les Livrets typographiques des fonderies françaises*, Paris, 1933

F.C. Avis, *Edward Philip Prince, type punchcutter*, London, 1967

Iain Bain, 'James Moyes's Temple Printing Office of 1825', *Journal of the Printing Historical Society* 4, London, 1968

Johnson Ball, *William Caslon master of letters*, Kineton, Warwickshire, 1973

Stephen Bann, ed, *Concrete poetry: an international anthology*, London, 1967

Giles Barber, ed, *Anecdotes typographiques où l'on voit la description des coutoumes, moeurs et usages singuliers des Compagnons imprimeurs by Nicolas Contat dit le Brun [1762]*, Oxford, 1980

J. Wesley Barber, *The Printers' text book*, Boston, 1875

Nicolas Barker, *A Specimen of types & ornaments, used in the printing-office of Joseph Aston, Exchange, Manchester (ca. 1808)*, facsimile, Berkeley [forthcoming]

Alan Bartam, *Fascia lettering in the British Isles*, London, 1978

_____, *Street name lettering in the British Isles*, London, 1978

_____, *The English lettering tradition from 1700 to the present day*, London, 1986

Fernand Baudin & Netty Hoeflake, *Type specimen of J.F. Rosart (Brussels) 1768*, Amsterdam, 1973

Dominique Baudouin, ed, *Dada et la typographie*, Paris, 1970

W.T. Berry & A.F. Johnson, *Catalogue of specimens of printing types by English & Scottish printers and founders 1665–1830*, London, 1935

_____, *Supplement* to the above, *Signature* 16, London, 1952

W.T. Berry & H.E. Poole, *Annals of printing, a chronological encyclopedia*, London, 1966

E.C. Bigmore & C.W.H. Wyman, *A Bibliography of printing* (3 vols), London, 1880–86

William Blades, *Shakspere and typography, &c*, London, 1872 (reprinted 1969)

_____, *Early type specimens of England, &c*, London, 1875

William Blake, *The Marriage of Heaven & Hell*, Lambeth, ca. 1790 (reprinted: *The Prophetic writings of William Blake*, vol. 1, Oxford, 1926)

C.H. Bloy, *A History of printing ink, balls & rollers 1440–1850*, London, 1967

Walter H. Blumenthal, *Eccentric typography & other diversions in the graphic arts*, Worcester, Mass, 1963

William Bowyer, *Account of the origins of printing, with remarks*, London, 1774

Charles Brightly, *The Method of founding stereotype* (Bungay, 1809) AND Thomas Hodgson, *An Essay on the origin and progress of stereotype founding* (Newcastle upon Tyne, 1820), with an introduction by Michael Turner, New York & London, 1982

Bertrand H. Bronson, *Printing as an index of taste in eighteenth-century England*, New York, 1958

David Bruce, Jr, *History of typefounding in the United States*, edited by James Eckman, New York, 1981

Henry H. Bullen, *Discursion of a retired printer*, Chicago, 1907

_____, *Duplicates of the type specimen books etc, U.S. & foreign for sale by the typographic library and museum of the American Type Founders Co*, Jersey City, 1934

_____, *Catalogue and list prices of duplicates of books, &c., offered for sale by the typographic library and museum of the American Type Founders Co*, Jersey City, 1936

_____, *The History of printing from its beginnings to 1930: the subject catalogue of the ATF library in the Columbia University libaries*, 4 volumes, New York, 1980

F. Burgess, 'Tombstone lettering on slates', *Typographica* (n.s.) 13, London, 1966

J. Callingham, *Signwriting and glass embossing: a complete practical illustrated manual of the art*, London, 1871

Harry Carter, *A View of early typography up to about 1600*, Oxford, 1969

_____, *The Type specimen of Delacologne [Lyons 1773]*, Amsterdam, 1969

David Chambers, ed, *Specimen of modern printing types by Edmund Fry 1828*, London, 1986

[concrete poetry] *Text Buchstabe Bild*, Zürich, 1970

Theodore L. De Vinne, *Historic printing types*, New York, 1886

_____, *The Practice of typography*, 4 vols, New York, 1900

_____, *Types of the De Vinne press*, New York, 1907

Dictionary of national biography, 22 vols, London, 1908

T.F. Dibdin, *Typographical antiquities; or the history of printing in England, Scotland and Ireland... begun by the late Joseph Ames, considerably augmented by William Herbert, and now greatly enlarged, with copious notes, &c*, London, 1810

_____, *The Bibliographical decameron*, London, 1817

David Diringer, *The Alphabet*, third edition, London & New York, 1968

John Dreyfus, *Aspects of French eighteenth century typography*, Cambridge, England, 1982

Kurt Faulmann, *Illustrierte Geschichte der Buchdruckerkunst*, Vienna, 1888

Paul Fisher, *An Uncommon gentry*, Columbia, Mo, 1952

Edmund Fry, *Pantographia*, London, 1799

Philip Gaskell, 'Photographic enlargements of type forms', *Journal of the Printing Historical Society* 7, London, 1971

_____, *A New introduction to bibliography*, Oxford, 1974

Albert J. George, *The Didot family and the progress of printing*, Syracuse, 1961

Al Gowan, *T.J. Lyons. A biography and critical essay*, Boston, 1987

J.B. Graham, *Handset reminiscences: recollections of an old-time printer and journalist*, Salt Lake City, 1915

Nicolete Gray, *A History of lettering*, London, 1986; Boston, 1987

_____, *Lettering on buildings*, London, 1960

_____, *Nineteenth-century ornamented typefaces with a chapter on types in America by Ray Nash*, London/Berkeley & Los Angeles, 1976

_____, 'Slab-serif type design in England 1815–1845,' *Journal of the Printing Historical Society* 15, London, 1980–81

Edmund G. Gress, *The Art and practice of typography: a manual of American printing, including a brief history up to the twentieth century*, New York, 1917

Ralph Green, 'List of type specimen books', *New England Printer*, April 1952

P.M. Handover, *Printing in London from 1476 to modern times*, London, 1960

_____, 'Letters without serifs', *Motif* 6, London, 1961

_____, 'Grotesque letters, a history of unseriffed typefaces 1816 to the present day', *Monotype News Letter 69*, 1963

_____, 'Black serif. The career of the nineteenth century's versatile invention: a slab-seriffed letter design', *Motif* 12, London, 1964

Luke Hansard, *The Auto-biography of Luke Hansard printer to the House, 1752–1828*, London, 1991

T.C. Hansard, *Typographia: an historical sketch... of the art of printing*, London, 1825*

_____, *Treatises on printing and typefounding*, Edinburgh, 1841

_____, *The Art of printing*, Edinburgh, 1851

Oscar Harpel, *Typograph*, Cincinnati, 1870
_____, *Poets and poetry of printerdom*, Cincinnati, 1875

Horace Hart, *Charles Earl Stanhope and the Oxford University Press* (with notes by James Mosley), London, 1966

Charles Hasler, 'The Emergence of the printer's stock block', *Typographica* 10, London, 1964

Nelson C. Hawks, *Explanation of the point system of printing type, with specimens*, Alameda, CA, 1918

Sir Francis Bond Head, 'The Printer's devil', in *The Quarterly Review*, London, December, 1839

Lafcadio Hearn, *Selected writings 1872–7*, Indianapolis, 1979

John Edward Hicks, *Adventures of a tramp printer 1880–1890*, Kansas City, 1950

John Hodgkin, *Rariora*, 3 vols, London, 1901

Dom Sylvester Houédard, 'Concrete poetry and Ian Hamilton Finlay', *Typographica* 8, London, 1963

Clarence P. Hornung, *Handbook of early advertising art*, New York, 1956

Ellic Howe, *The London compositor: documents relating to wages, working conditions & customs of the London printing trade 1785–1900*, London, 1947

Noel Humphries, *A History of the art of printing from its invention, &c.* London, 1868

Richard E. Huss, *The Development of printers' mechanical typesetting methods 1822–1925*, Charlottesville, VA, 1923

[W.H. Ireland] *Scribbleomania; or, the printer's devil's polychronicon. A sublime poem edited by Anser Pen-Drag-On, esq.* London, 1815

Frank Isaac, *A Catalogue of specimens of English & Scottish printing types*, Oxford, 1930

Peter C.G. Isaac, *William Davison of Alnwick pharmacist and printer 1781–1858*, Oxford, 1968
_____ et al, *Printers' trains*, Wylam, 1969

_____, *A Tentative checklist of Bensley printing*, Wylam, 1989
_____, *William Davison's new specimen of … ornaments*, London, 1990
_____, *William Bulmer, the fine printer in context 1757–1830*, London, 1993

Charles T. Jacobi, *Some notes on books and printing: a guide for authors and others*, London, 1892

Hugo Jahn, *Hand composition*, New York, 1930

Louis James, *English popular literature 1819–1851*, New York, 1976

Holbrook Jackson, *The Printing of books*, London, 1938
_____, 'Patterns in print', *The Dolphin* IV, part 3, New York, 1941

A.F. Johnson, 'Fat faces: their history, forms & use', *Alphabet & Image* 5, London, 1947
_____, *Type-specimens of Claude Lamesle (Paris) 1742*, Amsterdam, 1965
_____, *Type designs: their history and development*, third edition, London, 1966
_____, *Selected essays on books and printing*, Amsterdam, 1977

John Johnson, *Typographia, or the printer's instructor*, London, 1824*

Rob Roy Kelly, *American wood type: 1828 to 1900. Notes on the evolution of decorated and large types*, New York, 1969

Charles Knight, *William Caxton: a biography*, London, 1844
_____, *The Old printer and the modern press*, London, 1854

David Knott, 'Aspects of research into English provincial printing', *Journal of the Printing Historical Society* 9, London, 1973/4

Richard Kostelanetz, ed, *Imaged words and worded images*, New York, 1970

Ben Hur Lampman, *The Tramp printer. Sometime journeyman of the little hometown papers in days that come no more*, Portland, Oregon, 1934

David J. Lasko, 'Pin marks, nicks, & grooves: some notes on the history of

American typefounding', *Festina Lente*, Rochester, NY, 1980

L.A. Legros & J.C. Grant, *Typographical printing surfaces: the technology and mechanism of their production*, London, 1916

Charles G. Leland, *The Breitmann ballads*, Philadelphia, 1871

_____, *Pidgin-English sing-song*, Philadelphia, 1876

Henry Lemoine, *Typographical antiquities. Origin & history of the art of printing, foreign and domestic*, London, 1797

Roger Levenson, *'The Pressman's trade': a commentary on the traditional handpress*, Davis, CA, 1969

John Lewis, *Printed ephemera*, Ipswich, England and New York, 1962

William F. Loy, series of thirty-nine articles on American typefounders in *The Inland Printer*, 1900–5 [and forthcoming book with an introduction by Alastair Johnston and notes by Stephen O. Saxe]

Philip Luckombe, *The History and art of printing*, London, 1771*

Thomas MacKellar, *The American printer, a manual of typography*, Philadelphia, 1866 (Eighteenth edition: 1893)

[T.W. MacKellar] *100 years: MacKellar, Smiths & Jordan, 1796–1896*, Philadelphia, 1896

Gordon Martin, *The Playbill: the development of its typographic style*, Chicago, 1963

Robert Massin, *Letter & image*, New York, 1970

[Mayer] *publications by and works by edition hansjörg mayer*, The Hague, 1968

John McCreery, *The Press: a poem*, Liverpool, 1803; part 2, London, 1827

Mac McGrew, *American metal typefaces of the twentieth century*, second edition, New Castle, DE, 1993

Ronald B. McKerrow, *An Introduction to bibliography for literary students*, Oxford, 1928

Ruari McLean, 'An Examination of egyptians', *Alphabet & Image* 1, London, 1946

_____, *Victorian book design*, New York & Oxford, 1963

_____, *Victorian book design & colour printing*, second edition, Berkeley, 1972

_____, *Joseph Cundall: a Victorian publisher*, Pinner, 1976

John F. McRae, *Two centuries of typefounding*, London, 1920

R. Hunter Middleton, *Chicago letter founding*, Chicago, 1937

James Moran, *The Composition of reading matter*, London, 1965

_____, *Printing presses. History and development from the fifteenth century to modern times*, London, 1973

Edward Rowe Mores, *A Dissertation upon English typographical founders and founderies [1778]*, edited by Harry Carter & Christopher Ricks, Oxford, 1961

Stanley Morison, 'Decorated types', *Fleuron* 6, London, 1928

_____ et al, *Printing in the twentieth century a survey reprinted from the special number of* The Times *October 29, 1929*, London, 1930

_____, *John Bell, 1745–1831, bookseller, printer, etc*, Cambridge, 1930

_____, *Ichabod Dawks & his news-letter*, Cambridge, 1931

_____, *Richard Austin, engraver to the printing trade between the years 1788 & 1830*, Cambridge, 1937

_____, *Talbot Baines Reed, author, bibliographer, typefounder*, Cambridge, 1960

James Mosley, 'The Typefoundry of Vincent Figgins 1792–1836', *Motif* 1, 1958

_____, 'The English vernacular', *Motif* 11, London, 1964

_____, 'Trajan revived', *Alphabet*, London, 1964

_____, editor, *Fournier's Modéles des caracteres de l'imprimerie [1742]*, London, 1965

_____, 'XIXth century decorated types at Oxford', *Journal of the Printing Historical Society* 2, London, 1966

_____, *A Specimen of printing types by William Caslon [London, 1766]*, *Journal of the Printing Historical Society* 16, London, 1983

_____, *British type specimens before 1831: a handlist*, Oxford, 1984

_____, *S. & C. Stephenson a specimen of printing types and various ornaments 1796 reproduced together with the sale catalogue of the British letter-foundry 1797*, London, 1990

_____, *Ornamented types*, London, 1993

_____, *The Nymph and the grot: the revival of the sanserif letter*, London, 1999

Joseph Moxon, *Mechanick exercises on the whole art of printing* [1683], edited by Herbert Davis & Harry Carter, London, 1962

Percy Muir, *Victorian illustrated books*, London & New York, 1971

Joel Munsell, *The Typographical miscellany*, Albany, New York, 1850

Ray Nash et al, eds, *Printing and Graphic Arts*, Lunenberg, VT, 1953–65

John Nichols, *Biographical and literary anecdotes of William Bowyer*, London, 1782

Charles Olson, *Projective verse*, New York, 1957

W.Y. Ottley, *An Enquiry concerning the invention of printing*, London, 1863

G.W. Ovink, 'Nineteenth-century reactions against the didone type model,' 3 parts, *Quaerendo* I/2, 1971, I/4, 1971, II/2, 1972

Samuel Palmer, *A General history of printing*, London, 1732

David Pankow, 'Recast in an American image: the work of Hermann Ihlenberg, type designer,' *Ampersand*, XIII/3,4, San Francisco, 1994

[W.W. Pasko], *American dictionary of printing and bookmaking*, New York, 1894

Nikolaus Pevsner, *Studies in art, architecture and design*, New York, 1968

Frederic N. Phillips, *Phillips' old-fashioned type book*, New York, 1945

Graham Pollard, *Birrell & Garnett catalogue of typefounders' specimens, etc, offered for sale*, London, 1928

Sydney Pollard, *A History of Stephenson, Blake & Co. Ltd, 1818–1959*, Sheffield, ca. 1960 (copy of unpublished book at St Bride Library)

Mario Praz, *The Romantic agony*, Oxford, 1933

Frank Presbrey, *The History & development of advertising*, New York, 1929

Printing patent abridgements 1617–1857 [1859] (reprinted: London, 1969)

John J. Pullen, *Comic relief: the life and laughter of Artemus Ward, 1834–1867*, Hamden, CT, 1983

Talbot Baines Reed, *A History of the old English letter foundries* [1887], revised by A.F. Johnson, London, 1952

Jasia Reichardt, 'Type as art', *Penrose Annual* 58, London, 1965

_____, ed, *Between poetry and painting*, London, 1965

Hans Richter, *Dada: art & anti-art*, Cologne, 1964; London, 1965

J. Luther Ringwalt, *American encyclopædia of printing*, Philadelphia, 1871

Vivian Ridler, 'Artistic printing', *Alphabet & Image* 6, London, 1948

Lawrence B. Romaine, *A Guide to American trade catalogs 1744–1900*, New York, 1960

Daniel Roselle, *Samuel Griswold Goodrich, creator of Peter Parley. A study of his life and work*, New York, 1968

Charles Rosner, *Printer's progress 1851–1951*, London, 1951

John Russell, *An Address, presented to the members of the Faustus Association... at their annual celebration*, Boston, 1808

Michael Sadleir, *Nineteenth century fiction. A Bibliographical record*, 2 vols, New York, 1951

Henry Sampson, *A History of advertising from the earliest times, illustrated by anecdotes, curious specimens & biographical notes*, London, 1874

W. Savage, *Practical hints on decorative printing*, London, 1822

_____, *A Dictionary of the art of printing*, London, 1841*

Stephen O. Saxe, 'The Bruce legacy', in *ATF Newsletter*, Washington, 1984; *Bulletin* 16 of Printing Historical Society, 1985

John Sharkey, ed, *Mindplay*, London, 1971

Rollo G. Silver, *Typefounding in America 1787–1825*, Charlottesville, Va, 1965

———, *The American printer, 1787–1825*, Charlottesville, Va, 1967

Dame Edith Sitwell, *English eccentrics*, New York, 1957

Charles Manby Smith, *The Working man's way in the world* [1857], London, 1967

John Smith, *The Printer's grammar*, London, 1755*

Dan X. Solo, 'The Influence of galvanism on type design,' *The Kemble Occasional* 19, San Francisco, June 1978

Mary Ellen Solt, ed, *Concrete poetry: a world view*, Bloomington, 1968

John Southward, *Progress in printing and the graphic arts*, London, 1897

———, *Modern printing*, London, 1898–9

———, *Practical printing*, fifth edition, London, 1900

Martin K. Speckter, *A Disquisition on the composing stick*, New York, 1971

Herbert Spencer, *The Visible word*, London & New York, 1969

———, *Pioneers of modern typography*, second edition, London, 1982

Caleb Stower, *The Printer's grammar*, London, 1808*

F. Thibaudeau, *Manuel français de la typographie moderne*, Paris, 1924

John S. Thompson, *History of composing machines*, Chicago, 1904 (reprinted: New York, 1980)

Charles H. Timperley, *Encyclopedia of literary and typographical anecdote*, London, 1842 (incorporating *The Printer's manual*, 1838*)

———, *Songs of the press*, London, 1845

William B. Todd, *Directory of printers & others in allied trades, London 1800–1840*, London, 1972

Michael Turner, *The John Johnson collection*, Oxford, 1971

Paul Turner, *English literature 1832–1890 excluding the novel*, Oxford, 1989

Michael Twyman, *John Soulby, printer, Ulverston*, Reading, England, 1966

———, *Printing 1770–1970*, London, 1970; second edition: London & New Castle, De, 1998

———, *Lithography 1800–1850*, London, 1970

———, *The Landscape alphabet*, Hurtwood, Kent, 1988

Typographica 8, London, 1963

Carolyn F. Ulrich & Karl Kup, compilers, *Books & printing: a selected list of periodicals, 1800–1942*, New York, 1943

Daniel Berkeley Updike, *Printing types: their history, forms and use*, 2 vols, second edition, Cambridge, Ma, 1937

C.S. Van Winkle, *The Printer's 'guide,' or, an introduction to the art of printing: including an essay on punctuation, and remarks on orthography*, New York, 1818

Hendrik D.L. Vervliet, *Type-specimen of the Vatican Press (Rome) 1628*, Amsterdam, 1967

William Lightfoot Visscher, *'Vissch.' A Book of sketches, rhymes and other matters credited to Matthew Mattox, N.P.R.*, St Joseph, 1873

James Watson, *The History of the art of printing*, Edinburgh, 1713*

Roby Wentz, *Western printing: a selective and descriptive bibliography of books and other materials on the history of printing in the western states 1822–1975*, Los Angeles, 1975

Ralph Willett, *A Memoir on the origin of printing*, Newcastle upon Tyne, 1820 (facsimile reprint, New York, 1978)

Emmet Williams, ed, *Anthology of concrete poetry*, New York, 1967

Berthold Wolpe, *Vincent Figgins type specimens 1801 and 1815*, London, 1967

Robert Wood, *Victorian delights*, London, 1967

*facsimile edition published in London, 1965

Index